At Home with the Holocaust

At Home with the Holocaust

Postmemory, Domestic Space, and Second-Generation Holocaust Narratives

LUCAS F. W. WILSON

Rutgers University Press
New Brunswick, Camden, and Newark, New Jersey
London and Oxford

Rutgers University Press is a department of Rutgers, The State University of New Jersey, one of the leading public research universities in the nation. By publishing worldwide, it furthers the University's mission of dedication to excellence in teaching, scholarship, research, and clinical care.

Library of Congress Cataloging-in-Publication Data

Names: Wilson, Lucas F. W., author.
Title: At home with the Holocaust : postmemory, domestic space, and
   second-generation Holocaust narratives / Lucas F. W. Wilson.
Description: New Brunswick : Rutgers University Press, 2025. |
   Includes bibliographical references and index.
Identifiers: LCCN 2024021898 | ISBN 9781978839816 (paperback) |
   ISBN 9781978839823 (hardcover) | ISBN 9781978839830 (epub) |
   ISBN 9781978839847 (pdf)
Subjects: LCSH: American literature—History and criticism. | Children of Holocaust
   survivors, Writings of, American—History and criticism. | Home in literature. |
   Memory in literature. | Psychic trauma in literature. | Holocaust, Jewish (1939–1945),
   in literature. | LCGFT: Literary criticism.
Classification: LCC PS153.C444 W55 2025 | DDC 810.9/358405318—dc23/eng/20241031
LC record available at https://lccn.loc.gov/2024021898

A British Cataloging-in-Publication record for this book is available from the British Library.

Copyright © 2025 by Lucas F. W. Wilson
All rights reserved

No part of this book may be reproduced or utilized in any form or by any means, electronic or mechanical, or by any information storage and retrieval system, without written permission from the publisher. Please contact Rutgers University Press, 106 Somerset Street, New Brunswick, NJ 08901. The only exception to this prohibition is "fair use" as defined by U.S. copyright law.

References to internet websites (URLs) were accurate at the time of writing. Neither the author nor Rutgers University Press is responsible for URLs that may have expired or changed since the manuscript was prepared.

♾ The paper used in this publication meets the requirements of the American National Standard for Information Sciences—Permanence of Paper for Printed Library Materials, ANSI Z39.48-1992.

rutgersuniversitypress.org

For my dad, Keith Wilson

Contents

	Preface	ix
	Introduction	1
1	Postmemorial Structures: The "Space" and "Stuff" of Survivor-Family Homes	15
2	"Remember, my house it's also your house too": Postmemorial Structures in Art Spiegelman's *Maus*	32
3	Domestic(ated) (Un)fashioning: Sonia Pilcer's *The Holocaust Kid*	51
4	A Tale of Two Storeys: Upper and Lower Space and Postmemorial Divergences in Elizabeth Rosner's *The Speed of Light*	76
5	Pre/Occupied Longing: Toward a Definition of Postnostalgia in Jonathan Safran Foer's *Everything Is Illuminated*	101
	Conclusion	124
	Appendix	133
	Acknowledgments	135

Notes	139
Bibliography	161
Index	169

Preface

It was at Liberty University, of all places, where I was initially introduced to second-generation Holocaust literature. Few probably would expect a study on second-generation representation to include Liberty University in the first sentence of the preface, but the truth of the matter is that my love for Jewish literature, strangely, began at the world's largest evangelical institution of higher education. As an undergraduate at Liberty, I became interested in Jewish studies after enrolling in courses like Jewish Literature, History of Antisemitism, and (the unfortunately named) Old Testament Survey. It was after taking these courses that I, in all my young (evangelical) hubris, thought I knew all there was to know about Jews and that I had mastered the subjects of Judaism and Jewish literature. Perhaps in line with other undergraduate students who, after taking one class on a particular subject, believe themselves to be experts in that field, I was convinced that I knew all I needed to know in order to enter graduate school and write my thesis on Holocaust literature.

However, at McMaster University—where I did my MA in English—I was quickly corrected and informed that, in fact, I had *much* to learn when it came to not only Jewish studies but the study of literature in general. Because of my disappointing education at Liberty, I realized I was woefully underprepared for my graduate studies, causing me to seriously consider dropping out. By way of example, my master's-thesis proposal was rejected *seven times* before it was accepted on the eighth attempt—a story I discuss in greater detail in "Unlearning Evangelicalism: What a Poor

Education Taught Me."[1] Though I eventually wrote my master's thesis (with a focus on Elie Wiesel's *Night* and A. M. Klein's *The Second Scroll*), it was a sincere struggle. Not only had I little idea how to navigate writing a thesis because of my previous "training" (if we can be so generous with such a term) at Liberty, but my Christianized readings of Jewish texts proved to be a glaring issue in my writing. My thesis supervisor—for whom I still feel terrible, given how much on which he had to catch me up to speed—recurrently had to correct my Christianized misreadings. I still remember telling him at one point: "I promise that I'm not stupid; I just haven't been trained properly. Please help me!" And help me he did, despite what I assume to be much frustration on his part.

I soon after matriculated to Vanderbilt University to begin my MTS, though I was still a student at McMaster and was concurrently finishing my MA thesis as I began my second master's degree. As I started taking classes in Vanderbilt's Divinity School, I felt much better prepared to succeed because of my actual academic training at McMaster. I eventually defended my MA thesis successfully and continued in my studies at Vanderbilt, enrolling in courses like Hebrew Bible (the corrective to Liberty's Old Testament Survey), Reading the Bible after the Holocaust, Poetry since World War II, The Holocaust: Meanings and Implications, and Literature of Children of Holocaust Survivors. It was these last two courses—taught, respectively, by the inestimable Jay Geller and Adam Meyer—that crystallized my interest in Holocaust studies. I eventually wrote my MTS thesis on a piece of Nazi propaganda, Veit Harlan's film *Jud Süss*, under the direction of Geller. I chose to research the film in light of how I wanted to get into the heads of Nazis and Nazi collaborators, wondering how they could have ever believed such lunacy. Though I did not find the answers I was looking for (and, in truth, still have not found many satisfying answers), I had become preoccupied with the enduring effects of the Shoah after 1945. Mainly because of the Literature of Children of Holocaust Survivors course, which I took while writing my MTS thesis, I knew I wanted to pursue further study of the children of survivors. In this course, I wrote a paper on domestic space in Sonia Pilcer's *The Holocaust Kid*, and Meyer informed me that this paper could be augmented to become a much longer study of the second generation. This idea that I could write about domestic space in second-generation literature stuck in my head and began to germinate, so I decided that I wanted to pursue my PhD to explore this topic. But as it was too late to apply for PhD programs that year, I would wait a year before I could submit my applications.

In the meantime, I both taught at a small liberal arts college in Nashville and interned at the Tennessee Holocaust Commission. I was an adjunct instructor at Lipscomb University, a Church of Christ institution, and it was there that I was somehow allowed to teach a senior seminar on Holocaust literature. I have written about this experience teaching at Lipscomb where I had to teach my students how not to interpose their own Christianized misreadings into the texts at hand,[2] so I will not recapitulate that experience here. But suffice it to say that I tried to do for my students what my supervisor at McMaster did for me: to help resist Christian supersessionist readings of Jewish texts. Through the Tennessee Holocaust Commission, I worked with children of Holocaust survivors, along with the children of camp liberators. I was tasked with creating a group for the descendants of survivors and liberators that would hold space for them to share their experiences of growing up with parents who were directly implicated in the Holocaust and World War II. While working with these men and women, I witnessed how what I had learned at Vanderbilt played out in the daily lives of the second generation. I became increasingly familiar with the various ways by which their parents' traumatic pasts came to bear on their own psyches—how they suffered from psychological and emotional wounds in line with their mothers and/or fathers—almost as if they themselves were alive during and personally affected by the Third Reich. This work, in concert with my previous studies on the children of survivors, solidified my interest in the second generation, and I applied for my PhD with a project in mind that is, by and large, the same one as this very study.

This study is also an indirect response to my own personal biography. Ever since first reading Anzia Yezierska's short story "Children of Loneliness," I resonated with several themes in Jewish American literature, namely that of being caught between two worlds. Whereas for the protagonists in a number of Jewish American texts were caught between the Old World and the New World—or between the world of their families and the greater extrafamilial world—I felt torn between what seemed to be two uncompromising forces: my religious commitments and my sexuality. When I first began reading Jewish literature at Liberty, my sexuality was something that I tried to hide from those around me, especially those in my evangelical community. I felt as though I could not be both gay and a Christian.

Though I have no desire to be straight today (or tomorrow) and though I am no longer religious, at the time I thoroughly believed that I wanted to be straight (or, more accurately, *was told* I wanted to be straight). But I wasn't anything but queer, which precluded me from living comfortably as an evangelical man given how homosexuality is considered irreconcilable with living out one's so-called Christian witness. As such, I felt suspended between two worlds, and insofar as Jewish-American literature gave voice to such ontological suspension, I felt at home in the stories of Yezierska and others who addressed similar themes. My sense of feeling at home bled over into my experience of reading second-generation literature, largely because of how the authors' descriptions of their parents' mental health issues resonated with my own experience.

Indeed, my project is also an indirect response to my own family dynamics, particularly my relationship with my mother. Even though such dynamics are of course markedly different in many ways, this present study was in part conceptualized because I saw a number of similarities between my relationship with my mother and the family relationships I saw in second-generation literature. My mother, who struggles with her mental health, was a hoarder, which I have come to understand as an externalization of her internal, mental "clutter." As she held onto so many belongings—damaged, broken, or otherwise—she also held onto much emotionally and mentally. Her vexed and disorderly relationship to her home served as a guiding rubric for how I saw members of the second generation's relationships to their own homes. I could see how their postmemorial lives were registered in and through their domestic spaces, similarly to how I could see my mom's mental health issues reflected in and through her disarranged home. Of course, my personal experience of growing up in a home largely defined by my mom's mental health issues is not isomorphic with those of children of survivors, and I acknowledge the *significant* differences between these experiences. I want to be clear that in no way am I equating my mother's mental health issues with those of survivors; the levels, scales, and intensities of issues between both parties are qualitatively different, and no part of me is interested in claiming my mother's experiences to be on par with those of survivors. What I am claiming, however, is that because of my mother's mental health issues that shaped our family home, I became more attuned to how domestic spaces "speak" to mental health issues, which shaped my approach to this project.

In sum, my scholarship in Jewish studies has been shaped by my own domestic experiences, my relationship to my mother, my past and present relationships with children of survivors that I have cultivated over the years, and my academic training. But my research in Jewish studies has also led to profound changes in my life, including and especially in regard to how I relate to religion. After reading a number of Jewish authors, including several in this present study, I gave up my evangelical religious commitments in favor of a more honest way of living and being. It was in large part because of shedding such a restrictive theology that I was able to more fully live into my queer identity. Without the opportunity to think—and to think deeply—about issues that I believe to be important, some of which I discuss in this study, I am quite confident that I would be a very different person living a very different life than I am today. As a result, I am eternally grateful for both the Jewish texts that I have read over the years and this present study itself—all of which have changed me indelibly.

At Home with the Holocaust

Introduction

What does it mean for survivors[1] of the Shoah and their children to be "at home" with the Holocaust? Of course, this question does not suggest that survivor families lived comfortably with or found a sense of refuge in the memories, stories, or traumas from the Shoah post-1945. For survivors and their children, those known as the *second generation*, this was most certainly not the case; these two groups, affected both directly and indirectly, were not uncommonly traumatized by the murderous events that took place between 1933 and 1945. This question of being "at home" with the Holocaust instead refers to how the memories, stories, and traumas from the Holocaust took up residence, abided with, and haunted survivors and their children alike in their homes for years to come. For both groups, their domestic lives were in significant ways shaped by the Shoah, such that the Holocaust came home with them, so to speak, darkly coloring how they interacted with and inhabited their domiciles. Being at home with the Holocaust thus denotes a state of domestic existence that was (and is) imbued with the enduring legacy of the Shoah.

The experience of being at home with the Holocaust, though occurring worldwide for survivor families, was particularly notable in the United States. This was not only because of the sheer number of survivors who ended up in the United States but also because the U.S. cultural milieu sparked a growing awareness of the Third Reich's atrocities in the subsequent decades after they occurred.[2] Despite how some have claimed there to have been relative silence surrounding the Holocaust for many years,[3] a number of historians and cultural critics have established how it was indeed discussed, commemorated, and represented in U.S. public life, sometimes even before 1945 and increasingly so as time went on. In truth, in the late 1940s and throughout the 1950s, the Holocaust was not a *major* preoccupation or topic of conversation for the average person—not to mention how many were not prepared to speak about it. However, in the immediate decades after the "end" of the Holocaust, it was nonetheless a cultural and historical reference point with which many were familiar, and discussions of the topic were relatively easy to find. In regard to U.S. Jews specifically, *many* thought, spoke, and wrote about the horrors that had just happened in Europe.[4] And outside Jewish circles, the term *Holocaust* was being used in print by the 1950s, which suggests how the catastrophic events were more broadly recognizable to the general U.S. populace not long after 1945.[5] Awareness of and interest in the Shoah only continued to increase as time went on—including and especially for the children of Holocaust survivors—because of several publications, pivotal events, and cultural moments throughout the country and abroad.

From 1945 to the end of the 1970s, the period in which the majority of the second generation grew up,[6] there were numerous artistic representations of the Holocaust in the United States that raised children of survivors' awareness of the destruction that defined their parents' lives. In American letters alone, there were diffuse allusions to and detailed depictions of the Shoah (see the appendix), which made such representation accessible for children of survivors who sought it; some of these texts incorporated only passing references to the Holocaust, whereas others, such as Bernie Krigstein's "Master Race" (1955), Stanley Kramer's *Judgment at Nuremberg* (1961), and Susan Fromberg Schaeffer's *Anya* (1974), offered dedicated treatments of the Holocaust. This is not to mention works by Yiddish-speaking Jews that discussed the Shoah, the considerable number of survivor testimonies, or magazines with Holocaust-focused content.[7] Moreover, on television and the radio, there were several programs that either touched on the topic (e.g., *Star Trek*) or centered around it (e.g., NBC's wildly popular miniseries *Holocaust*, which garnered over 120 million viewers).[8] The Holocaust also took center stage, as it were, in theater and film productions like *The Diary of Anne Frank*. This substantial body of Holocaust representation, in concert with a growing number of academic studies, furnished the second generation with ample literary, artistic, testimonial, and scholarly touchstones that gave voice (and image) to what occurred—and what they imagined to have occurred—during Hitler's reign.

By the 1960s and into the 1970s, several pivotal events raised the second generation's consciousness of the Shoah even further, which in turn engendered a prominent framework—no doubt, one of many—through which survivors' children understood themselves. One major, if not *the* major, event that mobilized interest in and discussions of the Shoah was the Eichmann trial in 1961, which was featured on all three national commercial networks in the United States during their nightly prime-time news shows and special programs. The trial—treated in depth by Hannah Arendt in several articles in the *New Yorker*, which were later compiled in her influential (and controversial) book *Eichmann in Jerusalem* (1963)—reinvigorated discussion of the Holocaust for survivors and the wider public, thereby offering the second generation a larger platform to re-view Jews' systematic persecution and murder. Additionally, conflicts like the Six-Day War of 1967 and the Yom Kippur War of 1973 revivified and deepened the second generation's consciousness of the Holocaust, as they were repeatedly reminded of the Shoah and that threats to the Jewish people were still very much possible. These events, along with the other aforementioned cultural representations, in part framed the second generation's connection to the Holocaust. What also framed their connection to the Holocaust was, of course, their relationships with their parents—survivors themselves.

As survivors, an emphatically diverse group of individuals, were variously affected by their own Holocaust experiences,[9] survivors' children, also a markedly heterogeneous group,[10] were affected by their parents' traumatic pasts in a multiplicity of ways as well. Whereas some survivors were reportedly resilient after 1945, others were hospitalized for severe psychological disturbances. And while some were overall quite stable, though nonetheless struggled with recurring psychosocial difficulties, others experienced a period of latency where their traumas did not surface until years later.[11] Many survivors grappled for decades with issues that resulted from living through the Shoah, including chronic anxiety and depression, extended mourning, withdrawal, suspicion, hostility, recurring nightmares, insomnia, temporal distortions, moodiness, vegetative dystonia, psychic closing off, a sense of helplessness, despair, crying spells, feelings of emptiness, persistent tension states, reduction in memory, the inability to concentrate, psychosomatic manifestations, and hypochondria.[12] Many children of survivors—though certainly not all[13]—were likewise affected by their parents' Holocaust pasts *as if* their parents' traumatic experiences were their own. Marianne Hirsch refers to this intergenerational transmission of trauma and embodied knowledge as *postmemory*, a term she further defines as "the experience of those who grow up dominated by narratives that preceded their birth, whose own belated stories are evacuated by the stories of the previous generation shaped by traumatic events that can be neither understood nor recreated."[14] Despite how postmemory is not memory in and of itself, in many ways it functions as though it were, thereby burdening children of survivors with its emotional, cognitive, and sometimes overwhelming weight.[15] Members of the second generation adopted, to varying degrees, certain tendencies, anxieties, fears, and neuroses of their parents, along with related issues, that were a result of the Shoah.[16] As Helen Epstein, a prominent second-generation author, explains, those who were traumatically affected by their parents' pasts adopted "a particular worldview."[17] Of course, even within this particular worldview there was a range of experiences, but what united the sizeable subgroup within the second generation who were affected by postmemory was how "the Holocaust [was] *the* dominant psychic reality,"[18] if not *a* dominant psychic reality, for them.

The means by which children picked up on their parents' Holocaust experiences were legion. In excess of their epigenetic inheritances,[19] the second generation commonly learned of their parents' dark pasts from stories told (or, ironically, *not* told) by their parents and their parents' survivor friends; from their parents' dispositions and nonverbal cues; and from seeing or interacting with certain mementos, documents, or belongings from before or during the Holocaust, such as family photographs. Focusing her work primarily on photography's role in the transmission of trauma between survivors and the second generation, Hirsch asks: Which *other* "technologies," as she puts it, communicated, imprinted, and carried the traumas and embodied experiences from parent to child, thus leading to the creation of postmemory?[20]

One specific group of technologies integral to the formation of postmemory was survivor-family homes. To date in Holocaust studies, survivor-family homes have not been theorized as key elements in the creation of postmemory. Though many critics have examined the second generation and postmemory in depth, few have discussed, or even mentioned, survivor-family homes in their studies—perhaps because the domestic sphere might seem like an inconsequential object of analysis.[21] Despite how many have talked *around* survivor-family homes, only a handful have talked *about* such homes. And although some occasionally have touched on domestic life, markedly few have offered detailed treatments of how the physical homes themselves or domestic practices therein contributed to the formation of postmemory. Additionally, no scholar has fleshed out the particulars of how second-generation Holocaust representation depicts domestic space or its role in the intergenerational transposition of traumatic knowledge and embodied experience.

As survivor-family homes were central actants in the creation of postmemory, these homes serve as sites of inquiry into how traumatic knowledge and embodied experiences were passed from survivors to their children. In her study of the second generation, Janet Jacobs explains that many children of survivors' homes, where she conducted her interviews, functioned as "field sites in and of themselves" because they were imbued with family narratives of the Shoah that evoked and deepened interviewees' belated connections "to loss, survival, and calamity."[22] Describing these homes as spaces where Holocaust traumas were conserved in both "the material and emotional culture of the second generation,"[23] Jacobs is one of few, along with Nina Fischer,[24] who explicitly, albeit in passing, identifies survivor-family homes as possible avenues for scholarly inquiry. Serving as critical resources for understanding survivor-family homes as postmemorial technologies, narratives in both second-generation literature and oral history provide much insight into how the second generation found themselves at home with the Holocaust. To be fair, not all texts written by children of survivors include intricate depictions of the physical, affective, or psychosocial space of their homes, and not every oral history narrated by children of survivors includes a discussion of the physical home at length. And of course, given how not all children of survivors were postmemorially wounded by their parents' Holocaust experiences, it is necessary to note that not all survivor-family homes were or are postmemorial structures. But this study only includes treatments of literary texts and oral histories that represent or discuss postmemorial structures, so as to better understand how these homes functioned and continue to function in the transmission of traumatic knowledge and embodied experience.

Given the interconnection between home, self, and parent(s), second-generation literary representations and oral-history descriptions of domestic life operate as indirect, though densely layered, ways of describing their postmemorial relationships to the Holocaust. In order to situate my study, I focus on Hirsch's description of postmemory as "a *structure* of inter- and transgenerational return of traumatic knowledge and embodied experience."[25] She employs the term *structure* in reference to the arrangement of relationships between the past and present, specifically mediated by the family unit. But her description of postmemory qua structure lends itself well to understanding the actual homes of survivor families as *postmemorial structures*. The phrase *postmemorial structures* refers to how survivor-family homes—the very physical, domestic milieus the second generation inhabited—have operated as sites of traumatic transference. In line with Hirsch's work and Gaston Bachelard's notion that domestic spaces mirror the subjective psychological conditions of their owners,[26] there is an emblematic relationship between postmemorial structures and those who lived within them, as represented in second-generation literature and oral history. Sharing space and time in postmemorial structures, that is, living in such close relationship and proximity to survivors, traumatically marked many in the second generation. But postmemorial structures were not only the settings for the intergenerational transmission of trauma and embodied knowledge; they were, at the same time, also fundamental actants in how the second generation's postmemories were structured. Inasmuch as "the body is woven into its domestic environment" as James Krasner explains in a different context,[27] the domestic environments of postmemorial structures were woven into the bodies *and* minds of the second generation.

Postmemorial structures functioned as material archives of survivors' Holocaust pasts that in turn shaped the second generation's psychical and emotional relationships to themselves, their parents, and their parents' Holocaust experiences. As Krasner further notes, "We unpack our selves onto the home's material spaces and structures, and we draw our sense of identity from the home which supports our habitual motions through it and interactions with our loved ones."[28] The material and spatial aspects of postmemorial structures (i.e., the spatial arrangements and negotiations of family members, domestic activities, household objects, interior architecture, decoration, etc.) all carried postmemorial import to varying degrees. These tactile, visual, and physical aspects of the home, materially registering survivors' Holocaust traumas and experiences, engendered and perpetuated the perceived collapse of past and present that so defined and continues to define the domestic spaces of many in the second generation. In short, the "space" and "stuff" of postmemory in survivor-family homes—or, otherwise put, the domestic affect and materiality of intergenerational trauma and embodied experience—structured and continues to structure how the second generation related to the Holocaust in the past and how they relate to it today.

Second-Generation Literature and Oral History

With the inevitable passing of survivors, there has been a profusion of second-generation literature in the United States from the turn of the century until now, a corpus that explores the children of survivors' relationships to their parents and their parents' Holocaust pasts. This body of literature has become remarkably expansive—so much so that, as Bettina Hofmann and Ursula Reuter explain, it is "impossible for experts to keep up."[29] Putting aside Elie Wiesel's *Le serment de Kolvillàg* (translated into English as *The Oath* [1973]), *Le Testament d'un poète juif assassiné* (*The Testament* [1980]), *Le cinquième fils* (*The Fifth Son* [1983]), and *L'oublié* (*The Forgotten* [1992])—novels that implicitly validate the second generation's experience of growing up in the shadow of survivors' traumatic pasts[30]—the first literary works to explore second-generation experiences emerged in the 1970s, 1980s, and 1990s.[31] Most of the prominent early second-generation texts were published by authors from the United States, including Lucy Y. Steinitz and David M. Szony's *Living after the Holocaust: Reflections by Children of Survivors in America* (1975); Thomas Friedmann's *Damaged Goods* (1984); Art Spiegelman's *Maus I: A Survivor's Tale: My Father Bleeds History* (1986), based on the earlier comics he created in the 1970s; Carol Ascher's *The Flood* (1987); Barbara Finkelstein's *Summer Long-a-coming* (1987); Lev Raphael's *Dancing on Tisha B'Av* (1990); and Spiegelman's *Maus II: A Survivor's Tale: And Here My Troubles Began* (1991). This is not to mention Epstein's enormously influential investigative study of the second generation, *Children of the Holocaust: Conversations with Sons and Daughters of Survivors* (1979). These second-generation texts, along with those that came after, give voice not to the Holocaust itself[32] but to the children of survivors' inherited traumas and embodied experiences that were and are a result of it.

As a subgenre of Holocaust literature,[33] second-generation literature is defined by its representation of intergenerational trauma, which trauma theory helps illuminate. Cathy Caruth defines trauma "as the response to an unexpected or overwhelming violent event or events that are not fully grasped as they occur, but return later in repeated flashbacks, nightmares, and other repetitive phenomenon."[34] Caruth refers to trauma as an *unclaimed experience* because the violent, original event happens too quickly, too suddenly, for the psyche to register it either consciously or unconsciously, leaving the traumatized individual without the ability to recall and, therefore, articulate what happened. The violence of the original moment of wounding exceeds the mind's capacity to comprehend, process, and come to terms with what occurred in a meaningful way. Trauma can be understood as a breach in the mind's experience of time which disrupts the traumatized individual's sense of chronology and continuity with the past.[35] Since the violent moment of wounding takes place outside what Dori Laub refers to as "normal" reality[36]—which thereby leaves a gap in the individual's memory and understanding of that event— the psyche tries, often unsuccessfully, to fill in this gap through the repetition and re-enactment of the traumatic trace left behind. Belatedly essaying to capture and assimilate the traumatic scene into cognition, the mind attempts to master the narrative that so resists narrativization.[37] Laub, though speaking in the clinical context, suggests that one who listens to a traumatized individual narrate his/her/their trauma becomes "a co-owner of the traumatic event: through his very listening, he comes to partially experience [the] trauma in himself."[38] When those who are in close contact with traumatized individuals, particularly the children of traumatized individuals, hear their traumatic stories, they in turn are not uncommonly overwhelmed and thus also become wounded. Yet, the original wounding event is even more elusive, even more unknowable, given how it never happened to them. As trauma erases the history that it enacts, in tandem with how the original wounding event is at a generational remove for children of traumatized individuals, coming to terms with such inherited trauma is doubly difficult. Such is the case for children of Holocaust survivors who struggle with postmemory.

Second-generation literature depicts the transmission of trauma from survivors to their children in numerous ways, but one of the most striking means of depicting this transmission is through its representation of survivor-family homes. Second-generation narratives reveal how children of survivors related to and inhabited their homes in their childhoods—in tandem with how they construct, fashion, and describe their homes as adults—which mirrors how they related and continue to relate to their postmemories. This literature demonstrates how childhood *domestic* spaces, imbued with survivors' traumatic pasts, contributed to the *domestication* of second-generation psyches, thereby intensifying their relationship to the Shoah. In part, survivors' domestic practices rendered these homes spaces of traumatic transference, as their behaviors and nonverbals contributed to the second generation's postmemories. In truth, some of those behaviors and nonverbals were not limited to the domestic sphere, for they also took place outside the home; however, those behaviors and nonverbals that took place outside the home nonetheless shaped how the second generation inhabited and perceived their homes and how they lived with and understood their postmemories. Moreover, the very physical conditions of survivor-family homes—their material and spatial aspects alike—operated as extensions of survivors' wounded psyches that their children "inhabited"; indeed, their physical inhabitance mirrored the second generation's psychical "inhabitance" or "indwelling" of their parents' Holocaust pasts. This was because survivor-family homes functioned as screens onto which the children of survivors projected their postmemories that in turn perpetuated and amplified their inherited traumas and embodied experiences. Insofar as it was common for children of survivors to imaginatively transform their homes into the sites of their parents' Holocaust traumas—concentration camps, ghettoes, places of hiding, or otherwise—their homes became significant catalysts in their psychosocial domestication. Such imaginative transformations also occur in the space of their adulthood homes, as the second generation's childhood experiences and perceptions of their domestic spheres shaped how they perceive and experience their homes and their postmemories years after moving out on their own.

This study primarily includes representations and descriptions of postmemorial structures in the context of the United States. The focus is on postmemorial structures in the United States largely because of the qualitative differences between life in the United States and elsewhere. For instance, life in Europe after the Holocaust in countries like Germany and Poland was situated in the same geography where the Holocaust and World War II took place. This indelibly colored how survivors and their families perceived and related to their geographical surroundings, which impacted how they perceived and related to their domestic spaces. As for life in Israel, the decades following the Shoah were marked by war and conflict, which would have unquestionably affected home life for survivor families—especially, in no small part, as survivors' traumas from the Holocaust would have been reanimated in a qualitatively different way. These significant differences between countries shaped survivor-family life and how their lives unfolded in their domestic spaces. In truth, this theorization of survivor-family homes can be applied in part or in whole to postmemorial structures in other national contexts—especially in other English-speaking countries like Canada, Australia, and New Zealand. However, for the purposes of specificity and in order not to homogenize national contexts, I concentrate specifically on postmemorial structures in the United States.

The main selected works range from fiction (e.g., novels, story cycles, and short stories) to life writing (e.g., memoir, graphic narratives, and personal essays). Read together, these texts represent survivor-family homes on (at least) two levels: as lived spaces of domestic existence and symbolically, that is, as spaces that metaphorize the protagonists' relationships to their postmemories. Yet, with Spiegelman's *Maus* (1986, 1991) as the exception, the majority of the main selected texts are not autobiographical, even if based in large part on the authors' lives. As such, only *Maus* is both testimonial (giving voice to the author's own lived domestic experiences) and figurative (presenting the home symbolically), whereas the other texts are not, in a strict sense, testimonial. The other main selected texts—Sonia Pilcer's *The Holocaust Kid* (2001) and Elizabeth Rosner's *The Speed of Light* (2001)—offer fictionalized representations of survivor-family homes that operate on a figurative level, not to mention Jonathan Safran Foer's *Everything Is Illuminated* (2002), which provides a fictionalized account of one man's quest to find his family's homeland that also operates on a figurative level. Some may take issue with the breadth of the genres included in this study, but the selected texts exemplify in their own ways how postmemorial structures functioned and continue to function. I am less concerned with genre-specific, formal concerns and more interested in how these texts depict postmemorial structures. Fiction and life writing alike are capable of offering insight into postmemory, as Fischer, Hirsch, and Leo Spitzer note,[39] and of revealing what it was like to grow up with survivors in the intimate space of the home. Though the postmemorial structures I examine are heterogeneous across genres, they also certainly possess a number of commonalities; indeed, in these major texts—in concert with other minor texts—there are clear and consistent underlying continuities between how postmemorial structures are represented and how they operate in the narratives.

Although the primary focus here is most certainly second-generation literature, I also incorporate second-generation oral histories by U.S. narrators in order to ground my argument not in abstract theorization based solely on literary analysis. I triangulate my analysis, putting into conversation secondary research—both critical theory as well as studies on the second generation—with the literature and oral histories of the second generation. The benefits of including oral history are that narrators are able to ponder questions in real time, make connections, and respond viscerally and organically with less time to self-edit, along with the benefit of immediate feedback from a trained listener. The unedited and off-the-cuff nature of oral histories furnishes us with additional extemporaneous material, semiotic texts in their own right, to compare with the literature that is highly stylized, considered, and crafted. Notwithstanding the differences between second-generation literature and oral histories, I "read" these two media in a comparable way. In line with my approach to second-generation literature, I attend to the ways by which the oral-history narrators describe their homes in their childhoods and in their adulthoods, examining how their descriptions elucidate the ways by which their postmemorial structures functioned in the creation and amplification of postmemory. With the exception of Arlene Stein's *Reluctant Witnesses* (2014), there has been no substantial scholarship published on second-generation oral history. In response to this scholarly gap, I have not only conducted several oral histories of my own, which are housed at and accessible through the College of Charleston's Special Collections, but I examine one of these oral histories in depth in one of the following chapters. Moreover, I analyze one of Avinoam Patt's In Our Own Words Interview Project oral histories and Spiegelman's *Maus*, which is in part a work of oral history, in my study of postmemorial structures.

Given their capacity to register and represent inherited trauma, second-generation literature and oral histories are privileged vehicles to examine postmemorial structures. Like photography, postmemorial structures spatially and materially manifested and communicated survivors' traumas and knowledge of the Holocaust to their children. But unlike photography, postmemorial structures were and continue to be habitual, everyday points of contact for the second generation. As such, analyzing postmemorial structures serves as a fruitful entry point into understanding the intergenerational transmission of trauma and embodied knowledge from survivors to their children.

Chapter Breakdowns

At Home with the Holocaust is broken into five chapters. Weaving analyses of literature written by descendants of Holocaust survivors with supplemental discussions of second-generation oral history together, subsequent chapters present how children of survivors have navigated and interacted with their postmemorial structures throughout their lives, along with how the notion of "home" has become complicated for these descendants. Revealing both the commonalities between and divergences among second- (and third-) generation narratives, I analyze how survivor-family homes qua postmemorial technologies have shaped children of survivors' relationships to Holocaust traumas and stories, in addition to discussing how returning to the homelands of survivors alters descendants' understandings of what it means to be "at home" with the Holocaust.

Chapter 1 fleshes out the defining characteristics of postmemorial structures, which lays the groundwork for the remaining multi-text exploration of the topic. With an eye toward the physical space of survivor-family homes and the material belongings contained therein, this chapter establishes how the stories and traumas from the Shoah affectively permeated and were registered in the domestic sphere, along with how these homes then shaped the second generation's postmemories. As space and matter are dimensionally related to time, I connect my discussions of both the space of and belongings in survivor-family homes to the second generation's altered perceptions of chronology, continuity, and causality. These homes often contributed to the muddling of the second generation's perceptions of the past and present qua distinct temporalities—a consequence of their inherited traumas. Throughout this chapter, it becomes clear how survivors' pasts came to live within these homes as spectral presences and, in turn, how members of the second generation imaginatively "lived" within such haunting pasts in and through their homes.

Offering an illustrative depiction of one such domestic experience, chapter 2 takes up Spiegelman's watershed graphic narrative *Maus*. The subject of space in *Maus* offers insights into the ways that postmemory ineradicably shapes one member of the second generation's childhood domestic life. *Maus* further demonstrates how protagonist Artie's childhood postmemorial structure also determines the affective environment of his adulthood domestic—and, no doubt, extradomestic—lived experiences; in other words, his adulthood home becomes a postmemorial recapitulation of his childhood home. I provide a topoanalysis of Artie's childhood and adulthood homes, suggesting that his parents' Holocaust memories indelibly altered his perception of space, time, and matter, even after moving out on his own. I further argue that Artie's search for his deceased mother is a postmemorial search for "home." By offering a close reading of Artie's childhood and adulthood homes, this chapter underscores the foundational influence that postmemorial structures have on the intergenerational transmission of trauma and embodied knowledge from survivors to their offspring.

Chapter 3 centers on Sonia Pilcer's *The Holocaust Kid*, considering the various ways that the protagonist's parents postmemorially domesticate her. The atmosphere that protagonist Zosha's parents create, in tandem with the clothes that her mother tailors for her, constitute two domesticating features of her youth that directly and indirectly reinforce her imaginative connection to the Holocaust. In tandem with treating these domesticating practices within the home, I discuss how Zosha attempts to free herself from such domestication. One such attempt to loosen the grip of the Shoah, specifically her inherited (sexualized) trauma, that Zosha makes is through her erotic role-play in her postmemorial structure. Positioning herself in her apartment as a prisoner of a concentration camp, Zosha seemingly works through her postmemories and, in doing so, transforms her home into an imagined concentration camp of sorts. Such a transformation of domestic space into an imagined camp demonstrates how the home operates as both a generative space to come to terms with one's postmemories but also a space that exacerbates postmemories, thereby revealing the home's paradoxical postmemorial function for children of survivors. Pilcer's narrative illustrates the gendered intricacies of a second-generation response to survivor parents' traumatic Holocaust experiences.

Elizabeth Rosner's *The Speed of Light* has received surprisingly scant academic treatment to date, but chapter 4 rectifies this scholarly lacuna by analyzing the novel's presentation of how children of survivors' postmemorial responses can and do vary even within the same family. I treat the divergent postmemorial responses of two sibling protagonists to their father's Holocaust experiences, along with how their domestic practices and their relationships to their homes offer insight into their postmemories. After investigating how their relationships to their childhood home diverge, I examine the siblings' shifting responses to their father's Holocaust past as reflected by their changing relationships to their adulthood apartments throughout the novel. This chapter further examines how addressing postmemories for the first time as adults, as opposed to as children, leads to different effects than those who have actively acknowledged their postmemories since they were children.

Chapter 5 treats Jonathan Safran Foer's *Everything Is Illuminated*, theorizing how descendants of survivors—with an emphasis on the *third* generation—possess so-called nostalgic attachments to the homelands of their survivor-family members. This discussion includes not an analysis of physical homes but, more broadly, *notions* of home and family homelands. As many descendants have understood the Holocaust as the place/time of their families' origins, "finding" pre-Shoah family and Jewish life in their progenitors' homelands offers them occasion to come to terms with their inherited traumas as they attempt, imaginatively, to root themselves in such pre-Shoah family and Jewish stories. By physically positioning himself in the lands of his forebearers, Foer's protagonist Jonathan attempts to physically fill in absence, to piece together narrative fragments of family life, to reintroduce Jewish life where it was decimated, and to connect to his family's roots that were incinerated during the Holocaust. Of course, his "recovery" of pre-Shoah family life is always already partial, incomplete, and ultimately impossible. But his response nonetheless offers an avenue to generatively come to terms with his inherited legacy of loss.

In these literary representations of survivor-family homes and homelands, along with selected oral-history discussions of domestic space, it becomes clear how *space speaks*. As survivors' traumas and experiences of the Holocaust were imbued in their homes, such traumas and experiences were expressed in and by the affective space of the second generation's childhood and adulthood homes. Surrounded by their parents' Holocaust pasts that found affective, material, and spatial expression in their domestic milieus, children of survivors became aware of and subject to their postmemories of the Holocaust. Postmemorial structures were and are integral actants that affectively speak to the second generation about their parents' Holocaust experiences. This specific sort of speaking—this type of affective, material, and spatial communication—typified and, in many cases, continues to typify postmemorial structures, wherein the second generation have found themselves, in complicated and complex ways, at home with the Holocaust.

1

Postmemorial Structures

The "Space" and "Stuff" of Survivor-Family Homes

Offering but one literary example of how survivors' Holocaust experiences traumatically informed the second generation's perceptions of their spatial world, Thane Rosenbaum's short story "Cattle Car Complex" (1996) is a quintessential document of postmemory. The story's narrator describes the second-generation protagonist, Adam Posner, as one whose spatial awareness was profoundly shaped by what his parents went through during the Shoah. Referring specifically to cattle cars, the narrator states: "Adam himself knew a little something about tight, confining spaces. It was unavoidable.... *He had inherited their* [his parents'] *perceptions of space*, and the knowledge of how much one needs to live, to hide, how to breathe where there is no air."[1] The narrator expounds on Adam's inherited awareness and experience of space, describing how he suffered from claustrophobia and a fear of the dark, along with how he consistently positioned himself near the door at parties where he knew he could exit easily.[2] Adam's need to be transient and flee at the drop of a hat is a function of learning about his survivor parents' experiences of, in excess of being evicted from their homes, having been rounded up onto trains to be sent to a camp. His "unavoidable" perception of space, albeit largely specific to his parents' traumatic journeys in cattle cars, speaks to the experiences of many within the second generation. Adam, whose name in Hebrew translates to "man," is a second-generation *every*man, one who filters his perception of space through the eyes of his parents—an experience that is at the heart of inhabiting postmemorial structures.

Survivors' Holocaust pasts—or, more accurately, what the second generation *imagined* to be their parents' Holocaust pasts—not uncommonly became the very lenses, or at least significant lenses, through which their children experienced the spatial and material world. Indeed, the second generation's perceptions of their parents' Holocaust experiences—whether they took place in cattle cars or elsewhere—framed the second generation's individual paradigms, grounding how they sensed and made sense of the world around them. Though the traumas of survivors were spatially and materially registered in survivor-family homes, their Holocaust experiences were not always easily understood by their children—or at least not in a straightforward sense. From how survivors set up their homes to how they moved through their domestic spaces—in tandem with how, for example, they frequently monitored their children—survivors communicated their Holocaust pasts by how they managed their domiciles. Part of such domestic management included whether they shared their Holocaust experiences in explicit terms with their children. As some survivors refrained from telling their children about their traumatic pasts in hopes of protecting them from such knowledge, others *did* tell their children about their experiences, often as cautionary tales or warnings, in order to prepare them for any future persecution or similar onslaughts. Some survivors spoke often; others spoke rarely; and still others spoke not at all, especially if their traumas disabled them from narrating their personal histories. Whatever the case—and whether they were intentionally trying to protect their children—the ways by which survivors communicated their Holocaust experiences were numerous, and survivors' communication was often a combination of verbal and nonverbal cues. Such cues, constitutive components of shared domestic life, assisted in constructing the affective space of postmemorial structures.

A careful reading of second-generation narratives, represented in both literature and oral histories of children of survivors, reveals the affective contours and content of survivor-family homes and how they contributed to the intergenerational transmission of traumatic knowledge and embodied experience. This chapter establishes the defining features of postmemorial structures, offering an extended analysis of both the "space" and the "stuff" of postmemory—that is, an examination of the spatial and material aspects of these homes that shaped how children of survivors responded to their parents' traumatic pasts as children and as adults. The following discussion of the space and stuff of postmemory is further connected to the second generation's oftentimes nonlinear perceptions of time that are functions of their inherited traumas.

Historical, Cultural, and Literary Discussions of "the Home"

The home, the material and conceptual space where domestic life unfolds, is a basic feature of one's lived experience. The idea of the home as a space of privacy and retreat first emerged in the mid-eighteenth century in France and Britain among bourgeois households, followed by urban middle-class families in the United States in the mid-nineteenth century. Before that, many homes were inhabited not only by family members but also by workers and boarders unrelated to homeowners. This created a host of heterogeneous households that differed from many contemporary configurations of the home as a private space apart from non-kin.[3] For working-class families, it was not until the twentieth century that the home began to resemble what we commonly conceive with the term today.

In contrast to previous, less "homey" conceptions of the domestic sphere,[4] there are a number of positive characteristics and benefits that are common to many, though certainly not all, contemporary homes. In our historical moment, homes are often considered spaces of origins and roots,[5] in addition to spaces of identity formation and psychic self-regulation.[6] They typically function as interior, private spaces that enable personal boundaries, furnish inhabitants with a sense of permanence and continuity, and provide shelter or refuge from the outside world. All this engenders feelings of security, safety, and stability.[7] Variously described as nests, hearths, and even idealized paradises, homes are said to provide their inhabitants a sense of intimacy, control, and belonging. In one's childhood, the home frequently operates as a space of imagination and dreams,[8] and in one's adulthood, the home, depending on how it is designed and decorated, often becomes a reflection of its owner's or owners' tastes, ideas, and values.[9] This is why Carole Després refers to the home as "the most powerful extension of the psyche"[10] and why Mihaly Csikszentmihalyi and Eugene Rochberg-Halton describe the home as "an expanded boundary of the self... that includes a number of past and present relationships."[11] In light of these characteristics, the home is commonly perceived in positive terms for many, a place and space that makes room, so to speak, to develop and reinforce both inhabitants' senses of self and their interpersonal, especially familial, relationships.

Given the fundamental role of the home in identity formation and cultivation, it is unsurprising how prominently representations of homes figure in U.S. literatures, spanning as they do different time periods (the Gilded Age, the modernist era, the postmodern era, etc.), genres (fiction, poetry, nonfiction, drama, etc.), and literary traditions (African American, Asian American, Jewish American, etc.). Some U.S. literature even self-consciously notes the significant role of domestic space in American letters.[12] The vast amount of U.S. literature that centers on representations of and questions relating to "the home" suggests four (not mutually exclusive) categories of ways by which domestic life is typically represented: (1) representations of the home as a positive and crucial institution;[13] (2) ambivalent representations of the home;[14] (3) narrative hauntings of the home;[15] and (4) narrative flights from (and, in some cases, returns to) the home.[16] In regard to second-generation literature, literary representations of survivor-family homes can largely be classified within the second, third, and fourth categories. Some second-generation texts fall within the second category of ambivalent representations of the home (e.g., Lev Raphael's short stories in *Dancing on Tisha B'Av* [1990]) while others fall within the third category as they include narrative hauntings of the home (e.g., Rosenbaum's *The Golems of Gotham* [2002]). Still others align with the fourth category insofar as protagonists take flight from their homes and often return, even if reluctantly (e.g., Elizabeth Rosner's *The Speed of Light* [2001]).

Whatever the category to which they belong, second-generation texts, in line with the broader U.S. canon, present the home as a psychosocial space that often operates as a metaphor for the self or the psyche. Gaston Bachelard popularized the notion of the home as a metaphor for the psyche. Building on Carl Jung's earlier mapping of the psyche onto the home, Bachelard explains that it is sensible to say we read a house or a room, insofar as houses and rooms serve as "psychological diagrams" that inform representations and examinations of intimacy.[17] In his "systematic psychological study of the sites of our intimate lives"—a field of study that he refers to as *topoanalysis*[18]—Bachelard generalizes the home as a "*felicitous space.*"[19] He bases his notion of the home as a psychic/emotional space on a domestic model of bourgeois stability and safety; his investigation into the intimacy of domestic life maintains an idealized conception of the domestic sphere.[20] Bachelard is an important, if not central, theorist of domestic space, in light of how his topoanalytic approach to analyzing homes offers a generative framework that connects domestic space to inhabitants' imaginations, dreams, and psychosocial lives. Yet, despite the usefulness of Bachelard's poetics of space, his theory does not map neatly onto homes marked by great tension, tragedy, or trauma. Mary Douglas does well to highlight this reality that not all homes are as positively conceived as Bachelard presents them when she writes that, although there are those who allege the home stabilizes, deepens, or enriches their personality, "there are as many who will claim that it cripples and stifles."[21] The latter description of the home aligns with how a significant number of children of survivors represent and describe their homes.

According to many within the second generation, survivor-family homes were permeated with a dark, underlying "presence" that emotionally stifled and, in some cases, psychosocially crippled those who lived within. Indeed, postmemorial structures were characterized by great emotional flux, compounded by a sense of impending threat and difficulties circumambient to immigrant and refugee experiences. Many survivor-family homes were imbued, to varying extents, with senses of fear, anxiety, guilt, and shame that were commonly a function of their parents' Holocaust experiences (as well as, in some cases, a result of their parents' earlier traumatic experiences—in Russian and Eastern European shtetls, for instance[22]). Of course, home life in postmemorial structures was by no means entirely negative or damaging, for many such homes were also imbued with affective constellations of joy, intimacy, affection, happiness, and celebration.[23] However, a significant feature of postmemorial structures was the affective transmission of traumatic knowledge and embodied experience, which bleakly colored survivor families' domestic lives.

A topoanalytic approach to postmemorial structures offers a fruitful theoretical model to evaluate the second generation's affective projections onto and inhabitation of their domiciles. More specifically, Bachelard's suggestion that "the house image" becomes "the topography of our intimate being"[24] is applicable, even if complicated, for the children of survivors. Indeed, for many children of survivors, the house image of their postmemorial structures both mirrors and constitutively shapes their intimate, thorny, and traumatized relationships to the Holocaust.

The Space of Postmemory

Consistently reminded of survivors' painful pasts by way of stories and/or nonverbal cues, the second generation inhabited domestic spaces that communicated survivors' traumatic knowledge and embodied experiences throughout their youth. These children imagined what happened to their parents during the Holocaust in and through the space of the home, and the space of their childhood homes thereby became for many a part of these stories of suffering. That is to say, the second generation imagined their parents' experiences through the homes in which they grew up, projecting what they imagined to be their parents' traumatic pasts onto their postmemorial structures. From being forcibly evicted from their homes and being displaced from their countries of birth or residence to being imprisoned in concentration camps, survivors' experiences during the Shoah were filtered through the second generation's experience of their domestic spaces that were then imbued affectively into the space of the home. The stories survivors told—or, in some cases, did not tell—shaped how the second generation perceived and experienced home life, and their homes in turn shaped their parents' stories, creating a reciprocal relationship between traumatic narratives and domestic space. As a result, the second generation's relationships to their affectively charged homes reflect their traumatic relationships to their parents' Holocaust experiences.

Postmemorial structures operated as archives of survivors' experiences during the Shoah. But these domestic spaces not only archived survivors' traumatic pasts; they also traumatized their children. The word *archive* is derived from the Greek *archeion*, meaning a house or a residence.[25] Though an archive often reveals information about a particular subject, as Jessica Lang explains, an archive also "serves to shelter, to hide, and to conceal."[26] In line with the conceptualization of home qua archive, postmemorial structures functioned as archival spaces in which members of the second generation were raised. Yet, as much as postmemorial structures qua archives revealed about survivors and their Holocaust pasts, in line with Lang's suggestion, they simultaneously concealed survivors' Holocaust histories. It was this simultaneous revealing and concealing of survivors' Holocaust histories that assisted in the creation of postmemory, insofar as children of survivors constructed their parents' histories with whatever information they had (or did not have).

Many children of survivors in part learned about their parents' Holocaust experiences from their parents' explicit stories—whether they were fragmented, piecemeal, or more straightforward narratives. Though some survivors were silent, others were markedly and sometimes obsessively[27] insistent upon telling their children about their lives during the Holocaust, effectively forcing their offspring to function, in the words of Yael Danieli, as "a captive audience."[28] Discussing how stories function as the prisms through which individuals understand themselves and the world around them, Robyn Fivush avows that family stories provide "a framework" for self-understanding and "a stage" on which they predicate their lives.[29] Insofar as many understand themselves in relation to and through others' stories, particularly those relating to and told by family members, Fivush's meditations on family stories help shed light on the children of survivors' relationships to their parents' narratives. However, despite how narratives normally "organize event memories into comprehensible chronological and causal sequence of events in the world,"[30] survivors' personal Holocaust histories were not always easily comprehended by the second generation because of their enormous gravity. Due to their traumatic nature, such personal histories commonly defied linear temporality.

Traumatic family Holocaust narratives often overwhelmed and wounded the children who heard them, which darkly colored how the second generation inhabited the space they shared with their parents. Anne Karpf, a British child of survivors and author of *The War After* (1996), explains how she heard family stories about those who were murdered during the Shoah: "Death was alive and present in our home. My parents had a few rescued pre-war photo albums containing group pictures of chillingly merry people. They would point out who was who and how they died. With so few living relatives dead ones had to suffice, so my sister and I heard countless stories about the Jóseks and Jadzias, the Mileks and Natans. They were spoken of vividly, as if they might walk through the door at any moment. But these reminiscences only confirmed the deep caesura in the family's continuity."[31] The discrepancy between the "vividly" narrated stories and the glaring absence of those in said stories ("the Jóseks and Jadzias, the Mileks and Natans") prompted Karpf to imagine her family before and during the

Holocaust. This is because, in order for her to have made sense of this starkly contrasting discrepancy, she had to reconcile (or try to reconcile) presence with absence, along with negotiating attendant questions about life and death at such a young age. Her attempts to reconcile an animated past with a present void speak to the ways by which members of the second generation were forced to imaginatively construct and fill in narrative gaps in family histories. Such attempts also gesture toward how the second generation tried to bridge the temporal chasm between their families' histories and their own lives years later. These endeavors would be demanding for anyone, let alone a child without the emotional capacity or support to navigate such traumatically fraught waters. For Karpf and other children raised in postmemorial structures, the vividness of family narratives, compounded by the sheer number of times they heard them, increased their intensity and affective impact. It thus makes sense why Karpf posits: "The Holocaust was epic, but for us," referring to her and her sister, "*it was also domestic.*"[32] Of course, not all children of survivors were subject to such vivid, fleshed-out narratives that influenced their perceptions of their domestic spaces; some only heard snippets of their parents' narratives.[33] But in either case, children of survivors, who were commonly left to make sense of these overwhelming narratives by themselves, were compelled to imagine their parents' traumatic pasts in and through their homes. Attempting to understand these narratives required significant emotional labor as they imaginatively fleshed out and filled in the details of their parents' Holocaust stories. As these stories implicitly or explicitly bespoke survivors' Holocaust traumas, the second generation struggled to come to terms with these difficult legacies, thereby leading in many cases to the creation and intensification of their postmemories.

Along with hearing survivors' narrated stories, another means by which the second generation became aware of their parents' Holocaust experiences was, ironically, through what their parents did *not* say. Given how many survivors wanted to protect their children from the painful stories of the Holocaust and how their children did not want to upset their parents by asking about the Shoah, both parties commonly participated in what Danieli describes as a "conspiracy of silence."[34] Each recognized that they could neither understand nor alleviate the other's pain.[35] As Dan Bar-On describes the situation, "a sort of 'double wall' forms between the two generations: parents do not tell; children do not ask. Even if one side tries to open a window, they usually confront a wall."[36] Because of this double wall of silence, some within the second generation were not told directly about their parents' Holocaust experiences. However, many within this group explain that they nonetheless knew about the Holocaust for as long as they could remember; despite not always being told explicitly, many within the second generation knew from a young age that *something* happened to their parents "back then."[37]

This *something* was in many ways made known to them by way of their parents' nonverbal cues. Underscoring how not all survivors told their children about their Holocaust experiences *verbally*, Karpf succinctly explains, "There are different ways of talking."[38] Building on the work of Freud and Jean-François Lyotard, Claire Nouvet offers insight into these nonverbal ways of talking by way of affect theory. Nouvet refers to *the inarticulate affect* when discussing what trauma "says" when it "speaks." She suggests, along with Lyotard, that affect ought to be thought of as a "phrase."[39] As survivors' inarticulate affects were communicated to the second generation, such "phrases," though largely inscrutable and enigmatic, pointed to how whatever happened to their parents in the past was serious, immense, and grave. This is to say that whether survivor parents spoke verbally about their experiences, their traumas nevertheless spoke in a palpable way through their nonverbal cues—and many within the second generation could not help but listen.

Many second-generation descriptions of postmemorial structures, those which underscore the affective space of the domestic, suggest that the nonverbal cues of survivors at least initially catalyzed awareness of the Shoah. Some such nonverbal cues included survivors' emotional dispositions, facial expressions, bodily comportments, gestures, behaviors, habits, routines, and auras. In tandem with other contributing factors—such as the aforementioned explicit stories about the Holocaust—survivors' nonverbal cues that bespoke their Holocaust traumas were habituated, and postmemorial structures were thereby charged with energetic intensities that came to define the moods of such homes. Members of the second generation themselves note these moods, as when Naomi Berger describes a "terrible past [that] was hovering over [her] family like a cloud" in her childhood home[40]—or, put differently, a threatening "cloud" of inarticulate affect, to borrow Nouvet's term. Similarly, Karpf describes how, in her childhood, the Holocaust "just seeped into [her family's] home, like some peculiarly mobile fog, and took up residence."[41] Karpf's metaphorical "fog" connects to what Helen Epstein describes as an "extra presence in the air" in her childhood home,[42] an energetic intensity that one of her interviewees also notes: "I never needed to hear words. It was the looks, the vibrations which gave me the feeling I have."[43] Such descriptions show how, for children of survivors, postmemorial structures were haunted, as it were, by survivors' Holocaust pasts—pasts that were both unbounded within the domestic and then communicated affectively to the second generation.[44]

The affective environment of postmemorial structures created the conditions for blurred subjectivities between parent and child, resulting in the second generation's perception of space that was akin to how their traumatized parents experienced space. Describing how survivors' nonverbal cues spoke to their children, Epstein names survivors' affective communication as "wordless osmosis,"[45] a term that implicitly suggests how the ego boundaries between parents and children were permeable. Pushing against, for example, Freud's understanding of the self-contained ego as discrete and individually separate from others,[46] Epstein's idea of wordless osmotic communication is in line with affect theorists' notion that affective transmission is a fundamentally social phenomenon. Providing insight into the permeability of ego boundaries in relation to affect, Teresa Brennan explains that the transmission of affect is always interpersonal in nature and often results in bodily changes. Inasmuch as the transmission of affect can result in brief bodily changes, it can also produce longer lasting bodily changes: "In other words, the transmission of affect, if only for an instant, alters the biochemistry and neurology of the subject. The 'atmosphere' or the environment literally gets into the individual."[47] Brennan's argument that affect is relayed interpersonally, in concert with her idea that the atmosphere can and does enter the individual, fittingly applies to the experience of living within postmemorial structures. Karpf gives voice to this phenomenon as she describes her childhood home: "We [she and her parents] were so undifferentiated, so merged that what one felt, all felt: it was as if we held shares in each other's dejection and delight."[48] Karpf, in concert with the above descriptions of emotional intensities of postmemorial structures, points to the affective space of survivor-family homes that assisted in blurring the distinction between the second generation and their parents. Given how their subjectivities were often confused with their parents', as noted by Karpf and explored in Rosenbaum's "Cattle Car Complex," the transmission of traumatic, inarticulate affect was all the more prevalent than if the distinction between parent and child had been well-defined. As a result of the affective environments of postmemorial structures, children of survivors experienced space, both domestic and beyond, in comparable terms to their traumatized parents.

Yet, postmemorial structures altered not only the second generation's perception of space but also their experience of time. Within their postmemorial structures, the second generation experienced an incongruous experience of time—or, otherwise put, a recurrent, perceived collapse of past and present that created a space of precarious temporality, which typified their domestic lives. As trauma is always an issue of temporality—an issue of a past wound that endures and repeatedly calls out in the present—many children of survivors were taken out of time and struggled with their nonlinear positionality, resulting in a sense of temporal, as well as spatial, disorientation. The second generation's incongruous experience of time—that which extended the past into and perceptually ruptured the present—thickened, so to speak, the second generation's experiences of the here and now with a dual valence of temporal simultaneity. Indeed, the present not uncommonly became impregnated with, captive to, and haunted by the second generation's imagined constructions of their parents' Holocaust pasts. Shedding light on this blurring of temporalities for those impacted by the Holocaust, Eva Hoffman, a child of Holocaust survivors, describes in *After Such Knowledge* (2004) how her fear of atrocity became "unaccountably attached to mundane interactions taking place in ordinary time. The images of humiliation and physical pain repeating in the mind infect or drown out perceptions of the more benign reality of the normal, peacetime world."[49] Indeed, in postmemorial structures, the line between waking life and the dream world was often blurred, where the nightmarish past impinged upon the present and disrupted linear temporal order. Fantastical visions issued forth as members of the second generation attempted to navigate traumatic pasts that were never theirs. Not uncommonly, the temporal confusion and spatial distortion of/within postmemorial structures aided the second generation in imaginatively transforming the domestic (and, to be sure, the extradomestic) into the sites of their postmemories (e.g., hiding places, cattle cars, barracks, camp brothels, gas chambers). Whatever the site of trauma that the children of survivors imagined, their homes became stages to re-enact their inherited traumas and embodied experiences.

These temporal, spatial, and imaginative transformations of their domestic spaces contributed to many being stripped of the fiction that their homes were spaces of safety and protection. Largely a result of their parents having their homes invaded and then being forcibly evicted and uprooted during the Holocaust (or even after the Holocaust in some cases), the second generation not uncommonly shared an anxiety of their own homes being invaded; made real by their parents' experiences, the second generation came to the knowledge that their houses were also subject to potential incursion. This anxiety speaks to how many in the second generation were denied the chance to live in a world of childish idealism in their early years; their anxiety was a result of how they were made aware of the sobering reality that human evil is pervasive and any sense of absolute safety is ultimately chimeric. As "trauma is a piercing or breach of a border that puts inside and outside into a strange communication,"[50] it can be seen how the trauma from *outside* postmemorial structures—that is, how survivors' traumas of being expelled from their homes years earlier and of what happened during the Shoah—found expression *inside* postmemorial structures in the present. Despite the typical conception of homes as spaces of shelter from the outside world, postmemorial structures resisted such traditional associations. That the division of outside and inside was violated for their parents—which thereby stripped their parents of their homes that served as protective barriers—incited anxiety, belatedly, yet recurrently, for the children of survivors. Their homes thus served as constant reminders of vulnerability and threat.

The perception of space, both domestic and otherwise, as "unstable" is indeed a common experience within the second-generation. In *The Aftermath* (1995), Aaron Hass, a child of survivors himself, recounts an interview with another member of the second generation, one whose parents gave him the "international name" Joseph, so that if he had to flee his country at any point, it would be "easily translatable." Joseph's parents also repeatedly pushed him to become a doctor because they believed he could then practice medicine anywhere. He says: "My life has been a preparation for the potential need to uproot myself at a moment's notice. . . . Every day I heard about the Holocaust and I've been getting ready for it to happen again."[51] Connecting this lack of settledness to physical space, Victor J. Seidler, also a member of the second generation, explains in *Shadows of the Shoah* (2000) that he unconsciously believed it was dangerous to care about his surroundings too much because he never knew when he would have to leave. He often felt that space was unstable and still finds it a challenge to invest time or attention into his physical surroundings to make them beautiful. He concludes: "It seems to have something to do with the always temporary quality of existence."[52] Seidler's reticence to decorate his home, a product of his parents' anxiety surrounding the need for transience that he adopts for himself, is an expression of his postmemory, a response to his parents' unsettled and unsettling pasts. This feeling of constantly having to be ready to uproot, of instability, defines not only Seidler's lived experience. It is further discernable in a number of other second-generation testimonials and literary accounts.

This anxiety finds indirect expression in Rosenbaum's abovementioned "Cattle Car Complex." The narrator of the short story describes Adam's adulthood apartment as "voiceless" and "sanitized," a lonesome, not-so-homey residence where he lives by himself. The narrator also describes his apartment as "his very own place in the sky" (a traumatically informed spatial response to his aversion to "tight, confining spaces"?).[53] He spends little time in his apartment and instead devotes long hours to the law firm where he works. The narrator goes on to describe how when Adam returns home each night, he finds a dearth of creaturely company and the buzz of an empty refrigerator, physically and sonically pointing to the spatial and emotional emptiness of his home. Indeed, the barren refrigerator reveals how little stock, literally and figuratively, he invests in his domestic space. Indicative of his need to be transient—to move from place to place and to survive wherever he finds himself—his apartment lacks signs of imbued belonging or rootedness. He is not materially or spatially tied to his apartment; he can escape with much ease—which is in stark contrast to the elevator that traps him like the imagined cattle car at the end of the story—and if he were to escape, he would barely leave a trace of having lived there. The space of his apartment and his perception of it give voice, albeit obliquely, to his inherited traumatic knowledge and embodied experience, similar to other second-generation literary representations of anxiety surrounding the instability of space.[54]

Children of survivors' relationships to the space of their postmemorial structures mirrored their relationships to their parents, but more profoundly, their relationships to the space of their postmemorial structures reflected their belated relationships to the Shoah. Yet, their relationship to the Shoah was not only reflected by their relationship to their domestic spaces; it was also in turn *structured* by their domestic spaces. As their parents' traumas were archived in their postmemorial structures, children of survivors found themselves in domestic spaces that affectively communicated their parents' wounds. Postmemorial structures thus became spaces that contributed to the wounding of members of the second generation in their formative years, in light of how they "inhabited" their parents' spatialized and materialized traumas. For some like Artie in Spiegelman's *Maus I* (1991) who imagines Zyklon B coming out of the showerhead in his childhood home (see chapter 2),[55] survivor-family homes became spaces to re-enact imagined traumas; everyday sites of domestic life were transformed into the sites of their parents' lives during the Shoah, which reinforced their inherited traumas when they performed quotidian tasks like, for instance, showering. For others like Zosha in Pilcer's *The Holocaust Kid*, who consistently attempts to leave her childhood home (see chapter 3),[56] and Paula in Rosner's *The Speed of Light* (see chapter 4), who spends much of her time outside the house, survivor-family homes were places from which to escape because of the stifling atmosphere created within. In either case, postmemorial structures psychologically domesticated members of the second generation and (re)inscribed survivors' traumas. Thus, when members of the second generation represent and describe their homes, they also indirectly represent and describe their postmemorial relationships to the Holocaust.

The Stuff of Postmemory

Survivors' traumas defined not only the space of postmemorial structures but also the stuff contained therein. As postmemorial structures served as spatial containers and amplifiers of postmemory, they housed belongings that also gave voice to survivors' Holocaust pasts. In some cases, these belongings (photographs, legal documents, books, religious objects, clothing, items that were smuggled into or procured in camps, and so on)[57]—were testimonial in light of how they came directly from concentration camps or other sites of Holocaust memory. As Oren B. Stier rightly explains, such physical artifacts powerfully signify the Holocaust because they embody and testify to victims' "authentic experience."[58] Such testimonial belongings became, as Victoria Aarons helpfully suggests, proof of pre-Shoah Jewish and family life, as well as containers of bygone worlds and imagined narratives that represented "both presence and absence,"[59] as exemplified by Karpf's photo albums referenced above. These belongings, or talismans—imbued with "the affective weight of the past"—held the potential for members of the second generation to feel closer to those who were murdered.[60] In other cases, belongings housed within postmemorial structures were not overtly related to the Holocaust, as they were oftentimes purchased *after* the Shoah, but they nonetheless held the potential to engender postmemories. Regardless of their origin and their direct or indirect relationship to the Holocaust, a number of household belongings gave children of survivors insight, or at least an entry point, into their parents' Holocaust experiences.

Both of these above-described groups of belongings—those overtly related and those inadvertently related to the Holocaust—"connected" the children of survivors to their parents' Holocaust pasts. Such belongings qua tools or, à la Hirsch, *technologies*[61] were defined by their ever-incomplete ability to "connect" the second generation to their parents' traumatic pasts. In lieu of hearing stories about the Shoah, or to accompany the stories that they did hear, the second generation sought to find out more about their parents' lives during the Holocaust through these material mediators.[62] Both groups of belongings, or things, communicated survivors' traumas and embodied experiences from the Shoah to the second generation, albeit in transformed, distorted, and modified ways. The second generation's relationship to their parents' things names not only a subject-object relation as described by Bill Brown but also a subject-subject relationship between parent and child.[63] For many children of survivors, the power of things within the home issued forth from their relationship with their parents that they in turn projected onto such things. Household things often possessed "a metaphysical dimension," as if they were imbued with a sense of Holocaust "reality" that blurred the line between past and present, between unconscious and conscious, and between the fantastical and reality.[64] These things not uncommonly became one of the means by which the second generation tried to come to terms with their postmemories.

These things ironically also more firmly bound them to their inherited traumas, given how they were overloaded with postmemorial meaning. The second generation's interactions with such things often reinscribed the very anxieties and postmemories that they sought to eschew, insofar as these things directly and indirectly bespoke Holocaust-related absence, death, and destruction. Though they often interacted with these things in order to come to terms with their parents' Holocaust traumas, such things qua mediators often revivified the second generation's sense of loss that stemmed from the Shoah. Indeed, household belongings had the power to exacerbate the circulation of negative and traumatic affects. As a result, these things mirrored the precarious and paradoxical condition of growing up with survivors: as much as they were tied to their parents' memories of the Holocaust, they were also emphatically distant from such memories.[65]

Both the former group of belongings (those related directly to the Holocaust) and the latter (those not directly related), although functioning differently in their transmission of trauma and embodied knowledge, constitute what I term *postmemorial things*. As noted above, there is a qualitative difference between items that were found *during* the Holocaust (e.g., in a concentration camp in Poland) and those that were purchased *after* the Holocaust (e.g., in a department store in the United States). There was a tendency to view items that came from concentration camps or sites of atrocity as precious or even sacred,[66] whereas items that were purchased after the Shoah—though imbued with meaning, to be sure—were not viewed (and were therefore not treated) in the same way. The ways the second generation consciously (and unconsciously) perceived these two overarching categories of things differed, at minimum, affectively, contextually, and symbolically. For instance, how one perceived a striped uniform from Auschwitz versus how one perceived a three-piece suit from Macy's varied significantly. Despite how these things are both items of clothing, they of course are not isomorphic. Nonetheless, both things held the potential to contribute to the creation and amplification of postmemory. As a camp uniform's direct relationship to the Shoah would have offered a more straightforward material, archival "connection" to the Holocaust, a survivor's three-piece suit bought after the Holocaust (especially one that was clean and well pressed) may have also gestured toward the Holocaust *via negativa* and thus functioned as a postmemorial thing in a more figurative sense. This is because many survivors' immaculate appearances after the Shoah were sartorial responses to their overwhelming physical degradation, befoulment, or, in the words of Terrence Des Pres, "excremental assault."[67] Although the camp uniform more directly represents survivors' ruptured lives, the three-piece suit, which symbolizes a markedly improved quality of life post-1945, obliquely bespeaks Holocaust trauma. In either case—whether these postmemorial things were more testimonial or more figurative—each of these categories of things shared the capacity to create and contribute to one's postmemories, even if differently and to varying degrees.

Though analyses of the first group of postmemorial things contained within survivor-family homes appear in subsequent chapters, I focus more so on the second group: postmemorial things that do not have an overt or direct relationship to the Shoah. Studies of the first group of things have been explored in-depth, notably by Aarons[68] and Fischer,[69] whereas the second group of postmemorial things have not. Fischer explains that the first group of things provide guidance for descendants who seek both physical and metaphorical journeys into their families' pasts.[70] Aarons, in her insightful study of things directly relating to the Shoah, explains how such things "provide traces of past lives and stories, but they are just that: traces, hints, projected fantasies, their shapes altered to accommodate the requirements of those who come too late. To be sure, such 'texts' tend to be overinterpreted and thus their original meaning and function largely eclipsed."[71] Hirsch, as noted earlier, also discusses postmemorial things, specifically the relationship between postmemory and photography.[72] I, however, attend more so to the second group of postmemorial things in order to expand the conversation surrounding the relationship between the second generation, material culture, and postmemory (see chapters 3 and 4).

Conclusion

Survivor-family homes operated as material and affective repositories of Holocaust traumas, memories, and stories—storehouses of the past that surrounded and, in many ways, overwhelmed many children of survivors. The second generation carried and continues to carry into their adulthoods a number of anxieties and fears from their childhoods that were functions of their parents' experiences in camps, in ghettos, in hiding, or of escaping the Third Reich about which they learned at home. As a result, many of their adulthood homes have also functioned as postmemorial structures; that is, their adulthood homes have further mediated and reverberated the domesticating traumas that they inherited in their childhoods, though oftentimes to a lesser, but still significant, degree. And as the second generation's childhood postmemorial structures framed their adulthood postmemorial structures, so too did their postmemorial structures shape how they experience the physical world beyond the home.

2

"Remember, my house it's also your house too"

Postmemorial Structures in Art Spiegelman's *Maus*

A prolific artist, author, cultural critic, and editor, Art Spiegelman is one of the most globally eminent graphic-narrative creators.[1] Born in 1948 in Sweden, Spiegelman moved to New York City as a young child where he was raised by parents who survived the Holocaust and where he lives as of this writing.[2] Spiegelman is the author of three collected works, including *Breakdowns* (published first in 1977, later reissued in 2008), *The Complete Maus* (1996), and *In the Shadow of No Towers* (2004). But *Maus* is certainly his most widely read, has had the largest impact on other comics creators, was what won him a special 1992 Pulitzer Prize (among other awards), and is no doubt the best-known piece of literature written by a child of survivors. Spiegelman's most famous graphic narrative—and work of oral history—presents one of the first literary representations,[3] if not *the* first, that elucidates in detail how survivor-family homes operate(d) as postmemorial structures. *Maus* is comprised of both *Maus I: A Survivor's Tale: My Father Bleeds History* (1986) and *Maus II: A Survivor's Tale: And Here

My Troubles Began (1991)—parts of which appeared earlier in the alternative comics *RAW* and *Short Order Comix #1*—in addition to other shorter comics (or, to use Spiegelman's term, "commix") like the original three-page precursor "Maus" (1972) first published in *Funny Aminals* [*sic*]. *Maus* depicts protagonist Artie's[4] childhood and adulthood homes—domestic spaces that are affectively imbued with the traumatic pasts of his parents, Vladek and Anja Spiegelman, who both survived the Shoah. Though the pasts of Vladek and Anja are no doubt uninhabitable, Artie nonetheless imaginatively "inhabits" the traumatic stories of his parents in and through his various domestic spaces in New York.

The influence of Spiegelman and his work, specifically *Maus*, is far reaching, and there is a vast amount of scholarship on his graphic narrative. *Maus* has indelibly influenced the fields of Holocaust studies, memory studies, narratology, and auto/biography studies[5] while also foundationally shaping second-generation studies.[6] In the numerous scholarly treatments of *Maus*, one of the most consistent avenues of analysis is that of postmemory. In this scholarship, however, postmemory has never been anchored in or connected to any sustained exploration of survivor-family homes. Although the text's presentation of space—specifically its formal use of space as an artistic consideration—is not new in the scholarship surrounding *Maus*, the subjects of domestic space as metaphor for Artie's psyche and of domestic space as a significant contributing factor in the production of postmemory have not yet been broached. To address these lacunae, this chapter presents a detailed exploration of postmemorial structures as represented in *Maus I* and *II* and other related texts, examining how the space of such domiciles underwrites the intensification of the intergenerational transmission of traumatic knowledge and embodied experience.

In line with how, as Mihaly Csikszentmihalyi and Eugene Rochberg-Halton explain, the home is "the most powerful extension of the psyche,"[7] Artie's postmemorial structures operate as spaces that shape and are shaped by his parents' traumas and experiences in the Shoah. The Spiegelman-family home offers readers a generative topoanalytic entry point into Artie's postmemories, such that his childhood domicile functions as a "text" that reveals his affective connection to his parents' traumas and experiences during the Shoah. As he projects what he imagines to be his parents' Holocaust experiences onto his family's domestic space, his childhood home in turn functions as a site of postmemorial traumatization for Artie, including when he moves back home as an adult. A topoanalytic examination of Artie's adulthood apartment moreover reveals how his domestic space similarly maps, mirrors, and mediates his imaginative connection to the Shoah. Indeed, his adulthood apartment becomes a postmemorial recapitulation of his childhood home. In light of how the home often operates as a sign of the individual who dwells within,[8] *Maus* presents Artie's postmemorial structures not only as fitting metaphors for Artie's psyche but also as integral actants in the production and relay of traumatic knowledge and embodied experience. Overall, this chapter argues that Artie's childhood home serves as a foundational and paradigmatic postmemorial structure that shapes his metaphysical perception of space and time in his childhood and adulthood domestic spaces, demonstrating the foundational power of survivor-family homes in framing and reproducing the inherited traumas of the second generation.

Artie's Childhood Home

The prologue of *Maus I* establishes the affective climate of Artie's Rego Park childhood home that creates the conditions for the intergenerational transmission of trauma from parent to child. Spiegelman himself sheds light on how this first scene sets up the ways by which Artie's childhood (along with his adulthood) is molded by the recurrent intrusion of his parents' Holocaust traumas into the present. He describes how the prologue thematically functions "as a fractal of the whole book. It seemed that positing this sort of normal childhood moment with a chilling shadow cast over it was an appropriate lead-in."[9] In this opening scene, Artie trips while roller-skating with friends—friends who represent the social world writ large and who, like Vladek's social contacts during the Holocaust, are revealed to be untrustworthy. He then returns home, whimpering, and approaches Vladek who asks him to assist with some woodwork. He explains what his friends did, to which Vladek responds: "Friends? Your friends? . . . If you lock them together in a room with no food for a week . . . *then* you could see what it is, friends!"[10] Vladek's request for Artie to hold a plank of wood, to aid him with his *physical* woodwork, serves as a platform for him to implicate his son into assisting him with the *emotional* work of listening to him talk about his traumatic past. His physical labor parallels his emotional labor, illustrating how quotidian tasks and everyday events in the Spiegelman-family home consistently become vehicles for Vladek to talk about his Holocaust wounds and for Artie to assume such lingering traumas secondhandedly—like, for instance, when later in the narrative Vladek guilts Artie for accidentally dropping ashes on the carpet after he tells him how difficult it was to clean a horse stable under Nazi supervision.[11] Vladek's repeated references to the Holocaust documented in *Maus*, like the reference to being locked in a room with no food with friends, elucidate why Artie would later say that no matter what he accomplishes, "it doesn't seem like much compared to surviving Auschwitz."[12] Indeed, as Vladek disregards his son's pain and forces him into acting as his interlocutor—one who must listen to his stories from his dark past—the prologue sets up for readers how Artie functions as a sounding board for his father, whose pain is minimized in comparison to Vladek's and who must continually confront his father's horrific past throughout his youth (and into his adulthood).

The prologue further establishes how Artie relates to his postmemorial structure and how his relationship to his childhood home reflects his belated relationship to the Shoah. Though we do not actually see him departing from the house in the first two panels of the prologue, it is clear that he has recently left home and is heading elsewhere. His domestic departure in this scene functions as more than just Artie leaving to play with his friends. In truth, he may be trying to avoid helping his father with his woodwork, but his departure also reads as him escaping his house, his parents, and their traumas. However, as he must return home after his roller-skating accident, he must also confront the postmemories that his home both symbolizes and sustains; although escape from his postmemorial structure and his parents' traumas is desired as the rest of the text makes clear, he is woefully resigned (as represented by his tearful homecoming) to return to and confront both. As he approaches his father fixing something in front of the house, the text visually connects Vladek-as-builder to the building behind him. Such a connection codes the Spiegelman-family home in terms of Vladek's "construction"—or, more accurately, re-construction—of his Holocaust past, particularly in light of how he recounts his memory of hunger and imprisonment during the Holocaust in this scene. With Vladek's speech bubbles overlaying the façade of the home in these frames, the content of these speech bubbles colors how we are to "read" the Spiegelmans' domicile; insofar as the survivor's speech bubbles cover the home, their home is covered, as it were, in stories of the Shoah. The scene concludes with Artie's postmemorial structure—that which is defined by and imbued with his parents' Holocaust pasts—in the bottom frame looming large behind father and son. The size of the postmemorial structure in comparison to Artie suggests the enormity of how he must confront his parents' Holocaust traumas within—and, as is made clear, in front of—their home. By closing the prologue with the image of little Artie and Vladek in front of the large Spiegelman-family home in a frame that is twice the size of the other panels on the page, the text emphasizes the sizable role of Artie's postmemorial structure in the transmission of trauma and embodied knowledge from parent to child.

The 1972 "Maus" comic offers a portrait of Artie listening to Vladek's Holocaust stories, this time inside the home, but in this comic, Artie positions himself in such stories, which frames how he experiences his domestic space growing up. Artie—referred to in the 1972 comic as Mickey (a nod to the American icon Mickey Mouse)—lies in the safety of his father's lap before bed, listening to him recount stories from the Holocaust.[13] The way in which the narration of the past in the 1972 comic is structured—with Vladek's words not contained within the actual frame, that is, with his narration situated above and below the drawings themselves—demonstrates how although his father's stories buttress and largely inform Mickey's/Artie's imagination, it is *Mickey/Artie* who reconstructs his father's stories (and he does so imaginatively), which thereby creates room for him to adopt such imagined memories as his own. Clearly, the separation of his father's narration and the images themselves indicate, on one level, a temporal division between Vladek's retrospective recounting of the events and the events themselves. But the structuring of the narration in this bedroom scene holds additional implications. That his father's narration is outside of, though nonetheless connected to, the events/images that Mickey/Artie imagines affords him the space, so to speak, to position himself within his imaginative reconstructions of such stories.

Indeed, despite how the "M" on the mice's armbands likely stands for "Maus," the "M" moreover signifies "Mickey" in this imaginative reconstruction, illustrating how Mickey/Artie inventively places himself in the shoes of those who went through the Holocaust. His father even says to him: "Children like you still played in the streets sometimes. They played *funerals* and they played *gravedigger*!"[14] The comparison he draws between the children of the ghetto and his son serves as an invitation for Mickey/Artie to place himself in his bedtime story specifically and in the narrative of the Holocaust more broadly, which Mickey/Artie does as he imagines a small child playing gravedigger who strikingly resembles the Mickey/Artie we see in bed. Such an imagistic double for Mickey/Artie reveals how he figures himself into his father's stories that give voice—and, as it were, give *image*—to his postmemories.

As the stories he hears aid in laying the groundwork for his postmemories, his childhood home assumes the affective quality of what another member of the second generation refers to as a "concentration camp of the mind,"[15] thereby rendering the domestic a space that continually sustains the affective states of anxiety and fear for young Mickey/Artie. Contrasting how the 1972 "Maus" comic depicts Vladek offering a detailed story to Mickey/Artie, Spiegelman-as-author describes how, typically, his "parents didn't talk in any coherent or comprehensive way about what they had lived through. It was always a given that they have lived through 'the War,' which was their term for the Holocaust."[16] He goes on to explain that he was made aware of his parents' experiences largely "from passing references in [their] home."[17] Such indirect allusions to the Holocaust, which he also refers to as "free-floating shards of anecdote,"[18] in addition to the actual stories his parents told him,[19] contributed to his knowledge of and inherited trauma from the Holocaust. Moreover, particular household belongings—that is, postmemorial things qua mediators—in the family home offered Spiegelman visual/material connections to the Shoah. He explains how some of the books and pamphlets published in Polish and Yiddish that he found in his parents' den first alerted him to the fact that "something enormous and devastating had hit [his] family."[20] The presence of these postmemorial things—a presence that ironically spoke of profound absence—further assisted in the imaginative transformation of his home into a site of Holocaust trauma.

Artie, who parallels Spiegelman-as-author, explains how he imaginatively transforms his home into Auschwitz—a function of him grappling with his inherited traumas. He describes his childhood home to Françoise, his wife: "When I was a kid I used to think about which of my parents I'd let the Nazis take to the ovens if I could only save one of them."[21] This description uncovers how, in his childhood, his domicile stands as the imagined setting of a *Selektion* in a reversed *Sophie's Choice* scenario, a point which Daniel R. Schwartz also notes;[22] the home imaginatively becomes the concentration camp that traumatically defined his parents' lives and the site of atrocity where he belatedly deliberates over matters of life and death. This imagined deliberation—that which would have taken place at one of the ramps of Auschwitz—leads to the transformation of his bathroom into a gas chamber, where victims were sent after *Selektion*: "Don't get me wrong. I wasn't obsessed with this stuff.... It's just that sometimes I'd fantasize Zyklon B coming out of our shower instead of water."[23] Here, it seems as if Artie doth protest too much given how his childhood preoccupation with the Holocaust appears *quite* obsessive; he explains the ways by which his imagination collapses the past and the present and thereby transmutes the space of the home into a fantastical gas chamber. Such moments reveal how Artie's childhood home both catalyzes and exacerbates the intergenerational transmission of trauma. Akin to how Vladek turns everyday moments into occasions to talk about the Shoah, so too do daily commonplace activities like showering engender thoughts of the Holocaust, along with attendant postmemorial anxieties. The affective space that Artie occupies, a space where he is in close proximity to and in recurrent contact with his parents, indeed intensifies the intergenerational transference of trauma.

Living in His Childhood Home as an Adult

His conflicted relationship to his parents and their Holocaust pasts finds additional expression in the brief, four-page interlude "Hell Planet," wherein the text illustrates how, even as an adult, Artie struggles with the domesticating effects/affects of living with his mother and father in Rego Park. Of course, Artie is the one who agrees to return to his childhood home and live with his parents after his time in a state psychiatric hospital.[24] But as an adult, he is unable to move outside the emotional and psychological containment of the postmemories that his childhood home symbolizes and sustains. Examining Spiegelman-as-author's relationship to his parents' home and what eventually drove him to the psychiatric hospital, Michael Levine explains that in Spiegelman's essay "Mad Youth" (1992),

> Spiegelman describes the Rego Park house in which he grew up as a "two-family brick pillbox" (*Comix* 21). While the pun on "pillbox" depicts the family residence as a place where drugs and the trauma of "The War" cohabited, this same house is figured elsewhere as a suffocating womb. "What happened to me the winter I flipped out was that I had gotten the bends; I had surfaced too quickly from the overheated bunker of my traumatized family... into the heady atmosphere of freedom" (*Comix* 23). Not only is the

"pillbox" now an "overheated bunker," but Spiegelman's emergence from the oceanic depths of this home is a birth trauma inseparable from the trauma of his mother's death.[25]

Levine's discussion of the home qua womb points to the foundational role of the Spiegelman-family home in the formation of Artie's traumatized psyche—a point to which I will return in detail momentarily. But what is of immediate significance here is how Spiegelman describes his parents' home as an "overheated bunker." This description reveals, at least in part, how he conceives of his childhood home: a space of postmemorial enclosure. To describe his home, Spiegelman employs numerous metaphors throughout his body of work—many of which include sites of Holocaust trauma. Indeed, this description of domicile-as-bunker (a space of confinement and hiding), which Spiegelman describes elsewhere as "claustrophobic,"[26] connects to the other Holocaust comparisons throughout *Maus*: home-as-concentration-camp (a space of containment and enslavement) and home-as-gas-chamber (a terminal space with no escape).

Presenting Artie's childhood home as a concentration camp/prison, "Hell Planet" offers the story of Artie recollecting his mother's suicide as it relates to his inherited trauma. Prior to Anja's suicide, we see Artie as an adult wearing either a concentration camp or a prison uniform (though it is unclear which, and such ambiguity allows for a both/and reading of his clothing).[27] However, at this point, we do not yet see his home represented as a prison. It is not until he recounts his last interaction with Anja before her suicide that his bedroom transforms into a metaphorical prison-like mise-en-scène. Her suicide, overwhelming him with a large measure of guilt, is also the catalyst that intensifies his already obsessive preoccupation with death and his parents' experiences during the Shoah. But Anja's death is not that which figuratively incarcerates him in the first place. Rather, we see her reading to him in a concentration camp/prisoner uniform as a child,[28] signaling how his trauma finds its genesis much earlier in his childhood. Since Artie's childhood home serves as a spatialization of his traumas, cognition, and emotions, *Maus*'s representation of the Spiegelman-family home points to the domesticating—or, more appropriately in the context of "Hell Planet," the *imprisoning*—effects/affects of living in his childhood postmemorial structure as an adult.

"Hell Planet" offers a developed portrait of Anja's psychosocial imprisonment of Artie through the off-kilter photograph of him and his mother,[29] which is suggestive of the affective environment of Artie's childhood postmemorial structure. The body language of young Artie and his mother in the photograph taken at Trojan Lake, New York, at the start of the spliced-in comic points to the connection he has with her—a connection that Marianne Hirsch refers to in a different context as "a self-in-relation."[30] Spiegelman's choice to include *this* photo, with Anja physically touching him as a young boy, announces at the beginning of the comic how he is constitutively a product of both his childhood and his relationship to his mother. Yet, her hand atop his head does not simply signal a benign connection between mother and son, especially given the tilted orientation of the photo that gestures toward a destabilized relationship. The placement of her hand on his head "might be seen as a protective/repressive gesture,"[31] containing what Spiegelman refers to in regard to another photo as "some subtext,"[32] insofar as it points to his mother's cognitive control that (over)shadows his psyche. Spiegelman-as-author offers insight into his understanding of the photo of him and his mother, explaining:

> I thought that this image both had the innocence of childhood with my five-foot tall mother as a large figure with me kneeling next to her, but showed her hand on my head with a certain kind of body language that said: "Stay small, my boy. Don't grow up." If I try to understand what happened, part of her suicide had to do with feeling unmoored as I was breaking away from the nuclear family. Keeping a hand on a head is both a maternal gesture, but also a pushing down when somebody's trying to get up. It evokes my childhood in an economical way that has something in common with the two-page prologue to *Maus*.[33]

His personal reading of the "subtext" sheds light on the multiple ways by which the photo operates in "Hell Planet," but the placement of Anja's hand further illustrates her psychosocial power over her son's impressionable mind. As Anja and Artie's body language represent how she passes along her traumatic knowledge to her son through her contiguity to him, the photo reinforces how Artie is stunted psychosocially in an infantilized state of postmemorial struggle in the shadow of his mother. Of course, throughout the rest of the text Artie is depicted "in infantile attitudes and postures [of] petulance, anger, sulkiness, self-pity."[34] But the photo of him and Anja at the beginning of "Hell Planet"—given his childish deportment and her position of dominance—serves as the very lens through which we read the entirety of "Hell Planet." This photo casts Artie as one whose existence is defined by his relationship to the past, his relationship to his mother, and, by extension, her experiences during the Holocaust.

This photo, moreover, sheds light on Anja and Artie's interaction in his bedroom before her suicide—a scene which speaks to Anja's overwhelming influence on Artie's psychosocial domestication. The exaggerated body shapes and distorted representation of space, both domestic and extra-domestic, reveal how Artie becomes increasingly unstable after Anja dies. But such spatial embellishment and manipulation can further be seen in the frames that depict Anja *before* her suicide, demonstrating how living with his emotionally dependent and traumatized mother results in a distorted perception of reality while she is alive.[35] Anja's exaggerated size, which Hamida Bosmajian also notes,[36] as she enters Artie's room—starkly larger than the small, hunched-over Artie—almost filling the entire door frame both vertically and laterally, along with the size of her abnormally large hands, speaks to her immense, overbearing presence in the home, as well as her lingering presence after her death.

Indeed, insofar as the Spiegelman-family home stands as a postmemorial structure that symbolizes Artie's psyche, Anja's entrance into his bedroom—his most private space—reads as a psychological intrusion that mirrors her trespass into his private thoughts and emotions. Her looming presence as she inches closer and closer to him, dramatically illustrated as she kneels behind her son in the center middle frame, does not appear to be a new phenomenon for Artie, for he angrily turns from her after she invades his (psychosocial) space.[37] As he turns his back, both literally and figuratively,[38] he attempts to wall himself off from her domesticating presence, distancing himself in an act of emotional and psychological self-protection. Yet, his clothing, in tandem with how he describes being resentful for how she "tightened the umbilical cord,"[39] speaks to the seeming impossibility of completely separating himself from his mother's controlling influence. Levine explains how the strangulating umbilical cord, "introduced significantly in the penultimate moment before the mother's suicide, seems to function here less like a nurturing lifeline than a tightening hangman's noose."[40] The metaphor of Artie's biological connection to Anja (the umbilical cord) gestures toward how his mother continues to "feed" him her death-dealing trauma (epigenetically?). This bodily metaphor works in concert with his sartorial connection (the prisoner garb) to her, suggesting that he is symbolically a prisoner to the past like his mother, in light of how he "wears" clothing representing her past. Artie's attempt to wall himself off proves futile because the moment Anja exits the room, his guilt becomes evident again, leaving him alone to sort through his competing, ambivalent feelings toward her.

With Anja's closing of his bedroom door, ushering in the arresting transformation of his bedroom into an imagined prison,[41] the text reveals how Artie finds himself isolated and locked inside the prison of his postmemories that he must navigate by himself. Even though Artie attempts to separate himself from his mother, it is *Anja* who closes the bedroom door, the door to his "cell," thereby demonstrating the central role that she plays in incarcerating him in the postmemorial structure that she and her husband, albeit unintentionally, created. Indeed, his postmemories of the Holocaust and his conflicted response to her death converge in the top center frame on the last page of "Hell Planet," which Victoria Elmwood refers to as "a single, very cramped . . . square, suggesting the cramped, stifling 'headspace' in which this emotional struggle takes place."[42] Also discussing this "headspace," Hillary Chute explains that "Spiegelman obsessively layers several temporalities in one tiny frame, understood by the conventions of the comics medium to represent one moment in time."[43] The different drawing style of this top center "headspace" frame contains the bolded and capitalized phrases "**MENOPAUSAL DEPRESSION**," "**HITLER DID IT**," "**MOMMY**," and "**BITCH**,"[44] which distinguishes this frame from the others on the page; this crowded, cluttered, and disordered frame with its multiple temporalities gives both voice and image to Artie's troubled mental state.

However, insofar as this top center "headspace" frame represents Artie's psyche, so too do the frames that follow function as cognitive "spaces" that reveal the imagined collapse of past and present, reinforcing the notion that his bedroom operates as a postmemorial prison cell. The repeated shading of his bedroom walls, like the shading of the living room walls,[45] in a pattern that resembles thin prison bars—visual precursors to the prison bars we see in the last three frames of "Hell Planet"—again points to how Artie's postmemorial structure assists in incarcerating him. Such imagery represents the destabilization of both time and space in his parents' home. This destabilization is underscored by the comics medium itself. "In a medium where time and space *merge* so *completely*," Scott McCloud explains, "the distinction often *vanishes*," and both time and space are thus "*one and the same*."[46] This is not to say that there is *no* distinction between time and space in Artie's childhood postmemorial structure (nor is McCloud claiming that time and space are isomorphic, as spacetime theorists like Einstein are wont to posit). But there *is* a perceived collapse of time that throws into chaos a clear distinction between the there/then of the past and the here/now of the present for Artie.

This confused temporal division finds further expression through the image of the disembodied slit wrist on the last page of "Hell Planet." As Artie calls to Anja after her death, he accuses his deceased mother of murdering him[47] and announces how her emotional grip on him, compounded by her suicide, circumscribes his entire existence. This notion of his mother murdering him is reinforced in the top center frame of the last page of "Hell Planet," where we see a hand slitting a wrist;[48] it appears that Anja is slitting her own wrist in the bathroom, but by virtue of these hands/arms being disembodied, this image also operates as a depiction of Anja slitting *Artie's* wrist. Such a reading opens up multiple interpretations of whose wrist is being slit, thus speaking to the intergenerational transference of trauma and the knowledge that led to Artie's metaphorical death. Artie fights to keep his emotions and memories straight, as he struggles to ascertain *where* he is, *when* he is, and ultimately *who* he is, as the distinction between his historical moment and the defining historical moments of his parents' pasts is muddied. This image of the disembodied slit wrist therefore gestures toward Artie's struggle to separate his own subjectivity from the subjectivities of his progenitors, particularly in the space of the Spiegelman-family home.

Immediately after Anja's death, Vladek forces Artie to console him, obliging him to parent his parent and thereby function as his father's comforter—an additional indirect reminder of his father's Holocaust past. That Artie must occupy this parental role is not surprising, for it is quite common for members of the second generation to find themselves in such a position. For example, in Helen Epstein's *Children of the Holocaust* (1979), one child of survivors describes her relationship with her parents: "It was not as if they were the parents and we were the children. We became the parents sometimes and I didn't like that. I would throw tantrums and rebel against the idea of protecting them.... We often try to protect each other, even now.... We're always trying to shield each other from pain."[49] Similarly, as Vladek clings to his son and as he makes Artie sleep on the ground with him,[50] along with when he cleaves to Artie upon his arrival home,[51] the role reversal between father and son becomes painfully clear. Yet, the position Artie is in when he first greets his mourning father—that is, his stooped-down posture on one knee with his gaze directed straight into the eyes of the reader—is an imagistic citation of the position Artie assumes when looking directly into the camera in the 1968 photograph of him and his mother at Trojan Lake. This postural connection between childhood Artie and adulthood Artie speaks to the precarious roles he is expected to adopt: that of Vladek and Anja's son and, simultaneously, that of their comforter/consoler (exemplified by how he must both embrace his father and also offer his mother confirmation of his love[52]). Such an impossible dual role—of being simultaneously their child and their proxy parent—that Artie feels he must assume is one of the many ways he is reminded of his troubled relationship with his parents that is shaped by and in large part a result of the Shoah. This troubled relationship repeatedly compels him to confront and negotiate palpable "emanations"[53] of firsthand Holocaust memories that were never actually his but nonetheless wounded him as if they were.

Even without Anja present, the Spiegelman-family home functions as a womb-like space—a space that continues to assist in passing along her and Vladek's Holocaust traumas. The idea of domicile qua womb relates to the numerous biological metaphors used by children of survivors to conceptualize the intergenerational transmission of trauma within their families like Artie's reference to the umbilical cord in "Hell Planet" noted above; as Artie and the second generation developed in their mother's wombs—and, as research suggests, they inherited trauma epigenetically—they later grew up in their postmemorial structures that aided in the transmission of intergenerational trauma. Despite how children of survivors surely received (emotional) sustenance and were nurtured both in their mothers' wombs and in their postmemorial structures, their experiences in both were *also* often defined by loss and traumatic transmission. Although the womb and the home are ideally spaces of comfort, safety, and shelter, the second generation's experiences of both not uncommonly resisted idealization. The traumatic breach of the protective womb at birth mapped onto how the second generation, as represented by Artie, perceived their childhood homes through the stories of their parents' homes being breached. As Holocaust traumas expressed themselves biologically in/through the womb, survivors' traumas also found expression in/through their womb-like postmemorial structures.

Artie's diligent search for his mother in her death operates not only as a belated effort to reconnect with her—one whom he tried to (or had to?) keep at an emotional distance for much of his life—but also as an effort to feel at home even and especially as an adult. Dominick LaCapra, in agreement with Hirsch,[54] views Artie's central concern as the retrieval of Anja's story: "Anja seems to become a phantasmic archive that Artie hopes will provide him with a point of entry into the elusive, seemingly redemptive past that he tries to recapture. Indeed, at times she seems to *be* her lost papers, and when they are destroyed, she almost shares their fate."[55] Artie's emphatic preoccupation with his mother's story that he seeks to hear through his father's mouth operates in connection to the Oedipal conflict to which a number of scholars point.[56] His wish to better understand and imaginatively inhabit Anja's story gives voice to his desire to secure a fundamental sense of safety, security, and comfort of the maternal brand that he was unable to feel fully both as a child and as an adult. But in order to move forward and find a sense of at-home-ness, Artie must first go backward to "find" his mother and her traumas from the Shoah. Freud suggests that "the dwelling-house was a substitute for the mother's womb, the first lodging, for which in all likelihood man still longs, and in which he was safe and felt at ease."[57] The mother, as Yi-Fu Tuan further explains, "is the child's primary place" whose image "is one of stability and permanence."[58] However, in the context of *Maus*, Anja is not depicted as one who stands for "stability and permanence," nor did the Spiegelman-family home fully function as a space that felt fully "safe" or allowed Artie to be "at ease." The graphic narrative thus asks: What happens when the supposedly comforting world of the maternal womb, both figurative and literal, is itself traumatized by the experiences of the Shoah? Though the link between mother and home is something of a potentially problematic or controversial idea—and is by no means universal—this connection holds great currency when considering Artie's psyche. Artie's search for Anja speaks to Freud's notion of mother as metaphor for home, that is, of the womb as the first domestic space; however, Artie's search requires that he sort out—and come to terms with—the fears and anxieties that so pervaded his domestic existence for much of his life in hopes of reclaiming a sense of home for himself. His search for his mother is thus a search for home, and his search for home—for a sense of at-home-ness and all its comforting attributes—is indeed a search for his mother. Although Artie desires to free himself from the domesticating control of his parents' traumas as a child and as a young adult, his search for his mother after her death also functions as an attempt to free himself from her (and Vladek's) traumatic legacy.

Artie is resigned to search for Anja's stories through the mouth of his father largely in the Spiegelman-family home—an experience that further underscores his belated relationship to the Shoah. As he speaks to Vladek about wanting to record his account of the Holocaust, he takes a seat in his childhood bedroom while his father begins to pedal on his exercise bicycle.[59] Here, Vladek cycles while he recycles his stories from the Holocaust. Although Vladek works out on his exercise bicycle and narrates his oral history for his son, the rest of the text suggests he is unable to work out—or, as some like Freud are apt to say, work *through*—his traumatic past; his ability to exercise highlights, *via negativa*, his inability to exorcise his traumas from the Holocaust. *Maus* thus suggests Vladek is simply "going in circles" on his stationary bike—"spinning his wheels," to put it colloquially—without actually moving forward beyond his haunting past.

More germane to this study, however, is the framing of Artie and his father's tattooed arm in this scene. The framing of Artie and his father's tattoo presents how the Holocaust borders and surrounds, though does not actually touch, the second generation, similar to the separation of narration and image in the 1972 "Maus" comic explored earlier. Despite never having been physically present in the camps nor having been physically marked himself, Artie is "contained" within his father's traumas and sense of loss, symbolized here by Vladek's Auschwitz tattoo. As the tattoo looms above his head in the frame, so too does the past that the tattoo represents figuratively hang over Artie like a banner announcing his postmemories. It casts its dark shadow over his cognition throughout the narrative, particularly as he listens to Vladek tell his stories. This image that combines spatial enclosure and a visual symbol of Auschwitz points yet again to the postmemorial imprisonment that defined the habitual act of sharing space with survivors in their homes.

It is conceivable, then, why Artie chooses not to visit his father for almost two years after his mother's death.[60] His eventual return, however, is illuminated by James Baldwin's following declaration: "Though I may have dreaded *going* home, I hadn't *left* home yet."[61] In actuality, Baldwin is not referring to going to his childhood home, but the particular phrasing that Baldwin employs in a different context, considered in relation to *Maus*, sheds light on how even as Artie dreads *physically* returning to his childhood home to visit Vladek, he had not really left *psychically*. That is to say that life in the Spiegelman-family home arrested him in a continuous state of postmemorial confusion long after moving out. By spending two years apart from his father, Artie attempts to maintain a physical distance from Vladek in hopes of finding respite both from the domesticating effects/

affects of his father's presence and from the home in which he grew up that reanimates his parents' Holocaust pasts.

Artie's Adulthood Home

Regardless of such physical separation from his father and his childhood home, the text illustrates the enduring legacy of Vladek and Anja's traumas in Artie's life and how his adulthood home—his apartment in SoHo, to which we are first introduced in "Mouse Holes" in *Maus I*[62]—also functions as a postmemorial structure. His adulthood postmemorial structure indeed continues to sustain the transmission of his parents' traumas from the Holocaust, notwithstanding his attempts to put such inherited traumas and affects to rest. Although Artie leaves his childhood postmemorial structure, in many ways, he also never really does.

Though different from his childhood home, Artie's domestic space in SoHo shares several affective and psychosocial qualities that continue to mediate the traumas he assumed as a child in Rego Park. Spiegelman's representation of his adulthood domestic space largely parallels Gaston Bachelard's notion that people's first homes shape their domestic experiences in each home they indwell thereafter. Bachelard explains how people's memories of their first homes, primarily filtered through their imaginations, inform their perceptions and experiences of each subsequent home in which they live: "An entire past comes to dwell in a new house.... Through dreams, the various dwelling-places in our lives co-penetrate and retain the treasures of former days."[63] Although Bachelard's poetics of domestic space idealizes the home as a space of fond memories ("the treasures of former days")— which contrasts postmemorial structures in a number of ways—his argument that childhood homes "dwell" within latter day domestic spaces can also be seen in homes marked by traumatic legacies. Bachelard's idea that "former days" find expression in future domestic spaces holds double significance for many in the second generation: not only are their childhood homes haunted by vestiges of former days (i.e., emanations of their parents' Holocaust pasts), but their adulthood homes are haunted by their already-haunted childhoods.

This multiple haunting pervades Spiegelman's representation of his adulthood home, as it does in much of second-generation literature's representation of adulthood domestic spaces. In this light, Vladek's directive, in his accented English, "Remember, my house it's also your house too [*sic*],"⁶⁴ speaks not only to how Artie is welcome anytime but, more significantly, to how Artie's Manhattan apartment is, metaphorically, also Vladek's. Indeed, his adulthood apartment serves as a simulacrum of the family's home in Rego Park, a version of his postmemorial structure in Queens. Artie's relationship to and inhabitation of his childhood home shapes his relationship to his SoHo apartment as the trauma and knowledge that he inherited in his youth come to manifest spatially within his adulthood domestic space. The affective qualities of his childhood home—the anxiety, fear, and frustration—are in varying ways retained and perpetuated in his SoHo apartment. From the imagined tangled mass of dead bodies beneath his easel and outside his front door to the guard tower in plain view from his window, *Maus* visually registers Artie's emotional and psychological struggle with his persistent postmemories.⁶⁵ These postmemories continue to both populate and alter his perception of reality, within (as well as without) his adulthood domicile, regardless of his efforts to separate himself from his parents' traumatic pasts.

One particular feature of Artie's apartment that speaks to his disorderly relationship to the past, specifically his relationship to the Shoah, is the Picasso-esque portrait of a disjointed face hanging in his bedroom.⁶⁶ Many of the paintings of Pablo Picasso, the Cubist and surrealist artist well known for his anti-war painting *Guernica* (1937), are defined by fragmented or disjointed assemblages. Such assemblages, in part representative of a fragmented or disjointed worldview, also characterize the portrait we see above Artie's bed. This portrait is reminiscent, given its placement in Artie's bedroom, of the portrait hanging in Vladek and Anja's bedroom: that of Artie's murdered brother, Richieu. As these portraits hang in both bedrooms, the text again visually concretizes the connection between his childhood home and his adulthood apartment, reinforcing Vladek's abovementioned statement that his home is also Artie's. The abstract Picasso-esque portrait, though different in content and in style from Richieu's portrait, can thus be understood as an abstracted and indirect expression of Richieu's lingering postmemorial presence in Artie's adulthood home. Indeed, as Artie refers to "having sibling rivalry with a snapshot" of Richieu as "*spooky*,"⁶⁷ the Picasso-esque painting qua postmemorial recapitulation of Richieu's portrait symbolizes how Artie's murdered brother, along with the Holocaust more broadly, continues to haunt him and take up residence in his home. The portrait points to how Artie's decoration of his adulthood apartment materially registers and archives his postmemories, even if obliquely.

The image/symbol of flies throughout the "Auschwitz (Time Flies)" chapter offers further insight into how Artie's postmemories transform his apartment and other commonplace domestic spaces into fantastical sites of his parents' Holocaust traumas. Examining the image of the flies depicted on the title page of "Auschwitz (Time Flies)"—though the following analysis could be applied to the entire chapter in *Maus*—Erin McGlothlin insightfully observes: "They are *time* flies (the substantive phrase rather than the verbal phrase), buzzing reminders of time passed and a past time that carry the trace of the past into the present."[68] It is unclear whether or not the flies in the beginning of the chapter are imagined (as the pile of corpses surely is) or if they are real.[69] But if these flies are indeed flying around him in his SoHo apartment, this scene demonstrates how such an ostensibly insignificant occurrence assumes great postmemorial import. The buzzing of the flies indexically points to death—for in and of themselves the flies do not directly signify death, as do the dead bodies of which they are a function. The presence of the flies thus reveals how such a seemingly inconsequential moment engenders an incongruous experience of time, inviting a rush of postmemories to permeate the here and now with reverberations of death and destruction, defining hallmarks of the Shoah. The sight and sound of the flies trigger for Artie a descent into the past, where the very architecture of his home and the space therein are, once more, transformed into an imaginative concentration camp of sorts.

As the flies symbolize "the disturbing residues of a past that, like a pesky insect, will not go away,"[70] Artie's attempt to kill them at the end of the chapter mirrors his attempt to put his postmemories to rest. While these bugs conjure the presence of Holocaust death, his attempts to snuff them out, along with the postmemories they evoke, remain for the most part futile. The elusiveness of the flies and Artie's struggle to control their movement (that is, kill them) mirrors the elusiveness of his postmemories and his struggle to control them (that is, extinguish them). It is, therefore, ironic that Françoise expresses her incredulity at how the Holocaust was ever possible while Artie angrily swats at the buzzing insects: "Sigh. It's so peaceful [in the Catskills] at night. It's almost impossible to believe Auschwitz ever happened."[71] For Françoise the flies are simply flies, whereas for Artie they are also "residues of the past," signs that bring him out of the present and remind him that it is *very* possible to believe Auschwitz happened. That he dismisses her comment ("Uh-huh"[72]) gestures toward his mind being elsewhere. He is disturbed by the flies, that is, disturbed by the past's perceived presence in the present. Indeed, for Artie, though the past is not the present, the past is, postmemorially, present.[73] And although Artie does not and cannot live in the past, he seemingly struggles to live in the present beyond the postmemorial confines of his parents' Holocaust pasts.

Conclusion

The varied, yet seemingly constant, reminders of the Holocaust, the "residues of the past," that Artie and many in the second generation more broadly encounter resist spatial-temporal normalcy in survivor-family homes and beyond. Indeed, the continuous collapse of past and present typifies postmemorial structures, as well as other domestic spaces (as demonstrated by the flies on the porch in the Catskills), and precludes a defined division between the events of the Holocaust and the present. *Maus* presents Artie's childhood and adulthood homes as representative of his cognition and emotions, a reification of his interior psychological state that is made manifest in the interior spaces of his childhood and adulthood postmemorial structures. Yet, *Maus* is not only a document in the study of postmemorial structures as metaphors for a psychosocially and emotionally domesticated second-generation psyche. It is also an examination of how postmemorial structures functioned as catalysts for traumatic transference, enclosed spaces that were and are conducive to the transmission of survivors' senses of loss and absence. Tracing Artie's domestic experience from his childhood to his adulthood, *Maus* explores the ways by which his postmemorial structures, in both Rego Park and SoHo, reveal and mold his relationship to his parents' pasts. His childhood home functions as a creator, container, and invigorator of Artie's postmemories as he lives in close proximity to his parents and invests imaginatively in their Holocaust experiences. So, too, does his adulthood home assume similar affective qualities that perpetuate and sustain his postmemories. Within his adulthood home, Artie experiences a continuation of his childhood domestic experiences, where the inherited traumas of his childhood home are continually *re*lived. *Maus*'s illustration of the intergenerational effects of trauma depicts the complicated position of the second generation and how some continue to struggle to move outside the domestication of their inherited pasts, as they recurrently find themselves psychosocially imprisoned within the confinement of their postmemorial structures.

3

Domestic(ated) (Un)fashioning

Sonia Pilcer's *The Holocaust Kid*

Sonia Pilcer was born in 1949 to two Holocaust survivors in a displaced persons (DP) camp in Augsburg, Germany.[1] She and her parents moved to the United States, settling in the boroughs of New York City, where Pilcer grew up and continues to live as of this writing.[2] Based in large part on Pilcer's relationship to her parents, her semiautobiographical story cycle *The Holocaust Kid* (2001), an epitomic second-generation text, explores the impact of being raised by survivors. Following the precocious and strong-willed protagonist Zosha Palovsky—from her infancy in a DP camp in Germany to her adulthood in New York—*The Holocaust Kid* depicts a number of issues related to survivor families and their domestic lives, including and especially what may aptly be termed *postmemorial domestication*. Postmemorial domestication names the psychosocial experience of being co-opted, tamed, or colonized, so to speak, by survivors' Holocaust pasts—pasts which dominate the children of survivors' psyches and life narratives. Offering insight into the concept of domestication in more general terms, Rachel Bowlby avows that domestication often refers to a story "of a wild and natural identity, a full presence, subsequently, and only subsequently, succumbing to forces that deprive it of an original wholeness."[3] In the context of *The Holocaust Kid*, insofar as Zosha was born without any concrete knowledge of her parents' Holocaust experiences, her life before learning what her parents went through possesses an "original wholeness," unhindered by narratives of anguish and suffering. However, after becoming privy to her parents' traumatic pasts, Zosha, like many other children of survivors, "succumbs" to the domesticating effects of her family's painful legacy, as she is circumscribed, overtaken, and subdued by stories and traumas from the Holocaust that are communicated in and through her childhood home.

Pilcer's work connects this theme of postmemorial domestication to the theme of *fashioning*, that is, to how Zosha's parents, Genusha ("Genia") and Heniek Palovsky, "fashion" both the family home and their daughter. The domestic atmosphere that her parents, particularly her mother, create, in tandem with the clothes that Genia tailors for her daughter, constitute two domesticating features of Zosha's youth that directly and indirectly reinforce her traumatic connection to the Shoah. But *The Holocaust Kid* not only presents how Zosha is postmemorially domesticated throughout the story cycle; it also depicts how she attempts to free herself from such domestication. As the Palovsky-family home creates, feeds, and intensifies her inherited traumas and embodied experiences, Zosha leaves their family apartment for extended periods of time as a child in order to "undomesticate" herself from her parents and her postmemories. The themes of postmemorial domestication and fashioning find further expression when Zosha moves as an adult into her own apartment that is distinct and distant from her childhood home—another attempt to free herself from the control of her parents and her postmemories. Her success in freeing herself, however, remains questionable, in light of how she is consistently overtaken by her postmemories well into her thirties, as evidenced by how she re-enacts her inherited traumas in the space of her apartment. More specifically, as she acts out in her apartment that which she imagines to be her mother's sexualized violation in Auschwitz, her home is imaginatively transformed into a concentration camp, which thereby exacerbates her postmemories.

Despite being a rich, complex, and intricate piece of second-generation literature, *The Holocaust Kid* has received relatively little scholarly attention, with Nina Fischer's *Memory Work* serving as one of the few detailed treatments of Pilcer's work to date.[4] This chapter expands this scholarship by establishing how the Palovsky-family home catalyzes, arouses, and reinforces Zosha's postmemories. Examining the multiple ways that postmemorial domestication, the domestic, fashion, and the fashioning of both people and space operate in *The Holocaust Kid*, I discuss how the traumatic legacies of two survivors subdue and colonize their daughter psychosocially, along with her efforts to free herself. These discussions enable us to better understand survivor-family homes as postmemorial technologies.[5] With a particular focus on Zosha and Genia, this chapter centers on the family dynamics in Zosha's childhood and adulthood postmemorial structures, with an eye toward inherited (sexualized) trauma and embodied experiences.

Zosha's Childhood Postmemorial Structure

Throughout the story cycle, Zosha repeatedly attempts to resist being tamed by the traumas and stories of her parents—traumas and stories that their family home archives and indirectly communicates to her. She fights to assert her subjectivity in her childhood, carve out a space for herself, and distinguish herself from her parents while living under their roof. From spending much of her time outside her family's apartment—which is consistently frequented by her parents' survivor friends—to dressing in a provocative "cool" aesthetic like her friends, Zosha endeavors throughout her youth to separate herself from her overbearing parents and their traumas that find continual expression through the stifling domestic atmosphere of her postmemorial structure.

Despite her attempts to separate herself, Zosha remains psychically tethered to her parents' Holocaust pasts, which leads to a metaphysical confusion of what constitutes reality and what constitutes her imagination, thereby affecting how she perceives both space and time. She describes this split sense of reality, stating that she lives "*in two time frames. Normal, shared reality* [and] *the ghetto of the dead.*"[6] Zosha inhabits both the intersubjective world of post–World War II U.S. society and the imaginative space of her postmemories, thus rendering her suspended between two spheres of existence: the former being the communal sphere ("*normal, shared reality*") and the latter the private realm ("*the ghetto of the dead*"). This perception of a dual reality is quite common for those born to survivors; many children of survivors articulate a similar experience to Zosha. Variously describing themselves as being a part "of both worlds, but arguably fully a part of neither"[7] and possessing a "split subjectivity,"[8] members of the second generation occupy what Judith Kestenberg, a psychiatrist who focused much of her work on the children of survivors, identifies as "*a simultaneous double existence.*"[9] As survivors communicated their Holocaust experiences to their children both directly and indirectly, the distinction between reality and fantasy was troubled for many in the second generation, as is the case for Zosha. This unclear metaphysical distinction engenders for her a blurred consciousness that confuses the here and now of the New World and the there and then of the Shoah. As Zosha takes notice of her parents' Holocaust pasts, along with hearing the traumatic stories of their survivor friends, she becomes increasingly postmemorially domesticated throughout her youth.

Indeed, one of the foundational aspects of home life for young Zosha that postmemorially domesticates her, in addition to sharing time and space with her parents, is the seemingly continuous presence of other survivors in the home. Akin to many in the second generation, Zosha grows up surrounded by her parents' survivor friends, which assists in the creation of an affective environment that catalyzes and sustains the transmission of trauma in the Palovsky-family home. Her parents adopt a sizable and insular network of survivor friends in New York, such that all Zosha's adult influences are survivors (with perhaps the exception of her teachers?), thus creating a psychosocial space defined largely by the stories and traumas of the Shoah. This is in no small part because, as one of her parents' survivor friends says, no matter the initial subject of the group's conversations, they "always end up back at the Holocaust."[10]

The scene where Zosha listens to her parents and their friends discuss the Holocaust in the family's living room crystalizes how their traumatic stories are "fed" to her in her home as a child. She describes playing in her living room while her parents host their group of friends. She sits under the coffee table which holds "books about the Warsaw Ghetto uprising and Auschwitz with photographs of concentration camp survivors in torn shifts, shaven heads—amidst bowls of celery stalks, cream cheese with scallions and radishes, Ritz crackers."[11] Here, symbols of the United States and the Holocaust—Ritz crackers and books about the Shoah, respectively—are joined together, in tandem with the overlying conversation about their dark past, gesturing toward how the Holocaust was part and parcel of everyday life. The juxtaposition of these symbols suggests that as much as Zosha is fed hors d'oeuvres in this scene she is also "fed" stories of the Shoah; as she consumes these snacks, she simultaneously "consumes" the horrific narratives from before her birth. In tandem with other moments where the text connects the consumption of food and the consumption of Holocaust stories,[12] Zosha's description of her parents and their friends sharing "morsels of wartime gossip"[13] further bears out this relationship between gastronomical and narratival consumption. Moreover, the image of Zosha under the coffee table—that is, of her being spatially enclosed while the adults talk about the Shoah—underscores her postmemorial domestication. Such spatial enclosure speaks to how she is surrounded, literally and figuratively, by the narratives of the Holocaust. As much as "none of [the stories] escaped" her, the rest of the narrative highlights her inability to escape the stories that haunt her throughout her youth.

Along with how her parents and their friends' stories contribute to her postmemorial domestication, another central catalyst is the clothing in which Genia dresses Zosha—that is, the postmemorial things that indirectly give voice to Genia's Holocaust traumas. Genia is emphatic that Zosha maintains a "decent" appearance in and out of the home. Cleanliness, tidy appearances, and dressing well are important for her, as they were for many survivors, because of the pervasive befoulment of camps, ghettos, and places of hiding (see chapter 1). Along with how Genia's time in Auschwitz was defined by filth and mire, the story cycle suggests that Genia's emphasis on physical appearances and cleanliness was further compounded by yet another factor, namely that which Genia's mother told her before being deported: "You must keep yourself clean, no matter what."[14] This maternal injunction of course was not followed by Genia, given the sheer impossibility of remaining clean in the camps, and one can infer Genia's subsequent shame that would have issued forth from not being able to maintain a clean appearance—especially in light of how Genia came from a well-to-do Polish family of well-dressed individuals. Her shame was reanimated when Poles saw her and other survivors shortly after liberation; their "laughter stabbed" when "she looked down at her own clothes."[15] This stabbing—this shame—finds indirect expression years later when Genia says to Zosha, "You must look decent. They tried to destroy us. ... Now we must show how well we dress."[16] How she is instructed to dress herself thus becomes an oblique site of postmemorial negotiation, where clothing qua postmemorial things reanimates her mother's traumas and memories of the Holocaust, which in turn engenders postmemories for Zosha.

The scene where Genia makes matching garments for herself and Zosha further highlights this role of clothing qua postmemorial things, revealing how Genia tries to "fashion" Zosha in her likeness, a vicarious attempt to live out her stolen youth through her daughter. After Genia sews matching cotton dresses for the both of them, they model the dresses in front of a full-length mirror on the back of the closet door before she squeals with delight: "Look, Zosha, we're exactly the same."[17] As Genia dresses Zosha in an identical outfit to her own, she thereby twins herself and her daughter. Employing the imperative tense ("Look"), she commands Zosha to recognize their similarity in the mirror as she claims they are identical. This rhetorical collapse of difference between mother and daughter ("we're exactly the same") is mirrored, as it were, by their reflection to which Genia directs Zosha's attention. The mirroring of Genia's likeness through her daughter, along with the mirroring of their matching appearances on the back of the door, reflects how Genia sees herself in and through her daughter. By sartorially twinning herself, Genia renders an egoistic double onto whom she projects her desire to live out her stolen youth—especially since Genia spent much of her adolescence and young adulthood under Nazi control. Along with several other members of the second generation who mention similar mother-daughter dynamics to that of Genia and Zosha, Arlene Stein also describes the experience of being dressed by and like her survivor mother: "My mother clothed me immaculately: the child as reflection of the adult. I was to be a streamlined extension of my mother, but with all the opportunities that had been denied to her."[18] Like Stein, Zosha becomes the conduit through whom her mother can relive that which was lost to violence and destruction. As such, Genia's fashioning of Zosha in the same garments further "clothes" Zosha in the knowledge that her mother's youth was lost to the horrors of the camps. Employing a sartorial simile that speaks to this enmeshed relationship between herself and Genia, Zosha explains that her mother worried about losing her "like a loose button on her blue cardigan sweater."[19] This simile of Zosha-as-button and Genia-as-cardigan suggests that Genia conceptualizes her daughter as a part of her person onto whom she is "sewn" and with whom she is bound, not as separate or distinct; it suggests that Zosha is, as Genia would have it, her mother's possession. Such a comparison underscores the domesticated position of being "possessed," by both her mother and, as the rest of the text makes clear, her mother's past.

It is this comparison that illuminates how Genia sees herself physically and emotionally in relation to her daughter. Indeed, as she dresses Zosha like she dresses herself and as she conceptualizes her daughter as part of herself, Genia blurs the line between parent and child, in turn binding Zosha all the more to herself and her traumatic past.

That said, there is one way that Zosha explicitly and defiantly resists Genia's attempt to blur the line between herself and her mother: by refashioning herself in a "cool" aesthetic. Zosha joins a friend group, known as the Cleopatras, who sport teased-out hairdos with satin bows above the bangs and makeup akin to Liz Taylor's. Teasing her hair four and a half inches high and donning white lipstick, Zosha fits in with the group as she wears a tight black skirt and off-black stockings. Shedding light on Zosha's motivations behind her aesthetic of choice, Mihaly Csikszentmihalyi and Eugene Rochberg-Halton explain that the easiest way one can demonstrate one's self-control or independence of outside influences is by becoming "cool."[20] Throughout her childhood, Zosha *attempts* to use her cool aesthetic to assert her self-control and independence like her friends; yet, her aesthetic is more so a cover for—a covering over of—her dearth of autonomy and her inability to separate herself from her entangled relationship to her parents, particularly her mother. Her clothes, which emphasize her efforts to individuate, serve as symbols of rebellion against her parents. Indeed, Zosha's use of clothing-as-protest against Genia and Heniek is an outward expression of her inward struggle against their domesticating practices and is in line with other members of the second generation who mention a similar means of rebellion, including Lawrence Sutin who defied his survivor parents because his "options seemed either to be rebellion or engulfment by [his] parents' past."[21] Yet, Zosha's attempts to individuate, to untether herself from Genia and Heniek's controlling grip, are consistently frustrated, thereby sustaining her postmemorial domestication.

In the face of Zosha's efforts to be with her "cool" friends in the streets of New York, Genia attempts to keep her daughter inside and proximal to her, further compounding Zosha's psychosocial confinement. Describing her home during Rosh Hashanah in her youth, Zosha observes her parents, realizing that their remembrance of the past often led them to tears. As her mother paces from room to room, Zosha concludes that her parents did nothing but remember the past. When she asks to go outside, Genia turns to her and cries: "*Paskudynak!*" before telling her that it is the day she lost her entire family.[22] In the face of Zosha's desire to leave the family's apartment, Genia restricts her daughter's mobility to the confines of the postmemorial structure and within earshot of her mother's (and father's) tearful mourning of their dead relatives, additionally contributing to the maintenance of the *"ghetto of the dead"* that Zosha imaginatively inhabits.[23] Yet, this effort to coop Zosha up is not an isolated instance; it is part of Genia's sustained attempts to keep her daughter close to her, both physically and psychically, as she consistently turns "her immense energies terrifyingly toward [Zosha]."[24] Zosha functions as her mother's central preoccupation—the one on whom Genia obsessively fixates and to whom she unintentionally passes on her traumas—resulting in Zosha's literal and postmemorial domestication in their family home.[25]

In her attempts to escape her parents' domestication, Zosha shares a number of parallels with one member of the second generation in particular: Evaline E. Delson. Despite the fact that Zosha is a fictional character (even if semiautobiographical) and Evaline is not, the two possess several similarities in how they seek reprieve from their mothers' overbearing and overwhelming presences in their lives. I first met Evaline in 2019 when I was conducting a series of oral histories of children and grandchildren of Holocaust survivors in and around Charleston, South Carolina. Evaline's mother, Dientje Krant, was a child survivor who was hidden in a wardrobe in Holland by a woman Dientje remembered as a nun. As I asked Evaline questions about her mother's Holocaust experiences, her relationship to her mother, and her home growing up, her responses pointed to the ways by which her childhood home functioned as a postmemorial structure much like Zosha's childhood home. Early on, Evaline established that her mother was not allowed out of the closet much during the Holocaust. Evaline did not explicitly detail how being forced to spend extended periods of time in a wardrobe would have made her mother feel claustrophobic, nor did she describe feeling secondhandedly claustrophobic. However, there was a prevailing sense that Evaline felt constrained and confined—or, otherwise put, *domesticated*—in her home growing up. She detailed feelings of sadness in her childhood domicile as well as a recurrent sense of fright. One notable example is how her mother, upon hearing an ambulance siren, would start screaming, "They're after me. They're after me," and would then try to hide her daughter. Dientje would also, for no clear reason, sometimes have "a little freak-out." Evaline explained that watching her mother during one of these episodes would make her markedly afraid. Her dad would take her mother in the other room and try to calm her down, which Evaline also described as "very scary."[26]

Dientje's recurring episodes, along with how she tried to be more of a friend than a mother, pushed Evaline into wanting to leave home as a senior in high school. As Dientje liked to party with her and her friends, Evaline felt as though she needed space. She realized, particularly in comparison to her friends' relationships with their parents, that she was essentially functioning as her mother's babysitter. Her eventual decision to "go away to school, as far as [she] possibly could," was largely a product of how her mother clung all too closely to her in a reversed child-parent dynamic. This dynamic, often an outcome of survivors seeking out the relationship they lost with their parents because of the Holocaust,[27] resulted in Dientje constantly pushing her daughter to stay at home with her: "She didn't ever want us to leave. 'Oh, don't leave me. Don't leave me.' That kind of thing."[28]

Dientje's desire for her daughter to stay with her at home shares similarities to Genia's desire to keep Zosha proximal and emotionally close. Just before teenage Zosha is about to leave the family's apartment with her friends, Heniek fusses over her appearance and calls Genia into the room. He asks Genia if she is going to let Zosha out of the house looking as she does. She responds: "What do you want me to do? . . . Lock her up?"[29] Here, Genia's question ("Lock her up?") is not only rhetorical; her inquiry also gestures toward Zosha's postmemorial incarceration. No matter how much she rebels in her teenage years and attempts to free herself from the controlled confines of the family's home—that is, liberate herself from the postmemorial domestication of her parents—she struggles to emancipate herself from the *"ghetto of the dead"* that she so describes. Though Genia explicitly states that she never intended to wound her daughter,[30] the domestic space she sets up—the psychosocial space she constructs—contributes to the intergenerational transmission of trauma and embodied experience from parent to child; inadvertently, the affective domestic conditions that Genia creates in the present further bind her daughter to her Holocaust past. As Genia unintentionally fashions her home as a postmemorial structure, so too does Dientje. Indeed, Dientje's attempts to keep Evaline home in a space defined by sadness and fright speak to how she tried to domesticate her daughter, in a physical sense, throughout her childhood. However, Evaline's domestication, like Zosha's, constituted not just being manipulated into staying home through the application of guilt; such domestication was also deeply psychosocial.

At length, Evaline described panic attacks from which she suffered throughout her life—panic attacks that speak to and are functions of her postmemorial domestication. She explained that she began experiencing panic attacks in her adolescence into her teenage years and early twenties and still dealt with them occasionally as an adult. Her parents called these attacks her "problem," thinking that she might have epilepsy because she appeared to be having what looked like seizures. She said that she "would just start thinking about things, and then just freak out." She would try to escape, and no one would be able to hold her down. No one knew the cause of these episodes, until it was eventually diagnosed as a panic disorder. These panic attacks, she proposed, stemmed from her fear of death—of "what comes next?"—that she developed at a young age. Evaline's fear of death elicited a flight response to such an extent that she would start physically running as fast as she could. She remembered how the first of her panic attacks occurred on her way home with her mother at the age of about six or seven. She discussed how the road they were traveling on was dark, perhaps representative of death for young Evaline. Her location (a dark road), in tandem with her travel partner (her mother, the source of her postmemories), appears to have contributed to her first panic attack. But what is perhaps most notable is her response in and of itself: how she felt compelled to run. In light of how Evaline stated earlier in the oral history, "most of the times I do suppress my fears," her running constitutes a psychosomatic response to her postmemories, where she both literally and figuratively attempted to flee from her inherited traumas and embodied knowledge of the Shoah. The issue of course is that one cannot run from oneself or one's inner world. Insofar as trauma cannot "speak" directly, it finds expression in indirect ways—and in this case, Evaline's traumas found expression in and through the practice of running. But what is further notable, and more germane to this study, is Evaline and Dientje's destination: their home. That they were heading back to the family home points to how her postmemorial structure shaped—at least in part—her psychosomatic response to her fear of death. She explained further: "I wasn't afraid of the boogeyman. . . . I was afraid of Nazis coming into my house, tying me up, and having me watch them kill my family in front of me. That's what I was afraid of growing up."[31] It is thus not coincidental that her first panic attack took place on the way home to her postmemorial structure, the space that helped engender her nightmares. Her running from the Holocaust is not dissimilar to Zosha's attempts to leave her apartment, to go outside her home, as much as possible. Though Zosha does not have a psychosomatic response to her postmemories like Evaline, the desire to be separate from her parents and their home as a child finds a number of commonalities.

How Evaline described her childhood home (or, more accurately, failed to describe her childhood home) further speaks to her postmemorial domestication and her relationship to the Shoah. After interviewing Evaline for several minutes, I asked her to offer a fleshed-out portrait of what her home was like growing up. In response, Evaline provided very little detail about her home itself. Briefly, she mentioned that, similar to the Palovskys, her parents were often present, only to go on and describe how her family frequently traveled to Florida, North Carolina, and Harrisonburg, Pennsylvania. She then noted how, when they were not on vacation, they would go to the beach and how she and her siblings played outside a lot. In other words, she did not actually engage with my original question about her home. So, I followed up: "Based on your description you just gave—almost everything you had pointed out was outside." She responded:

> Oh yeah? Well, inside it was sad [*laughs*], I guess. My mother was in the bed a lot, I mean—but also, that's what we did. We had to finish our homework before we were allowed to go outside and play. That was the rule. My dad bought us these desks, these schoolhouse desks. We would sit at our desks, do our homework, and we would go outside, and we had to come home when the streetlights came on. That was it. That was the rule. And we would. That was just what we did. It was fun.[32]

As is clear, Evaline did eventually respond (briefly) to my question, only to go on and talk again about her life *outside* the home. This redirection of the question paralleled her attempts to evade her postmemories ("most of the times I do suppress my fears"). The sadness she identified with her home contrasted with the "fun" she described outside her home. As she unconsciously connected her home to the Shoah, Evaline avoided describing her postmemorial structure, akin to how she tried to be outside her home as much as possible in her youth and to how she ran from what her parents euphemistically called her "problem." Evaline's discussion of her home, like *The Holocaust Kid*'s presentation of Zosha's childhood postmemorial structure, demonstrates how children of survivors' descriptions of their homes correlate to how they relate to the Holocaust.

In line with Evaline's compulsion to run from and be outside her family home, Zosha's childhood routine of sitting on the fire escape of her parents' bedroom is symbolic of her attempts to escape her postmemories. Zosha explains that as often as she is at home, she is out on the fire escape of her parents' bedroom, metaphorical of how she seeks refuge from that which threatens her inside. Indeed, as the term *Holocaust* refers to a wholly burnt sacrifice in the original Greek, her use of the fire escape functions as a figurative attempt to flee from the conflagration of her postmemories that find expression within and through her childhood home. This metaphor follows the literary precedent set by Tennessee Williams's *The Glass Menagerie* (1944), namely the play's inclusion of a fire escape in the Wingfield-family home that is described as "a structure whose name is a touch of accidental poetic truth, for all of these huge buildings are always burning with the slow and implacable fires of human desperation."[33] Inasmuch as she repeatedly attempts to escape the domesticating control of her parents and their memories, Zosha is forced to navigate the "implacable fires" of trauma and sadness inside her family domicile. And in doing so, she must continuously return to the space that both catalyzed and sustains her postmemories throughout her youth.

The Holocaust Kid's representation of domestic space and domestic activities in the Palovsky-family home presents readers with a tragic irony: in Genia's perpetual attempts to maintain a strong bond with her daughter—as seen through her negotiation of how Zosha navigates domestic space—she unknowingly postmemorially domesticates her daughter while also pushing her further away. Though Genia attempts to establish a more intimate connection with her only child, she nonetheless repels her, creating an even wider emotional chasm between the two—similar to Dientje's efforts with Evaline. And though she desires to "shelter" Zosha from her Holocaust past, Genia and her management of their home inevitably subsume her daughter within her traumas from the camps. Genia's traumas profoundly truncate Zosha to the point where Zosha purports to have "spent years within [Auschwitz's] architecture,"[34] that is, to have imaginatively lived inside her mother's (and, in a different sense, father's) Holocaust past(s). The architecture of Auschwitz that Zosha first imagines as a child largely structures her interior world, shaping her cognition to such an extent that she claims to have postmemorially inhabited the site of her parents' traumas; such an avowal, to have lived within Auschwitz, reveals how she obsessively dwells on the Holocaust to the point of "dwelling within" it belatedly and imaginatively. Indeed, the space of her childhood postmemorial structure, like that of her adulthood postmemorial structure, imaginatively assumes affective qualities of the death camp her parents survived. As she "recreates" the space/architecture of Auschwitz in her various homes, these homes in turn concurrently reanimate her parents' Holocaust pasts. Eventually, as an adult, Zosha moves out on her own, but Zosha's postmemorial domestication is not so easily shaken. The effects of living with Genia (and Heniek) endure, as her parents continue to disallow her to maintain physical and psychic distance from them.

Zosha's Adulthood Postmemorial Structure

In "The Idea of Home," Mary Douglas posits, "Even its most altruistic and successful versions [of a home] exert a tyrannous control over mind and body. We need hardly say more to explain why children want to leave it and do not mean to reproduce it when they set up house."[35] Douglas's observation supports the idea that Zosha's childhood postmemorial structure contributes to her psychosocial domestication, which is in no small part because of the Holocaust's haunting presence. In line with Douglas's observation concerning children's desire to leave home, Zosha not only routinely escapes her postmemorial structure as a child, but she also eagerly moves out on her own as an adult, doing her best not to "reproduce" or replicate the home in which she grew up. She creates a domestic space that is distinct from her family home largely to separate herself from her parents and their pasts.[36] She explains her desire to claim her own identity upon moving out as an adult, stating that when she left home, she planned "to create a self that had nothing to do with [her] parents' past."[37] Attempting to establish herself in her adulthood apartment, beyond the reach of her parents and their Holocaust traumas, she moves a distance away from them—into a building without an elevator, making it difficult for them to visit—and endeavors to arrange, decorate, and maintain her domicile qua refuge in sharp contrast to the postmemorial structure in which she was raised. Indeed, unlike her childhood home, her adulthood apartment is dusty, disorganized, and devoid of knickknacks. But despite how she seeks to create a home distinct from the one in which she grew up, as an adult she nonetheless brings the Holocaust home with her, so to speak, which is compounded by how the Holocaust is brought home to her by way of her parents' repeatedly intruding upon her domestic space. In this way, her adulthood apartment becomes a space where her inherited traumas continue to be reanimated. This revivification of her inherited traumas is perhaps most dramatically portrayed during her sexual rendezvous with a professor of Holocaust studies, Uly Oppenheim. This encounter renders her home a site of imagined sexualized trauma. How her parents intrude upon her domestic space and how she imagines her home as a site of sexual exchange during the Shoah each contribute to Zosha's continued postmemorial domestication, thereby disallowing her to come to terms with her inherited traumas and embodied experiences.

Despite Zosha's attempts to maintain distance from her mother, Genia and Heniek continue to domesticate their daughter by recurrently imposing themselves on Zosha in her apartment, precluding her from maintaining a separate psychosocial space distinct from them. Angry that Genia and Heniek unexpectedly invade her apartment one morning, Zosha vents that they had no respect for her privacy.[38] Their lack of boundaries, in tandem with their frustrating presence, serves as a reminder for Zosha, albeit indirectly, of their Holocaust past, as is made clear when she locks the bathroom door behind her before turning on the hot water and entering the shower: "I didn't want to move. *Heal me, I am broken*. I started to cry. . . . I wished I could stand still forever. . . . Free of them and their painful history."[39] That Zosha locks the door, barring herself from her parents' intrusive company, underscores her psychosocial confinement. She becomes a prisoner in her own home in a double sense: in addition to having her space overtaken to the point that she must tearfully relegate herself to the bathroom in isolation, she again becomes captive to "their painful history," recatalyzed by their intrusion and their overwhelming, controlling presence. Genia then oversteps her boundaries minutes later when she sneaks into Zosha's bedroom and reads her daughter's manuscripts about the Holocaust.[40] Her physical and readerly intrusions echo her psychological intrusion throughout Zosha's life. This unwelcome invasion of Zosha's private space mirrors how she and her enduring traumas figuratively take up residence in Zosha's psyche against Zosha's will. Indeed, when Genia brings a housecoat and slippers to make herself at home, lugs in several containers of food to fill Zosha's fridge, and even breaks into her daughter's apartment multiple times to clean and organize when she is not home, we see how Genia repeatedly takes over and controls Zosha's domestic space, paralleling how she takes over and controls Zosha psychically and emotionally.

Such parental intrusions persist, albeit in a different form, when Genia continuously calls her daughter, resulting in the shortening of the psychic and emotional distance between the two. In addition to phoning her at work—always refusing to leave a message, so that Zosha must call her back to find out the reason for her call—Genia often rings Zosha at home, even one time trying to chat with her after it is clear that Zosha has a date in her apartment. Offering insight into how phone calls hinder one's sense of privacy, Stephen Kern explains how the barriers of distance are broken down by telephones and how the protections of doors, waiting rooms, guards, and the like are eliminated by the ring of a telephone.[41] Kern suggests that "the intrusive effect" of a telephone ring compels recipients of the call to stop whatever they are doing and answer. They are forced into "a passive role," insofar as they cannot necessarily prepare for the conversation ahead of time and control it from the onset as much as the caller can.[42] Similarly placing Zosha in a passive role and sonically controlling her daughter in the space of her apartment, Genia consistently imposes herself, disallowing the psychic and emotional distance that Zosha so desperately seeks.

The story cycle extends the theme of control by connecting the telephone with images of bondage, further underlining Zosha's postmemorial domestication. Assuming the role of omniscient narrator, Zosha describes her mother on the phone with her friend—a description that reads as Zosha projecting her experiences with Genia onto this imagined exchange. Indeed, though Zosha is referring to a conversation between her mother and her mother's friend, the following description sheds light on how Genia uses the phone as a tool of control with Zosha: "She wound the phone cord around her wrist.... The yellow wall phone jerked as she moved around with the long cord following like a leash."[43] The image of Genia winding the phone cord around her (singular) wrist resembles a sort of self-bondage, where she seemingly handcuffs herself with the cord. Yet, Genia's binding of only *one* of her wrists with the cord suggests that she is not binding just herself but is also, metaphorically, shackling herself to the party on the other line. This implied bondage gestures toward the control Genia consistently asserts over her daughter by way of calling her. Zosha's domestication is emphasized in how the phone cord follows Genia "like a leash." The leash, however, is not controlling Genia. Rather, it is Genia who makes figurative use of the leash to control her interlocutor. The image of the leash, in concert with the image of the cord-wrapped wrist, serves to reinforce the idea that the telephone functions as a domesticating tool that Genia employs to keep Zosha at a close psychic and emotional distance. Otherwise put, the leash simile and the image of the bound wrist doubly stress the invasive and controlling presence of Genia in Zosha's adulthood apartment, even when she is not physically present.

Yet, it is also Heniek who postmemorially domesticates Zosha—albeit by way of silence, especially during his and Genia's surprise visits to their daughter's home—to which Zosha gives voice by comparing him to a symbol of colonization. Explaining how colonization constitutes a form of domestication, Bowlby notes, "In one French usage, *domestiquer* means quite simply the subjugation of a tribe to a colonizing power. To 'domesticate' is to bring the foreign or primitive or alien into line with the 'domestic' civilization and power, just as a 'domesticated' animal is one that has been tamed into home life."[44] Domestication qua colonization finds expression in *The Holocaust Kid* by way of intertextual reference to Sylvia Plath's poem "The Colossus" (1957). Zosha describes looking at her parents when, all of a sudden, she "had a vision of a colossal stone statue, centuries old. The imposing monarch, his smaller, narrow-hipped queen next to him, and, carved between them, a tiny slip of a princess."[45] The association of Heniek with "a colossal stone statue" and Genia with "a narrow-hipped queen" first suggests that her parents are living "memorials" to the Holocaust. Second, the comparison draws upon the imagery of the despotic father in Plath's confessional poem (though of course, and the irony is, Plath's father was pro-Nazi, unlike Zosha's father who fell victim to Nazism). The speaker in "The Colossus" explains the emotional distance and lack of communication between herself and her father, avowing: "Thirty years now I have labored / To dredge the silt from your throat. / I am none the wiser."[46] The speaker's statement allows for at least one of two possible interpretations: either he refuses to communicate with her, or she is indeed successful in dredging up the silt from his throat, but his "mule-bray, pig grunt and bawdy cackles"[47] disallow her to discern the meaning of his vocalizations. Regardless of which reading one prefers, Heniek's silence parallels the colossus statue's silence in Plath's poem. Observing her father sitting across the room on one of her parents' surprise visits in her apartment, Zosha tries "to make sense of this totally incomprehensible stranger" as she notes how he is rarely without some sort of reading material in his hand to preoccupy him, whether it be a newspaper, a magazine, or a book about the Holocaust.[48] Heniek is both incomprehensible and a stranger to Zosha because, as Genia makes clear, "it's just too painful for him. He tries, but he just can't talk about some things."[49] His silence is a continuation of his sustained silence throughout Zosha's childhood, which precludes Zosha from knowing the specifics of his

Holocaust past. Not passing on the details of his Holocaust experiences leaves Zosha with the sorry task of imaginatively filling in the gaps of her father's traumatic history, which further engenders her postmemorial domestication.

In tandem with her parents' domestic(ating) incursions, Zosha's sexual rendezvous in her apartment reveals how her home functions as a space to negotiate her postmemories. Indeed, Zosha attempts to control her post-memories in and through her adulthood apartment—a space that, through fantasy and role play, she imaginatively transforms into a site of sexual exchange between a Jewish prisoner (her) and a Nazi (Holocaust studies professor Uly).[50] In general terms, erotic fantasy and role play are aspects of domestic life that, for many, allow participants to express their sexual desires and proclivities in the privacy of their own homes, even if those desires and proclivities are not necessarily known explicitly or straightforwardly by the participants themselves. Indeed, as the repressed contents of the unconscious are not known to the individual—and as traumas are commonly not known by the individual—fantasy and role play allow individuals the space and time to act out or express those repressions or traumas. Fantasy and role play can transform the taboo into the innocuous, thereby relieving the tensions between id and superego, which in turn engenders the integration of one's personality. For Zosha, her sexual rendezvous with Uly affords her the space to express the taboo content of her unassimilable knowledge—or, paradoxically and perhaps more accurately, her *lack* of unassimilable knowledge—of sexual violation. Through their erotic encounter, this (lack of) taboo knowledge is recognized and validated by Uly—one who functions as a witness and contributor to Zosha's taboo desire—which allows Zosha to integrate said taboo knowledge into how she self-identifies. But this erotic encounter is not just fantasy and role play; it is also a function of her inherited traumas, insofar as it gives voice and, as it were, *body* to what she imagines her mother to have gone through during the Shoah. This erotic experience in her apartment allows her to indirectly address and negotiate her inherited sexualized trauma that, up until that point, remains unspeakable.[51]

The term *inherited sexualized trauma*, inspired by Brigitte Halbmayr's term *sexualized violence*, is helpful when discussing Zosha's erotic encounter because it broadens the notion of inherited sexual trauma. Halbmayr defines the term *sexualized violence* as "direct physical expressions of violence that are bodily attacks, an unauthorized crossing of body boundaries."[52] Sexualized violence, contrasting sexual violence, points to how male violence against women is less about sexuality and more about a demonstration of power on the part of the perpetrator. This broadening capaciously includes more than vaginal penetration and thereby signifies any and all violations that could be understood in sexualized terms. And as sexualized violence comes in a multiplicity of forms—like sexual advances, transactional sex, bodily violation, humiliation, forced sterilization, forced abortion, sexual bartering, coerced prostitution, nonconsensual sex, instrumental sex, and rape[53]—so too does inherited sexualized trauma. For children of survivors, their traumas are shaped depending on the act(s) victims were forced to perform—or what they imagine their parents, specifically their mothers, were forced to perform. Many within the second generation, with Zosha as one (literary) example of many,[54] describe a nagging fear that their mothers may have experienced sexualized violence.[55] Fischer describes this assumed and unnamed fear "the specter of sexual[ized] abuse," that which leaves members of the second generation with the question of whether their mothers were victims of sexualized violence. These children of survivors do not ask questions for fear of what they might discover and of what the consequences might be for asking about such a shame-inducing subject.[56] It was thus not uncommon, as Janet Jacobs observes, for women descendants to imagine themselves as victims of rape and sexual threat. Such traumatic identification reveals the forceful impact of atrocity narratives to produce "a complex through which confusion between self and other becomes possible[,] if not inevitable."[57] Throughout *The Holocaust Kid*, this confusion of self and (m)other, of Zosha and Genia, particularly in terms of sexualized trauma, suggests the intimate ways Genia's Holocaust past domesticates her daughter.

Although it is never explicitly stated whether Genia was sexually violated, it does not seem to matter for how it affects Zosha; the threat of sexualized violence in and of itself becomes the specter that plagues and in turn traumatizes her. Kestenberg describes how her second-generation interviewees had "the need to discover, to re-enact, or to live [their] parents' past.... This need is different from the usual curiosity of children about their parents. These children feel they have a mission to live in the past and to change it so that their parents' humiliation, disgrace, and guilt can be converted into victory over the oppressors."[58] Similar to Kestenberg's interviewees, Zosha identifies with and re-enacts what she imagines to be her mother's experience of being coerced into sexualized activity during the Shoah. Evincing how questions of sex during the Holocaust preoccupy her, Zosha rhetorically asks early in the story cycle: "Would I have traded my body for bread? Fucked Nazis?"[59] These questions foreground the subsequent narrative moments when Zosha associates herself with her mother-as-prisoner and engages in erotic fantasy and role play with Uly. However, Zosha does not have a script from which to navigate her inherited sexualized traumas, so she draws upon her affiliative postmemories.

The scene between her and Uly functions as a form of postmemorial address that bespeaks what may or may not have happened to her mother. Sitting with Uly on her living-room couch, Zosha thinks to herself: "*He had selected me from the others. If I made him love me, he'd take me through the war. I would survive.*"[60] The language of *selection* she employs in her apartment echoes back to how earlier that night Uly notices her out of the group of fawning women who approach him after his book talk. Upon explaining how "he appraised [her l]ike chicken in plastic wrap,"[61] Zosha states: "He could have had any woman in that room, but he had selected me."[62] Her repeated use of the verb *selected*—in tandem with his dehumanizing appraisal of her ("like chicken")—points to how, from Zosha's perspective, her life parallels what she imagines to be one of her mother's Holocaust experiences. Indeed, her attribution of Uly as the one who selected her connects to her repeated references to her mother being chosen to live during the process of *Selektion* by a concentration camp guard (who, as it happens, wore "tall black boots"[63] like those Uly wears). As Zosha struts her "smart stuff" toward Uly in the lecture hall, wearing a small leather skirt and a red sweater that clung to her body,[64] her attractive appearance echoes back to her mother's at the moment of *Selektion*, insofar as Zosha believes that the soldier who selected her mother thought Genia "was too cute to gas."[65] This reveals how Zosha comes to embody her mother's Holocaust experiences in and through her sexual activity, though not in any direct sense—characteristic of how trauma expresses itself.[66] The text further fortifies this connection between Zosha and her mother when Genia calls Zosha's phone at the time that Uly is visiting her apartment during their one-night stand; as we are reminded of Genia in this moment, the narrative links Genia and Zosha together, prompting an association between mother and daughter. These various connections, among others,[67] establish how Genia's Holocaust experiences inform, albeit seemingly preconsciously, Zosha's sexual encounter in her apartment.

As this scene in her living room progresses, Zosha becomes fixated on Uly's Nazi-like boots, which ushers in the transformation of her apartment into the imagined site of trauma. She recounts that before he lounged on the couch, "he had taken off his black boots, which stood up straight, invisible legs inside them."[68] The image of Uly's boots—which Zosha identifies as a stock symbol of the Shoah[69]—appear to have "invisible legs inside them," suggesting that they are being filled by a ghostly aura, a haunting manifestation in the intimate space of her home. That they are standing "up straight" further codes the boots as phallic objects, thereby coloring their erect shape as a "penetrating" presence that invades the private, womb-like space of her home. This imaginative penetration parallels the postmemorial penetration of her psyche while also foreshadowing the sexual exchange that is to come. Zosha continues to explain that as she takes a seat on the couch, she is unable to take her eyes off the tall black boots, imagining an SS officer sporting them while also "wearing a long coat, a swastika armband on his sleeve. Uly pulled [her] to him."[70] As she cannot stop staring at and thinking about the boots that occupy the physical space of her living room, it becomes clear that they occupy her psychological space as well—that is, they preoccupy her with a rush of postmemories that bring her "back" to the camps, as if she were once there herself. In this moment, Zosha describes an SS officer and then immediately refers to Uly; this syntactical juxtaposition points to how Zosha conflates the two as she looks at the boots. And as the text makes clear, this Nazi-prisoner dynamic is nothing new for Zosha. Describing her former German lover, Ludwig, Zosha says: "He was my Nazi. I loved him with a wild passion."[71] With such an earlier sexual precedent set, Zosha speaks to Uly in Polish as they sit on her couch, situating herself as a concentration camp prisoner in order to help set the erotic mood and scene. By speaking in Polish, it is *Zosha* who initiates the performance of roles for her and Uly. Pinpointing the moment of Zosha's initiation reveals her active decision to assume the role of prisoner. This decision imaginatively renders Zosha's apartment the site of sexualized trauma; however, Zosha neither desires nor directly experiences trauma in this encounter. Rather, she rewrites the script of what she imagines to be her mother's experiences in the camps.

Her self-positioning in this erotic exchange operates as a retroactive effort to reclaim female agency during the Shoah—a belated attempt to assert female bodily autonomy in a time when nearly all autonomy was stripped from her mother. Referring to Uly in this erotic role play, Zosha thinks to herself: "He was the master. *Ubermensch*. Superman. So powerful. It was

1942. I was a prisoner. Jew. Whore."[72] As she is thinking this, the end of his tie swishes against her thighs, and she clasps it between her legs. Uly pulls it tighter, caressing her softly, and she presses his hands hard against her breasts. As she imagines herself in this erotic exchange, the titles she uses to describe Uly seem to indicate that she is his subordinate, that is, his powerless sex slave who is subject to his control and whose body is for his pleasure. However, she consents to his dominance, thereby allowing herself to be acted upon in the first place while also acting herself. Indeed, Zosha merely submits to the *illusion*, or *fantasy*, of Uly's dominance while, in reality, she is the one who maintains control throughout their encounter. Despite how she assumes the submissive role of a woman prisoner, it is *Zosha* who retains control in their erotic tryst. After he says her name, that is, after he recognizes her personhood (something that would have likely remained unrecognized in Auschwitz because of her Jewishness), she says: "I relaxed into his arms, letting him take off my sweater. 'Let's get rid of these too.' My leather skirt. He nearly ripped my lace panties."[73] It is important to underscore here that without Zosha's allowance, Uly would have no dominance to assert from the onset of this encounter. It is she who gives him permission to take off her sweater, and this action affords him subsequent permission to remove other articles of her clothing. Without her initial direction of him to take her clothes off,[74] there would be no sexual exchange at all—a point which again highlights Zosha's control in this scene by way of her gendered corporeality, not to mention her willingness to be there.

This scene further reveals how Zosha vicariously attempts to "make up for" what she imagines to be her mother's loss of power in Auschwitz (though, of course, one could never actually make up for such loss). Like many daughters of survivors who "inferred the violence of sexual abuse and rape ... [and] allowed for a more empowered interpretation of women's agency in which sexual exchanges and bartering were among the few instrumental acts of survivorship in which women could and did engage,"[75] Zosha acknowledges a more empowered interpretation of her mother's agency during the Holocaust. Despite how Uly qua Nazi holds Zosha qua prisoner's life in his hands, her embodied womanhood maintains power over him to such an extent that her physicality, in concert with her strategic use of it, functions as the key to her life and endurance in the imagined camp. The crux of this erotic scene occurs when Zosha realizes her power upon feeling Uly's erection through his pants. She says: "At that moment, I felt my power. I could do what I wanted with him. It was a delicious thought:

how much he needed me. I could withdraw my hand. I could tell him to go to hell. I could, but I didn't. He could kill me. I placed myself squarely on top of him, grinding into his hardness."[76] Her realization ("I could, but I didn't") again demonstrates how Zosha asserts her agency by way of sexual interaction. This expression of agency, however constrained (though nonetheless complex), is underscored by Zosha's above-cited thought, "*If I made him love me, he'd take me through the war.*" Utilizing the subjunctive mood highlights how Zosha as prisoner first critically evaluates the situation, in which she then acts by having sexual relations with Uly qua Nazi. Here, Zosha imaginatively makes intentional use of her body as a tool for survival, thereby integrating what she imagines to be her mother's traumatic past into her erotic life and identity as a second-generation woman. As the story cycle positions Zosha as the embodied, vicarious site of her mother's sexualized humiliation, disgrace, guilt, and shame, Zosha's postmemorial domestication informs the complex power dynamics of her fantasy and role play with Uly.

By sleeping with him, Zosha belatedly attempts to un-domesticate herself postmemorially. This attempt to un-domesticate herself is reinforced by how Zosha describes Uly's aesthetic as "feral,"[77] which in line with her attraction to him, obliquely suggests that Zosha longs for that which is untamed and wild; she desires Uly, who embodies freedom, one who has seeming mastery over the subject of the Holocaust—particularly in light of his profession—as opposed to Zosha who is mastered by her postmemories. In either case, this scene in Zosha's apartment highlights how postmemorial structures reflect members of the second generation's traumas and embodied experiences while also shaping their postmemories. Indeed, as her apartment functions as the setting of an imagined sexual exchange, it enables her to live out her fantasy because of the privacy it affords her.

Akin to Spiegelman's *Maus*, *The Holocaust Kid* elucidates how the second generation's postmemorial structures in their adulthoods operate as extensions of their childhood domiciles qua traumatic archives. In the closing of the "Our Father, Our King" story/chapter, Zosha describes her father at a parking meter, putting in two quarters before the light turns green and he crosses the street. She then states, "Though I left years ago, I follow behind him."[78] It is unclear if this chapter is imagined or if Zosha is actually outside her family apartment as she watches him. Regardless, Zosha's statement gives voice to the enduring impact of her childhood postmemorial structure on her cognition. Despite having moved away as an adult,

Zosha continues to metaphorically "follow behind him"—or, otherwise put, she imaginatively continues to go home to the space of her childhood apartment, regardless of wanting to escape its control. Similar to how Vladek says to Artie in *Maus*, "Remember, my house it's also your house too [*sic*],"[79] Zosha gestures toward how she continues to "inhabit" her childhood home. Thus, although Zosha physically left her childhood postmemorial structure, she, like Artie, psychically returns regularly, highlighting the profound postmemorial domestication of her psyche.

However, the end of *The Holocaust Kid* suggests that it is by having a child (though, not with Uly) that Zosha begins to un-domesticate herself while, ironically, becoming a more traditional domestic subject herself. As she leans into her role as a mother, one who becomes more of a homebody as a result, Zosha begins to reconceptualize her relationship to the domestic, to motherhood, and eventually to her parents' traumatic pasts. Before having a child, she expresses to her parents her desire to know more about her murdered family whose names she does not know, saying that she wants to make a Palovsky family tree.[80] This double entendre communicates not only that she wants to draw out a genealogical chart that represents her family. It also speaks to her desire to build part of the family tree herself, to continue the Palovsky-family line by having a child. As their family tree is almost completely devoid of branches or leaves,[81] Zosha seeks to extend her lineage because of how, she explains, she was raised to bear children and give them names of her murdered family members.[82] This responsibility to bear children is given further expression in her dreams, when she hears the voices of family ghosts who cry out, *"Name me. Give me your child. Resurrect our lost lives. Breathe life into your life, Zosha."*[83] Though she is postmemorially haunted by her murdered relatives, burdened by a history that relentlessly pursues her, her journey into motherhood allows her to begin detoxifying her relationship to the past. As she looks at the television monitor while undergoing amniocentesis, she sees a filament swimming with "its heartbeats exploding in tiny stars."[84] Her association of heartbeats with exploding stars is a reappropriation of a symbol of death. The explosions of stars, occurrences known as supernovas, are the deaths of such stars, but such explosions also result in the emission of light millions of times their normal levels. *The Holocaust Kid* employs this metaphor of bright eruptions to illuminate, so to speak, how Zosha's baby becomes a light, a hope, for the future. This metaphor of heartbeats as stars holds an additional valence of significance given the requirement for Jews to wear the Star of David during the Shoah. Zosha's metaphor reappropriates the symbol of the star, representative of death and destruction, to describe heartbeats, those which are indexical of burgeoning life. As she rubs her belly after waking up from a nightmare, she says that she could feel within herself a house being built for new life.[85] Like how Zosha herself becomes her baby's home, so does her home itself become renewed, reconfigured to make room for new life. Indeed, after having her son, her apartment becomes increasingly more focused on new life and less defined by her parents' Holocaust experiences. This is not to say that she is able to untether herself completely from the past and simply move forward, as if that were possible. Instead, by becoming pregnant and having a child, she is no longer immobilized *in* the past as much as she is able to carry the past forward *with* her in and through her various domestic (and extra-domestic) spaces. It can thus be said that having a son becomes the central means of postmemorially un-domesticating herself.

Conclusion

This chapter, as its title suggests, explores the multiple ways that domestication, the domestic, fashion, and the fashioning of both people and space operate in *The Holocaust Kid*, with a particular focus on how gender, sexuality, and embodiment inform Zosha's experiences of her various domiciles. Zosha struggles against being domesticated by her parents both physically and psychosocially in the home. But as this study makes clear, the physical (that is, the material space of the home) and the psychosocial are intertwined and animate one another; as postmemory qua structure[86] shapes the structure of the home, the structure of the home also shapes postmemory qua structure. Thus, Zosha's containment in her family home throughout her childhood amplifies her postmemorial domestication, resulting in her being tamed by her parents' pasts and having her cognition colonized by her postmemories. Her postmemorial domestication finds further expression in Genia dressing or fashioning her, making Zosha in her own likeness both aesthetically and postmemorially. As survivors' fashion choices commonly communicated Holocaust trauma indirectly, Genia's fashioning of her daughter in front of the mirror symbolizes how she clothes her daughter in her traumas. Zosha rebels by way of her fashion choices and in how she fashions her own apartment that sharply contrasts their family home. Yet, what happens is that Zosha is postmemorially fashioned by her adulthood home similarly to how she is fashioned by her childhood home; the space of her adulthood apartment becomes the space onto which she projects her postmemories, and the space itself in turn shapes said postmemories. Though she intends her adulthood domestic space to become the vehicle to undomesticate herself—given how her apartment is that which is supposed to help separate her from her parents and their pasts—it nonetheless postmemorially domesticates her, including when she has sex with Uly and he unfashions or undresses her in their erotic role play. This postmemorial domestication, however, is alleviated at least in part when she becomes a mother herself. These various representations of fashion, fashioning, the domestic, and domestication provide insight into how postmemorial structures shape the psychosocial lives of the second generation.

4

A Tale of Two Storeys

Upper and Lower Space
and Postmemorial
Divergences in Elizabeth
Rosner's *The Speed of Light*

Born in 1959 in Schenectady, New York, Elizabeth Rosner is a novelist, a poet, an essayist, and a short fiction writer.[1] The second of three children raised in a Jewish Orthodox household, Rosner is also the daughter of Holocaust survivors. Much of her work centers on the aftermath of the Shoah, largely reflective of her attempts "to come to terms with the impact of her parents' experiences on her own life, the indelible imprints of their history on her language, her identity, and her imagination."[2] Of all her writings, the text that speaks most to the relationship between survivors and their children is her novel *The Speed of Light* (2001)[3]—a text which presents detailed portraits of postmemorial structures that significantly differ from one another, despite belonging to siblings born to the same survivor parent.

The Speed of Light is the story of how two siblings, Paula and Julian, emphatically diverge in their relationship to their postmemories which stem from their father Jacob Perel's traumatic past. Born in Hungary, Jacob was sent to Auschwitz at the age of seventeen and became a part of a *Sonderkommando* (special command unit), that is, a group of Jewish prisoners who were required to work in the gas chambers and crematoria.[4] Jacob's work in a *Sonderkommando* forced him to witness and participate in the deaths of hundreds, if not thousands, of victims. This understandably left myriad psychosocial scars that led to a profound psychic closing-off—a self-protective retreat inward that resulted in an all-consuming state of affective dullness and a profound inability to emotionally connect with others, including his family. In his post-Shoah life, Jacob creates a home that is invariably defined by emotional depletion, resignation, secrecy, and silence about his traumatic past,[5] which Paula and Julian deal with in two dramatically different ways as both children and adults. Whereas young Julian parallels their father by retreating inward and emotionally isolating himself in the space of the Perel-family home, Paula leaves home to live with her music teacher at an early age in hopes of escaping the haunting legacy of their father. Highlighting the contrast between the siblings' coping strategies, Sola Luz Ordonio, Paula's housekeeper who becomes Julian's romantic love interest, describes Paula as constantly smiling and moving, which is in sharp contrast to Julian, who is stoic, largely static, and trapped within the traumatic dreams of their father—one whom Sola describes as "ready to disappear."[6] Throughout *The Speed of Light*, the Perel siblings' differing relationships to their father's traumas are made clear in multiple ways.

One of the most prominent expressions of how they relate to their postmemories is how they inhabit their various domestic spaces. How Paula and Julian perceive and experience their childhood postmemorial structure shapes how they later indwell their adjoined apartments as adults. Shedding light on the relationship between childhood homes and dreams, Gaston Bachelard explains that the house in which one is born is "imbued with dream values which remain after the house is gone."[7] In *The Speed of Light*, insofar as the Perel-family home becomes imbued with the dreams of what the siblings believe to have happened to Jacob during the Shoah, such dreams also shape how they relate to their domestic spaces in their later years. Similar to how Paula seeks refuge from her childhood home, she constantly travels and is thus rarely at home in her adulthood, which indirectly speaks to her desire to escape the postmemories that have defined the domestic for her. But despite how Paula essays to distance herself from their father's Holocaust traumas throughout much of her life, her eventual discovery of his work in a *Sonderkommando* results in her becoming not only paralyzed by his traumatic past but also a domestic shut-in at the end of the novel. Julian, on the other hand, spends the vast majority of his time within his home in the beginning of the narrative; his obsessive indwelling of his apartment mirrors his constant "inhabitation" of his inherited Holocaust traumas and embodied experiences. Yet, as the narrative progresses and he spends more time with Sola, he begins to open up and come to terms with his postmemories. In other words, whereas Paula initially attempts to avoid learning or speaking about the Holocaust until she is later consumed by their father's traumatic past, Julian finds himself domesticated from a young age by their father's experience in the camps but then begins to move beyond the restriction of his postmemories—and domestic space—by the end of the novel.

A topoanalytic examination of Paula and Julian's respective adulthood domestic spaces offers insight into how they relate to their postmemories in markedly different ways. Expanding the shockingly minimal scholarship on Rosner's work—with little more than a master's thesis on the novel to date[8]—this chapter establishes how the Perel-family home operates as a space that in part catalyzes the siblings' postmemories in their childhoods and shapes their subsequent relationships to their adulthood apartments. The spatial locations of the siblings' adulthood apartments—with Julian's atop Paula's—symbolizes how they navigate their father's Holocaust traumas. Insofar as Paula inhabits the main-floor apartment, she initially lives in a less heady and more "embodied" (lower) space that reflects her attempts to escape her postmemories by constantly keeping busy, specifically by singing. And as Julian occupies the upstairs apartment largely in reclusion, his constant domestic occupation serves as a metaphor for how he continuously occupies an isolated, "heady" (upper) space of postmemory that imprisons him within his father's past. The shift in Paula and Julian's responses to their father's Holocaust legacy are then registered in and through their shifting relationships to their apartments. Such shifts in how the two siblings individually relate to their father's Holocaust traumas, as mirrored by their relationships to their respective domestic spaces, constitute two interconnected *postmemorial divergences*. By postmemorial divergences, I mean to communicate the turning points for Julian and Paula when they change how they relate to their inherited Holocaust traumas and embodied experiences. With these interrelated plots operating in *The Speed of Light*, the siblings' postmemorial divergences speak to the range of ways that members of the second generation navigate their relationships to the Shoah, even within the same family. This chapter is the first in this study that centers specifically on the differing effects of postmemory on siblings, revealing how the Holocaust shapes domestic space for those within the same family and, inversely, how domestic space shapes siblings' postmemories in divergent ways.[9]

The Perel-Family Home

The Perel-family home, like many survivor-family homes, functions as an affective archive of Holocaust traumas and embodied experiences. As Jacob's traumatic past takes up residence and finds expression in the space of the family home, Paula and Julian's childhood domicile is rendered a space of disrupted and disruptive temporality. For the Perels, particularly for Jacob and Julian, the space of the domestic collapses their sense of past and present, such that the distinction between Auschwitz and the United States are temporally and spatially muddled. Indeed, as the material culture and the space of the home are imbued with Jacob's persistently haunting past, the novel underscores the ways by which survivor-family homes communicate Holocaust traumas to the second generation, which in turn create affective environments that can traumatize children of survivors. Jacob's silence and emotional distance from his children, along with his domestic eating habits, create a home environment that re-animates his traumas for Julian specifically, despite Julian having little actual knowledge of these traumas.

Although he does not want to pass on his sadness and grief to his children, Jacob transmits his traumatic past largely by way of silence in the Perel-family home, creating an affective domestic space that, ironically, communicates his Holocaust past to his son and, in a different sense, his daughter. Julian explains that, growing up, he and his father would sit together "in a room thick with silence" since Jacob would not say a word to his son.[10] His description of silence as "thick" points toward the sensorial intensity of the space they share, a palpable affective heaviness that defines the oppressive atmosphere they both indwell. Julian says that though he never heard his father's stories explicitly, it was clear that Jacob held within himself "shards of glass," that is, difficult memories that "cut him to pieces." Julian continues: "When he looked at me, it was not so much into my eyes as through them, as if I were a clear window to the past. I looked back at him, I listened to the wordless dark."[11] Contrasting Artie in Spiegelman's *Maus*, Julian is not privy to his father's Holocaust experiences, leaving him with the difficult task of piecing together the fragments ("the shards of glass") of Jacob's "wordless dark." But similar to second-generation protagonist Yaakov/Jason in Thomas Friedmann's *Damaged Goods* (1984) who avows, "my father speaks to me with silence,"[12] Jacob also communicates with Julian through his muteness. Julian, despite not knowing specifics, swallows his father's fragmented personal history,[13] forcing him to digest, so to speak, that which wounds him. Yet, it is particularly noteworthy that Jacob looks through Julian and that Julian describes how his father sees him as if he were a "window to the past." It is unclear to which past he refers—whether it be Jacob's pre-Shoah life or his life during the Holocaust. But in either case, the fact that Julian feels that he is not seen by his father—and is instead being looked *through*—points to that on which Jacob is fixated: the Holocaust, not his son. Feeling invisible in comparison to the Shoah, he remains at an unbridgeable distance from his father. Julian wonders if his father's silence was an exercise in "erasing his past," an effort "to stop the current" that nonetheless flowed "electric and relentless" in Julian.[14] Despite how his father may have attempted "to stop the current" through his silence, it is his silence itself that ironically feeds and indeed increases the current. The affective space of their home yokes father and son with a (post)memorial interconnection that transcends language. Louise Kaplan notes how survivors' silence often became "a Holocaust monument" that cast its shadows over the lives of their children.[15] Like many other members of the second generation, Julian struggles with the intangibility of his father's muteness, unable to grapple with the amorphous "monument" that ironically gives shape to his postmemories. He describes the transmission of his father's wordlessly articulated traumas by using lacerating imagery, stating that he "was cut open by that silence."[16] As he is emotionally and psychologically wounded ("cut open") by his father's mutism, his body is figuratively opened up and becomes porous to such an extent that the traumatic "current" runs throughout the home and flows through Julian seemingly osmotically. Paula, however, one who also notes Jacob's Holocaust past being "wrapped in silence,"[17] avoids the traumatic current by remaining largely outside the family home, separating herself from such affective transmission. Yet, for Julian and Paula alike, their childhood home stands as not just an archive of Holocaust trauma but also a conduit to pass along this trauma.

For Julian specifically, Jacob's traumatic past, communicated by way of his silence, blurs the line between the past and the present in their home, which exacerbates Julian's postmemories. Enumerating day-to-day sounds that throw into confusion the line between his daily life and his father's traumatic history, Julian states: "His nightmares lived in daylight too. . . . A certain kind of barking dog, a backfiring car, an explosion of fire in a chemistry lab. Reality came too close sometimes, reaching through skin and bone."[18] That the text describes these events as both "nightmares" and "reality" points to the hazy distinction between fantasy and the workaday world—not to mention between past and present—for both generations. The barks of their neighbors' dogs become the barks of camp guard dogs that threaten to attack; internal combustion engines become the sounds of Nazi Volkswagens; and explosions become reminiscent of the bombing that took place during the war. For Julian, quotidian sounds take on a postmemorial quality to such a degree that the everyday is not and *cannot* be taken for granted as mundane or banal. Instead, commonplace sounds transform the ordinary into the exceptional, wherein Julian's everyday sonic experience incites severe temporal and spatial disruption. As Julian does not identify the spatial or temporal nature of this reality, it is unclear if he is pointing to the camps or to his life in the United States. He further fails to specify for whom this "reality came too close"—whether it is for his father or for himself. With no such established partition between whose reality he is referencing and with no indication of its specific spatiality/temporality, Julian collapses the distinction between the past and the present and between father and son, revealing the unstable boundaries of their intersubjective psychosocial domestic world.

Julian's confusion of time and space—and of himself and his father—is compounded in and through the Perel-family home. After hearing an unnamed survivor's story about the Holocaust, Julian says that when he looked down at his own wrists, he saw Jacob's "fragile bones; in my eyes I saw his haunted look. At night I heard him sometimes whimpering in his sleep and instead of my mattress I felt hard wooden planks. His dreams were woven into mine."[19] Here, Julian's affiliative postmemory maps onto his familial postmemory. The unnamed survivor's story gives young Julian concrete details to come to terms with his nebulous postmemories that, despite being epistemically *un*known to him, were already deeply, and paradoxically, "known" in an affective sense. The role of these stories in helping Julian flesh out, so to speak, his father's past operates on two levels: not only do these stories furnish Julian with the imaginative fodder to fill in the narrative gaps of his untold stories from Auschwitz, but they also shape his perception of his own flesh. Insofar as bones provide the human form bodily structure, Julian's imaginative assumption of his father's "fragile bones" suggests that his father's traumatic past—that which made him emotionally and psychologically fragile in the first place—structures his embodied experience as a survivor's child. But more germane to this study is Julian's discussion of how his bed imaginatively transforms into a barracks bunkbed ("hard wooden planks"). Such a transformation points to how the Perel-family home functions as a screen onto which Julian projects his inherited traumas. The space of the home in turn reinforces these traumas, as it is the space in which Julian imaginatively animates the physical conditions of the barracks where he sleeps, thereby altering how he perceives and experiences his domestic space.

Julian, like his home, thus becomes a receptacle of Jacob's Holocaust traumas and embodied experiences. Julian states, "I was my father's grief."[20] His equation of himself as his father's grief speaks to how Jacob's Holocaust past not only affects him but, as Katharina Koerfer notes, "is the very essence of [Julian's] life."[21] Conceptualizing himself as his father's grief, Julian perceives himself as the embodiment of Jacob's traumas, the corporeal container of his father's Shoah experiences. Julian is in line with a number of children of survivors who describe being or containing within them receptacles of their parents' traumatic histories. Helen Epstein, for instance, describes having deep within her "an iron box,"[22] which "became a vault, collecting in darkness, always collecting, pictures, words, my parents' glances, becoming loaded with weight."[23] Similarly, Julian takes stock of Jacob's nonverbals and comes to share a number of commonalities with his father that are functions of Jacob's Holocaust past, including insomnia,[24] a fear of the smell of grilling meat,[25] and a protracted state of anxiety, depression, and psychic closing off.[26] By living within the space of the Perel-family home qua Holocaust archive, so too does Julian's body archive his father's traumas.

Eating together as a family becomes an especially troublesome site of traumatic transmission, where Jacob's eating habits further speak of his Holocaust past that his children are forced to witness. Julian recounts how for years the entire family was vegetarian because Jacob could not stand the taste or smell of meat since both made him feel sick.[27] Jacob's detestation is a function of his time as a *Sonderkommando*, one who was forced to smell burning human flesh up close. His prohibition of meat in the home serves as an additional wordless reference to his survival during the Shoah—that is, a gastronomical reminder of his unspoken traumas from Auschwitz. Paula describes how they ate in silence as a family and how Jacob would commonly descend into a "trance of inhaling" food.[28] Explaining that their father's mealtime ferocity made her lose her appetite and that she would not eat as a result,[29] she further explains that he hastily swallowed his food in order to fill a void—that is, "the memory of hunger"[30]—that could never actually be filled. Time at the family dining table forces Paula, along with Julian, to become a spectator of Jacob's embodied memory of hunger. His eating habits communicate how he survived in Auschwitz, thus reanimating, at least in part, his desperate condition in the death camp. Food and eating, therefore, take on postmemorial significance for both Perel children, thereby intensifying the emotionally fraught environment of the family home.

The affective state of their postmemorial structure that Jacob creates through his sustained silence and his eating habits is further intensified by the presence of other survivors in the home. Similar to Zosha in Pilcer's *The Holocaust Kid*, who is repeatedly surrounded by survivors growing up, Paula and Julian are forced to listen to other survivors' stories about the Shoah. In line with Julian's memory of there being more survivors who passed through their home than he could count,[31] Paula explains how she hated the seemingly endless testimonies of survivors who came through their house, which left her feeling as if they were trapped in "a permanent funeral," where guests would continuously mourn, recount stories of those who were murdered, and cry to such an extent that she would repeatedly make excuses in order to leave the table before finishing her food.[32] Here, Paula connects her recollection of living in "a permanent funeral" to her memory of leaving the dining table. This connection is suggestive of how Paula refuses, unlike young Zosha, to "consume" these survivors' traumatic stories, akin to how she refuses to eat much in the presence of her father. Yet, as Paula was in many ways (though not in every way) able to avoid "consuming" many of these stories, Julian contrastingly is consumed by such narratives. The space that Jacob creates for other survivors to give voice to their Holocaust experiences renders Paula a prisoner in her own home while engendering affiliative postmemories for Julian.

The Perel-family home is defined by and imbued with Holocaust traumas, a space that structures how Julian as well as Paula relate to their domiciles for years to come. The fact that much of the discussion in this chapter thus far is comparable to what has been explored in the previous chapters points to the many commonalities between children of survivors and their domestic experiences. Though Paula and Julian differ in how they relate to their father's Holocaust past, both share a number of parallels with other members of the second generation. As Paula attempts to run from her father and his traumas, she resembles *The Holocaust Kid*'s Zosha and oral-history narrator Evaline E. Delson. Yet, Julian, who is consistently consumed by his postmemories, also finds parallels to Zosha and Evaline, not to mention *Maus*'s Artie—all of whom find themselves overwhelmed by their inherited traumas and embodied experiences, including and especially in their childhoods. As these continuities and divergences between these characters and texts suggest, there are many experiences of postmemory. But what differs significantly from *Maus* and *The Holocaust Kid* are the postmemorial divergences represented in *The Speed of Light*, including when Paula is first overtaken and immobilized by her inherited traumas as an *adult*, as opposed to as a child.

Paula's Adulthood Apartment

Offering insight into how some members of the second generation did not begin to come to terms with their parents' Holocaust experiences until their adulthoods, Anne Karpf maintains that she considered herself "somewhat superior" to other children of survivors who only began to contemplate how their parents' Holocaust experiences affected them as adults: "I'd been thinking about the subject for several years now, in my therapy and outside it. If I wasn't special, I was at least advanced."[33] Karpf's observation—that there were many members of the second generation who had not meditated on the effects of their parents' Shoah experiences—suggests how Paula's avoidance of the Holocaust is not an uncommon experience for the children of survivors. Paula thus represents a notable demographic within the second generation, as she does not begin actively considering the effects of the Shoah on her life until well into her adulthood. Although as a child she contemplates her father's Holocaust past,[34] she intentionally focuses her attention on singing—an embodied, corporeal practice—so as not to be consumed psychologically by the Shoah. This avoidance of the Holocaust becomes reflected in how she sets up and inhabits her adulthood apartment—an apartment that stands in sharp relief to the home in which she grew up. It is brightly lit and open, contrasting the Perel-family home's dark and claustrophobic interior. Moreover, the messiness of her adulthood home is reflective of her "messy" psychological interiority; as postmemories are out of place almost-memories that throw into confusion members of the second generation's individual subjectivities, the disorderly state of her adulthood home reveals her "messy" postmemorial connection to her father's traumas. But even though she decorates her apartment in marked distinction from the house in which she was raised, the space of her adulthood apartment is nonetheless shaped by her childhood home. The memory of the Perel-family home, imbued with enduring "dream values" as Bachelard puts it, keeps Paula from spending much time in her adulthood apartment. Thus, Paula's time spent outside the home metaphorizes her refusal to be postmemorially domesticated as an adult, similar to how she separates herself from her father and his Holocaust past in her childhood.

Contrasting the interior aesthetics of the Perel-family home, the cheerful décor of Paula's apartment reflects how she attempts to present herself as happy and lighthearted, free from her father's dark past. Throughout the novel, her apartment is referred to as "bright,"[35] "filled with color and light and beautiful objects,"[36] and "open."[37] These cheery descriptions are indicative of how Paula attempts to remain focused on the positive aspects of her existence, refusing to pay any mind to anything sad, depressing, or painful. Like how Paula decides to leave her role in an opera company in northern Ontario because it is "cold and dark,"[38] she also flees, both literally and figuratively, from that which is not bright and warm as much as possible. As a result, she creates an aesthetically beautiful and well-lit interior in her apartment, paralleling her self-presentation as happy and buoyant. But both her home décor and her carefree persona are later revealed to be veiled attempts to convince herself and others that nothing is wrong, that all is well below the surface. Sola's description of Paula's apartment underscores the relationship between Paula and her domestic interiors; she explains that there are many mirrors in Paula's home that are strategically situated to catch the light from outside—all in order to "make the rooms feel wider, more open with space."[39] Insofar as Paula attempts to open up her apartment with the light reflected by her mirrors, she also tries to open herself up by singing, which keeps her (in her estimation) "in the air, buoyant with sound."[40] However, in line with the idiomatic expression of someone being said to be all "smoke and mirrors," Paula's bright, open, and mirror-filled decoration is a cover for that which is dark below the surface, similar to how the persona she presents to others is a cover for that from which she is running. The novel draws the connection between Paula and her apartment so as to illustrate how, despite sunny appearances, there is much that is unseen that is less than cheery, specifically her postmemories.

The novel further establishes the metaphorical relationship between Paula and her domestic by how her apartment is described—messy and disorganized—which speaks to the postmemorial "mess" that threatens to dis-order her psychosocial life. Not only does Paula refer to her own apartment as a "mess,"[41] but so too does Sola[42] who even labels it "a circus."[43] Sola goes on to explain that the first time she came to Paula's apartment, she thought it would be impossible to clean because there was too much disorder.[44] Helping us understand Paula's messy apartment, James Krasner explains that "personal history becomes carried by, hidden in, and materially experienced through disorderly accumulations."[45] As the mess of Jacob's Holocaust traumas threaten to temporally and spatially dis-order the present for him and his children, the mess in Paula's apartment functions as a disorderly accumulation that represents her postmemories. Regardless of her efforts to present herself as carefree and happy, Paula nevertheless holds within her the "mess" of Holocaust stories she heard as a child, those which she actively avoids and from which she continues trying to run as an adult.

That she spends little time in her domestic space—a space colored and shaped by her childhood postmemorial structure—speaks to how she seeks reprieve from her father's traumatic past. She explains that when she sang as a kid, she "was practicing leaving, practicing [her] flight into [her] own life."[46] What is noteworthy is her description of taking flight into her own life. Insofar as having postmemories constitutes being under the sway and control of a survivor's traumas and embodied experiences—that is, being postmemorial domesticated—Paula's flight from her childhood home is an attempt to free herself from Jacob's domestic postmemorial tyranny. She thus describes singing as a way to save herself, in that it enabled her to flee from her childhood home: "My voice was a ticket of escape, one way to anywhere but where I was."[47] The language of "escape" suggests a level of severity, where the Perel-family home functions as a space of postmemorial captivity—similar to that of the Spiegelman-family home in *Maus* or the Palovsky-family home in *The Holocaust Kid*. Therefore, in light of how one's adulthood home carries with it dream values from one's childhood home, it is understandable why Paula is rarely there. While the postmemorial structure in which she grew up made palpable the emanations of her father's Holocaust experiences, her adulthood apartment—despite its bright aesthetics and in all its messiness—threatens to do the same.

Julian's Adulthood Apartment

In sharp contrast to Paula's adulthood domestic space, Julian's apartment in his adulthood falls within the postmemorial ambit of Auschwitz, wherein his life is circumscribed by Jacob's Holocaust traumas. His father's traumatic past shapes how Julian organizes, decorates, and operates within his home. In the beginning of the novel, his domestic space—which is consistently closed up, obsessively ordered, and only selectively open to others—speaks to his overwhelmingly traumatized psyche that results in debilitating agoraphobia. His meticulous and obsessive curation of his home, particularly his compulsively organized collection of TVs qua postmemorial things,[48] is an expression of his desire for order, that which stands in stark contrast to his frenzied and disordered inner life. His compulsive ordering of his home parallels and is a function of his continuous attempts to assert some semblance of control in the face of being controlled by his father's traumatic past. His apartment, however, does not function as a domestic space that postmemorially incarcerates him in the same way as Artie's postmemorial structure in *Maus* or Zosha's in *The Holocaust Kid*. It nonetheless functions as a psychosocial space that bears witness to his postmemorial domestication. Both Artie and Zosha's adulthood apartments are spaces in which their parents' Holocaust traumas are reanimated, where their parents' experiences in the camps seemingly come to life and thereby further imprison them in their postmemories. Dissimilarly, Jacob's Holocaust traumas are not necessarily made manifest *through* the space of Julian's adulthood apartment; rather, Julian uses his apartment to try to keep his postmemories at bay, to maintain a safe distance from triggers that threaten to dredge up his father's past. But regardless of how Julian attempts to block out the Shoah by creating an isolated domestic space, his isolation nonetheless creates the conditions necessary for him to remain trapped within his mind and his adopted traumatic past.

In part a function of epigenetics[49] and in part a result of continuously sharing time and space with Jacob for years, Julian in his adulthood continues to live in a domestic state of temporal and spatial confusion that disallows him to separate the past from the present. Julian explains that time never made sense to him the way it seemed to make sense to other people.[50] Because of his postmemories, any linear perception of time and defined perception of space are profoundly jumbled; his postmemories throw into confusion a clear distinction between past (during the Shoah) and present (in the time the novel is set), not to mention any definite division between here (Northern California) and there (Auschwitz). In line with Stephen Kern's discussion of protagonist Marcel in Marcel Proust's *In Search of Lost Time* (1913), Julian's "body [keeps] its own time"[51] throughout the majority of *The Speed of Light*. As Julian spends much of his day (and night) in his apartment—sleeping, eating, and working inside—he does not participate in public time (the societally shared, collective experience of time). Instead, his reclusive domestic life creates the conditions for him to exist in a closed-off private sphere, apart from the greater social world. Like how he largely stays in his room as a child[52]—in order to be apart from his father—he obsessively remains within his adulthood apartment.

To create a sense of security and safety, Julian isolates himself in the enclosed space of his apartment, out of reach of the threats he imagines to be beyond his doorstep that are products of his postmemories. In his attempts to create for himself a space that protects him from extra-domestic threats or, as he describes them, "terrors of possible encounters,"[53] he not only tries to teach himself not to feel[54] (a form of self-protection), but he also secludes himself in his domestic space. In sharp contradistinction to how Paula is first depicted in the novel, Julian is initially portrayed as a domestic shut-in, one who attempts to shelter himself "in the safe embrace of [his] apartment."[55] Remaining within the fixed boundaries of his home, he lessens the frequency of encountering the aforementioned sonic triggers (i.e., dogs, engines, and explosions) that menace to drag him back into his adopted past while also reducing the possibility of chancing upon what he believes to be threats to his wellbeing. This reclusion affords him the space to maintain a sense of internal stasis as he tries to control and limit his exposure to that which he fears. In his efforts to retain such a sense of control, as well as a sense of order, he keeps his windows and doors closed when at all possible—efforts to seal himself off from the public sphere. This preoccupation with domestic boundaries and separateness from others parallels the somatic boundaries he maintains in order to prohibit others' entrance into his inner world. After Paula leaves for Europe, he avows that he knows how to keep "the rest of the world from entering." He continues: "I had practice reinforcing the boundaries of my skin. I could lock [Sola] out."[56] His description of keeping Sola and the rest of the world out holds multivalent significance. It is unclear if Julian is speaking about disallowing others to enter his life figuratively or if he is referring to physically barring others from entering his apartment, but this ambiguity underscores the conception of his home as emblematic of him and thus a psychosocial space. Epstein takes up this idea of "psychic closing off," describing it as "an inability to feel or project emotion in the ways survivors had been able to do prior to their war experience. In the camps or forests, 'psychic closing off' had been a survival skill, a way to get from one day to the next without losing one's life or mind."[57] Like his father who kept those around him at a distance, Julian is similarly able to keep others out of his shared, social world. He goes on to explain that invisibility was not as much a choice as it was a necessity: "I wanted to watch, not be watched. I wanted to keep an eye on the edges of things, the distances between myself and everyone else."[58] With "an eye on the edges of things," along with such distinct "boundaries of [his] skin," Julian attempts to remain distant from and out of sight of others, so as to place himself in a position of ocular control. His desire for control ("to watch, not be watched") functions as an additional response to his fear of being dominated or mastered, even if only by way of others' gazes. His attempts to separate himself from the outside world, in order to self-protect, ironically render him imprisoned within both his body and his home.

Paula's description of her brother and his apartment sheds further light on Julian's insular daily existence, further demonstrating how Julian's apartment stands as a metaphor for his traumatized psyche. Paula describes her brother: "His own mind was world enough, or so it seemed."[59] That she identifies his mind as his world points to the headiness of his existence. The world he sees and experiences, though, is largely contained within his apartment; as he consistently remains at home, his apartment thus in many ways *is* his world. As such, the walls of his apartment not only represent his walled-off-ness, but the walls themselves are also actual barriers that isolate him in his mind world. Paula says that she could not fathom "what it must be like to be closed up so tight" and that just thinking about it made her "feel suffocated."[60] That she remains ambiguous about what is "closed up so tight" gestures toward the interchangeability of Julian's psychosocial state and his apartment. Her aversion to such restricting containment elicits for her a suffocating sensation, drawing attention to the palpable affect of her brother's apartment and his constant containment within it. The effects of living in his apartment are disabling for Julian, as evidenced by his difficulty to move literally and figuratively outside it. Yet, he nonetheless remains within his psychosocial domestic space, in part, because he has lived such a domesticated existence for as long as he can remember, and to live differently would require both change and vulnerability—foreign concepts for him as they were for his father.

His organized domestic interior counterpoints his psychological interior—an interior that lacks a defined sense of temporal and spatial order. Despite his attempts to maintain order, the tidiness of Julian's apartment stands in contradistinction to the "disorder" of his postmemories, that is, to the temporal and spatial confusion caused by his inherited Holocaust traumas and embodied experiences. Shedding light on her own insistence upon order as a child, Epstein notes: "Putting things in order was my way of pretending that nothing was wrong. It was the tactic I often used to ward away pain."[61] Such a tactic is a common phenomenon in the second generation, as evidenced by Robert M. Prince's study of the second generation. Prince explains: "The need to control the self and the need to control the environment, based on fears of losing control, were prominent themes in the lives of the subjects."[62] Similarly for Julian, his lack of control in his psychosocial life manifests by way of his attempt to control his domestic space. Sola describes Julian's controlled domestic environment, stating that each room is "so tight with order" that it seems as if he uses glue to keep things in their place and a ruler to line up the edges of the neat piles of paper on his desk.[63] Julian's obsessive organization of his space speaks to his desire for orderliness since his daily psychic experience lacks any such tidiness and possesses no distinct separation between imagination and reality. Such fastidious domestic positionality is symptomatic of his deep yearning to keep the past in the past and master the postmemories that have mastered him his whole life; by putting everything in its place, Julian obliquely endeavors to arrange the disarray of his adopted past and create a sense of defined order in the face of chaos. His punctilious attempts to maintain order of and to control his almost-memories, however, are continually frustrated in light of how postmemory resists orderly temporality. Since postmemory transgresses temporal boundaries, indiscriminately interposing the past into the present, Julian's attempts to isolate himself and sort out his postmemories prove unsuccessful as he struggles with his inherited traumas, which force him to explore an alternative path to move beyond his psychosocial domestic space.

Yet, as Sola subtly suggests, such domestic order represents, *via negativa*, Julian's internal disarrangement and his inability to keep his father's Holocaust traumas separate from his own psyche. The text signals through the mouth of Sola that, below the surface, Julian is not nearly as "orderly" as his outward appearance would suggest. Sola posits that under his fingernails, he holds "the dust of the past."[64] This "dust of the past" beneath Julian's fingernails, representative of the traces of his inherited Holocaust past, speaks to the internal disorder that is nonetheless visible to those around him. Mary Douglas offers insight into how dust, like dirt, can be theorized. Douglas avows: "Dirt is essentially disorder."[65] Insofar as dust and dirt are "matter out of place"[66]—those which offend against notions of purity, cleanliness, and order—what Julian holds under his nails functions as a material parallel to what he holds within his psyche: out of place "memories." The dust under his nails undercuts the clean, orderly, and organized picture we otherwise have of both him and his physical world, enabling us to see how despite his domestic orderliness, that which is below the surface is defined by disorder.

His collection, organization, and viewing of his TVs qua postmemorial things further enables him to find some semblance of order and assert ostensible control in the face of his uncontrolled internal world. Julian stacks his collection of TVs with precision, two rows of four and one of three, placing his chair directly in front of the collection as though he "were the conductor instead of the audience,"[67] before stating that everything he watched on his televisions "was small enough, as quiet or loud as [he] chose."[68] Julian understands his organization of his TVs as an activity in which he is actively in charge (as the conductor). Yet, at as Mihaly Csikszentmihalyi and Eugene Rochberg-Halton remind us, the act of watching TV is largely a passive and pacifying pastime,[69] that which "is essentially a vicarious social activity, because the viewer is almost constantly confronted with representations of other people engaged in various types of interaction."[70] Thus, in addition to affording him the belief that he is in control, watching TV for Julian allows him also to avoid actively and directly confronting his postmemories. He explains that when he spirals into fits of anxiety stemming from his inherited traumas, he turns on his TVs to redirect his attention. After describing thoughts of explosions, the smell of burning flesh, and the incineration of human bodies, which plague his mind, he posits that the only way to free himself from his nightmares is to turn up the volume of the TVs and concentrate his attention as much as possible on what he is viewing. He notes that watching his TVs allows him to peel himself out of his own skin and alleviate the terror he has within himself.[71] But watching TV in his apartment also enables him to remain distant from the greater social world that terrifies him *because of* his postmemories. As such, his TV collection becomes an additional literal and figurative wall to the outside world, that which shields him from the potential chaos beyond his doorstep. His interaction with his TVs, like his organization of his apartment, speaks to his lack of and need for control, which issues forth from his postmemories.

His collection of TVs moreover keeps him company throughout much of the novel, accompanying him in a way that Jacob never did and thereby functioning as a stand-in for his emotionally absent father. Julian discusses how, in the wake of Paula leaving home to study music as a child,[72] he began to watch TV, keeping it on all the time, even while asleep; he states that he needed the "low voice" and the "predictable and comforting rhythm" of the TV to "soothe" his dreams.[73] The "low voice" of the TV speaks, as it were, more to Julian than Jacob did, allowing him to find comfort in his TVs as a child and as an adult, contrasting his inability to find comfort in his father. As Julian explains that his TVs "soothe" his dreams, they ostensibly become dreamcatchers of sorts, those which stand in sharp contrast to his silent father who is the very source of his nightmares. He thus relies upon his TVs to forefend against the nightmares that haunt him and in doing so creates a substitute "father," one who becomes a proxy paternal figure that is in many ways the opposite of Jacob. Discussing the role of things in daily life, Bill Brown helpfully asks: "What desires d[o] objects organize?"[74] For Julian, not only does he organize his collection of TVs, but his collection of TVs organizes his desire for an ameliorated relationship with his father. Noting how the TVs offered him "company,"[75] Julian explains further that he would spend the majority of his days watching the moving images, which distracted him "from every terrible truth."[76] Differing from Jacob who never tells Julian any stories of his past, the TVs furnish him with narratives, including those that offer a temporary diversion from the "terrible truth" of his father's memories that haunt him. Julian thus redirects his desire for his father's attention and affection—precluded because of the Shoah—toward his TVs. He is able to turn up the volume as a way to "hear" retroactively from his father, a preconscious expression of his desire to interact with Jacob who remained largely silent throughout his life. Julian's attempts to repair his TVs can further be understood as expressions of his desire to "fix" his psychologically damaged father, even if indirectly and belatedly. Thus, the TVs function as screens, literally and figuratively, onto which Julian projects his desire for his father's company and psychological repair.

Julian's apartment and his belongings contained therein seemingly function as technologies that he uses to keep his postmemories at a distance, but as the novel makes clear, these postmemorial things nonetheless amplify his inherited traumas. His isolated detachment—both his somatic and psychic separateness—from the greater social world becomes imprisoning in and of itself. Julian describes his reaction to when Paula took him to a park for his birthday. He says, "I felt my heart thrashing against the bars of my chest," before explaining that he wants to grab onto the door frame as they are leaving so as to remain inside.[77] His description of the bars of his chest, suggestive of prison bars, points to the ways by which he feels incarcerated in his own body and corresponds to how Sola describes him as continuously keeping everyone at bay while, as Sola puts it, "locking himself up in his apartment."[78] Though Sola's diction is in reference to his distance from the social world writ large, her statement also suggests that he is very much jailing himself, interning himself in a space of death-dealing quarantine. Assuming the same position as his father who lives in an ossified state of silence, Julian also constructs his adulthood apartment as a space of muteness and isolation. Although his apartment is seemingly secure and safe, it nevertheless perpetuates his continued nightmares—for muteness forecloses the opportunity to give voice to and thus exorcize his postmemorial demons. As Julian keeps silent about his postmemories, he thereby persists in a state of postmemorial struggle within the space of his own home.

Postmemorial Divergences

Although Julian and Paula navigate—or try to avoid navigating—their postmemories in the beginning of the novel, they both experience a profound shift in how they relate to and are affected by their father's Holocaust traumas. *The Speed of Light* represents these shifts, the siblings' postmemorial divergences, by way of their relationships to their domestic spaces. The novel's descriptions of Julian and Paula's adulthood apartments, along with the siblings' inhabitations of their respective domestic spaces, reflect the changes in how they come to relate to Jacob's Holocaust traumas.

Although Julian confines himself in the upper psychosocial space of his apartment for much of the novel, Sola's entrance into his apartment disrupts his space, which offers him a new way to begin to move beyond his postmemories. Sola, who stays in Paula's apartment during the time that Paula is in Europe, remains in close proximity to Julian for the majority of the novel. During her stay, she helps him to begin coming to terms with his postmemories, tutoring him in how to navigate the Holocaust traumas and embodied experiences he inherits (she is able to do so in large part because of her own traumatic experience of her family and community being barbarically slaughtered in her native [unnamed] country). Not only does Sola help Julian emancipate himself from his apartment, from that which ostensibly functions as his protective sheath and seemingly shelters him from external threats, but she also draws Julian out of his apartment, which metaphorizes how she draws him out of himself and enables him to open up psychosocially. The opening of Julian's domestic space, which theretofore was closed-up and walled-off—along with how he begins to move outside it more regularly—symbolizes how Julian begins to exhume and externalize his postmemories. Indeed, how Sola enters Julian's domestic space and interacts with the various architectural features of his apartment, specifically his windows and doors, illustrates how she enters Julian's life and offers him the opportunity to exit his postmemorial state of fear, anxiety, and silent suffering.

Not long after meeting Julian, Sola opens his living-room window, which unseals his closed-up space, representing how she opens him up to the shared social world beyond his isolated state of being. As she walks into Julian's apartment, Sola, in her non-native English, asks: "It is not closed up in here? Perhaps there is not enough air."[79] In accordance with Paula's aforementioned description of Julian's apartment as suffocating, Sola's question and statement point not only to the presumable stuffiness of such a confined space but also to the above-cited stifling affect of his domicile. As Sola opens the window, Julian thinks to himself, "The breeze touched my face with a rush; the window hadn't been opened in years, and it was as if the room had been waiting for a chance to inhale. I smelled fresh-cut grass and something sweeter, a flower I couldn't name."[80] Her entrance into the apartment and her opening of the window animates the inanimate, figuratively filling the lungs of Julian's breathless domestic space. As the apartment begins to "breathe," the space becomes enlivened and takes on an olfactory likeness to the outdoors, symbolically augmenting the space of his apartment to include the expansiveness of the open air. The literal opening of Julian's space via the opening of the window and the opening of his space to Sola are parallel instances of Julian's apartment, and thus Julian, being unsealed. These coinciding images of openness reinforce one another and sharply diverge from the suffocating state of Julian's apartment up until this point in the novel. Describing Sola after she opens the window, Julian expresses his anxiety surrounding the unsealing of his apartment: "Sola's smile looked so benign I could almost believe that the gaping hole behind her was harmless, too."[81] Despite the sweetness of the breeze and his almost-belief that the window is "harmless," the "gaping hole" presents for Julian a threat to his sense of stability that he finds in his isolation—a threat he begins to address in the days and weeks after Sola's initial entrance.

As Sola begins to frequent his apartment more often, she increasingly opens up about her traumatic past, which in turn offers Julian an invitation to reciprocate and share his. When he asks her what the word for *angel* is in her native language, she responds that she cannot say it, before quickly leaving the apartment and forgetting to close the door.[82] After her family was massacred, Sola stopped speaking her mother tongue as a way to divorce herself from her painful history. Julian's question, as a result, proves triggering. For Sola to speak in her native language would be to enter symbolically back into her past, so instead of responding, she leaves his apartment but fails to shut the door. That she leaves the door open gestures toward how the knowledge of her trauma provides for Julian a point of connection, a past to which he can relate that offers him "entrance" into community with her. The open door is a spatial connection between Julian and Sola that represents the opened pathway their respective traumas provide; as Julian describes Sola's sadness as "a bridge between [them],"[83] the open door metaphorizes this unifying bond.

The scene where Sola bids Julian to come downstairs in the heat of the summer serves as an additional metaphor for how she begins to help him exit his heady existence of postmemory. This moment of departure from his apartment is precisely that: a departure, an exit from the imprisoning and stifling confines of his psychosocial domestic reclusion. This is not to say that suddenly when he comes downstairs Julian is finally part of the greater social world or comfortably extricated from his heady closed-off existence. However, his domestic exit *does* mark a new era in his life when he begins the process of coming to terms with his postmemories in community with Sola. But before he leaves his apartment, he stops at his door and surveys his space: "The eleven TVs were empty shadows, a wall of dark silence. I thought I saw a heat shimmer rising from my chair. So I turned around again, and stepped across the threshold."[84] His description of his wall of TVs as "empty shadows" suggests that, though solid objects, these TVs are of illusory value—or, more specifically, they hollowly offer him the illusion of company and comfort. Akin to Plato's Allegory of the Cave, the "empty shadows" are insubstantial substitutes for that which they represent. Although for years Julian's TVs seemingly offered him company in lieu of his father, his burgeoning friendship with Sola proves to be of actual substance, which in turn reveals the emptiness of the TVs qua company (though Julian is not yet made fully aware of the TVs' emptiness at this point in the novel). In either case, this scene is a watershed moment for Julian, especially in light of his invocation of the "threshold" when describing his descent. By leaving his apartment and going downstairs for the first time in as long as he can remember[85]—a release from his heady, upper space—Julian enters a new era of postmemorial emancipation.

Julian's subsequent interactions with his collection of TVs further reveal how he begins coming to terms with his inherited traumas and embodied experiences. After one of his TVs turns black and no longer works, he notes that he surprised himself by his lack of interest in fixing it. Describing the broken TV, he says: "Its dark face reflected the room; from certain angles I could even see my own face, a blurry pale oval."[86] His lack of desire to fix the TV gives voice to his decreased need to assert control and create order, especially given how he begins to control—that is, starts addressing—his postmemories at this point in the narrative. His contentment with not fixing the broken TV further signals how he no longer feels the need to repair his relationship with his father in the way he once did (and such a task would of course be impossible given his father's death). Of additional significance is how he sees his own reflection in one of the blank TVs. That he is able to see himself (even if only as "a blurry pale oval") in what used to symbolize his father demonstrates how Julian begins to recognize himself over and above his father's past. Insofar as he begins coming to terms with his postmemories—realizing that he is able to "carry the past inside the present,"[87] as opposed to losing the present within the past—no longer do his father's Holocaust experiences overshadow him as they once did. In this scene, the TVs themselves are not only powered off, but they are also in turn revealed to have no power to help Julian address his inherited traumas and embodied experiences. In the novel's penultimate scene, when Julian is leaving to go on a hike with Sola, his TVs are again turned off,[88] concretizing the idea that Julian trades in the company of his TVs for that of Sola. The metaphorical function of TVs in the novel, in concert with the symbolic role of domestic space, serves to represent how Julian begins to address his postmemories.

Sola and Julian's trip outside his apartment solidifies the ways by which she both opens him up to the greater social world and enables him to begin addressing his postmemories. Describing the first walk he takes with her outside, Julian says that he watched his and Sola's feet and matched the size of their steps.[89] Inspecting and mirroring Sola's gait, Julian is learning to walk, so to speak, and take his first steps in becoming comfortable outside his isolated state of reclusion; taking him beyond the realm of the familiar, Sola begins to teach him how to find his stride, that is, how to navigate the greater social world beyond his closed-up interiority and postmemorial incarceration. Julian's scientific definition of relative velocity that he writes for his *Dictionary of Science* earlier in the novel parallels how Sola helps him find forward momentum beyond the confines of his heady existence: "the velocity of one body relative to another is the rate at which the first body is changing its position with respect to the second."[90] This scientific definition maps onto their relationship, where Sola's "velocity"—that is, her forward motion in the wake of her traumatic past—changes Julian's "velocity," allowing him to gain momentum in his quest to work through his inherited traumas and embodied knowledge. His increased physical mobility alongside Sola symbolizes how he starts to move forward, beginning to free himself from his once debilitating postmemories.

However, as Julian begins to come to terms with his inherited past, Paula becomes overwhelmed by hers. Her return home from Budapest signals a shift in her relationship to her father's Holocaust experiences, forcing her to begin acknowledging her latent postmemories. Describing her time in her father's hometown of Budapest, Paula says that she kept thinking how all the men of a certain age vaguely resembled her father and that she imagined someone dropping a net around her or shooting her in the back of the head.[91] Imagining this, Paula begins reanimating what happened on Hungarian soil during the Shoah. Though she alleges that she had never considered her father's past before,[92] she elsewhere states that she did in fact think about the Holocaust as a child,[93] in no small part because of being surrounded by survivors telling their stories as noted above. Staying in Budapest reinvigorates said childhood imaginings, confronting her with her postmemories and forcing her to finally reckon with her father's Holocaust experiences that, despite preoccupying her as a child, were nonetheless largely unknown to her.[94] After finding out her father was a member of a *Sonderkommando*, Paula says that she could not stop thinking about him, specifically about his hands that had held her as well as dead bodies. She further explains that she hears Hungarian voices in the hallway and a distant radio playing a waltz. For the first time in her life, music hurts her, and she only wants silence.[95] As she begins contemplating her father's forced labor in the crematoria and gas chambers, her surroundings become temporally unstable—that is, Jacob's traumatic past begins to bleed into her present, resulting in an incongruous experience of time. The soundscape that surrounds her functions as a postmemorial punctum[96] or, otherwise put, a trigger of symbolic noises that transports her to the time and place of the Shoah. That "the music hurt" points to how the surrounding soundscape reanimates traumatic wounds for her—where the waltz (a traditional German genre) functions as a "distant" echo of the Third Reich, not to mention how Hungarian voices become those of Nazi collaborators. Her desire for silence, stemming in tandem from her discovery of how Jacob was in a *Sonderkommando* and the postmemorial soundscape of Budapest, suddenly likens her to her silent father. She even goes on to describe her fear of losing her ability to sing, that which has defined her throughout the majority of the novel.[97] This fear operates on multiple levels: not only is she becoming like her father (one who did not speak much), but she fears losing her voice (symbolic of losing her identity). As she learns of Jacob's traumatic past, Paula's figurative and literal loss of her voice suggests that the distinction between her and her father becomes blurred, where his past overtakes her present and eclipses her subjectivity. With such an overwhelming discovery of the details of her father's Shoah experiences, Paula is compelled to begin facing her inherited traumas.

Her time in Budapest transforms—and is reflected in—her relationship to her postmemorial structure. Paula, one who is rarely at home throughout the majority of the novel, takes shelter in her apartment after returning to the United States and becomes a domestic shut-in like Jacob. Again desiring silence after discovering her father's dark past,[98] she is described as sitting curled up on her couch.[99] This posture is similar to how she responds when she first hears about her father's experience in Budapest; she sits folded with her head near her knees, wanting to curl herself up into a ball.[100] Here, Paula assumes the fetal position, signaling an infantile state of helplessness, a state of postmemorial undoing, where she begins regressing to a time in her childhood in the Perel-family home, surrounded by Jacob's silence and other survivors' Holocaust narratives. Her apartment—with her living room curtains closed, thereby blocking out the light[101]—further underscores the fetal imagery, where the dark, enclosed interior becomes a womblike space in which she reverts to a childlike state because of what she learns. As the novel consistently describes her curtains as open until this point in the narrative, her closing of the curtains, along with her bodily comportment, signals a significant shift in how she navigates her apartment and in turn relates to her father's traumatic past.

Paula's transformation further resembles the Julian we meet at the beginning of the novel: a domestic recluse debilitated by Jacob's past. When Paula visits Julian in his apartment after she returns home from Hungary, Julian stands up from his leather chair (inherited from Jacob) when she enters, goes to the kitchen, and offers her water. Paula accepts and replaces him in the chair.[102] In this scene, Julian and Paula physically trade places, but as Julian stands up from his father's chair and as Paula takes his seat, the novel uses the physical switching of spots to symbolize how they change positions in regard to how they relate to their father's traumatic past. As the chair represents Jacob by virtue of it having belonged to him, Julian's departure from it and Paula's sitting in it reveal how their relationships to the Shoah are reversed. Paula takes a more passive position (sitting) while Julian assumes a more active position (standing). This trading of passive and active positions points to how, respectively, Paula becomes the helpless recipient of a flood of her father's traumas and Julian becomes one who begins to find distance from his inherited past. This changing of positions in the domestic indeed signals how Julian and Paula come to diverge in response to their father's Holocaust past.

These postmemorial divergences are solidified in the concluding scenes of the novel. Recounting the morning she watches Julian leave with Sola for their trip, she stands at her living room window and notes that it is a Wednesday, just as it was a Wednesday when she had left for her work trip weeks prior.[103] Her domestic positioning in front of the window and the day when she watches her brother are almost direct citations of how Julian watches Paula leave for Europe at the beginning of the novel (from his window, also on a Wednesday). Mirroring how Paula assumes a similar ocular view to Julian from the window, she also assumes a similar postmemorial view of the world, one that is fearful, anxious, and consumed by emanations of the Shoah. This scene reveals how when individuals avoid their haunting pasts for extended periods of time, they risk becoming psychosocially domesticated by the history they seek to avoid. What is further revealed, by way of Julian and Sola traveling together, is the generative power of community when working through haunting histories.

Conclusion

The building in which the two siblings live as adults has two storeys: the upper storey belonging to Julian and the lower storey belonging to Paula. Yet, there are not only two storeys or physical levels in their building. There are also two stories or narratives contained within the building—stories of two differing postmemorial relationships to the Shoah. The novel employs Paula and Julian's inhabitations of their respective apartments in their adulthoods, in tandem with their inhabitation of their childhood home, as metaphors for each character's postmemorial relationship to the Holocaust. But both Perel siblings are also subject to postmemorial divergences, shifts in how they relate to their father's Holocaust past. Though Paula and Julian's homes function differently than other adulthood postmemorial structures examined in previous chapters, the siblings' relationships to their domestic spaces offer insight into how they relate to the Holocaust. How they position themselves in their homes and in relation to certain objects in those spaces reveals their postmemorial positions, that is, how they connect and are connected to their father's Holocaust traumas. Similar to but also divergent from the portraits offered in *Maus* and *The Holocaust Kid*, Rosner's text provides us with yet another portrait of the intricate and intimate relationship between domestic space and children of Holocaust survivors. In doing so, the novel further underscores the heterogeneity of postmemorial responses to the Shoah even and especially in the same family.

5

Pre/Occupied Longing

Toward a Definition
of Postnostalgia in
Jonathan Safran Foer's
Everything Is Illuminated

Throughout *At Home with the Holocaust*, I have discussed how the *space* of survivor-family homes has structured and continues to structure children of survivors' relationships to the Holocaust,[1] examining these homes as postmemorial structures in response to Marianne Hirsch's inquiry concerning which "technologies... mediate the psychology of postmemory, the continuities and discontinuities between generations, the gaps in knowledge, the fears and terrors that ensue in the aftermath of trauma."[2] In this penultimate chapter, however, I offer a focused exploration of how *place* connects descendants of survivors—both the second *and* third generations, with an emphasis on the latter—to their survivor families' pasts. For both generations, the idea of "home" extends beyond the domestic sphere, insofar as members of the second and third generations are commonly attached affectively to the places where their survivor-family members once lived before the Shoah. Their family's former home(land)s—the places where survivors and deceased family members previously resided—indeed structure the descendants of survivors' relationships to their families' Holocaust and, to be sure, pre-Holocaust pasts. As these home(land)s function as "technologies" in their own right, traveling to the places their relatives once inhabited serves as an avenue for the descendants of survivors to address the intergenerational transmission of traumatic knowledge and embodied experience.

With numerous similarities and continuities between the second and third generations, any study of the children of Holocaust survivors would be incomplete without discussing how their inherited traumas and embodied knowledges have affected and are negotiated by survivors' grandchildren. Jonathan Safran Foer's *Everything is Illuminated* (2002), an epitomic third-generation novel, gives voice to how one grandchild of survivors negotiates his traumatic legacy. Foer's work represents the ways by which the third-generation protagonist's grandparents' former home(land)s complicate his personal understanding of where and what is "home."

Theoretical Frame

As Anne Buttimer explains, individuals' personal and cultural identities are intricately bound to their "place identity."[3] Though many descendants of survivors understand the places in which they were born and raised as home, they often concurrently perceive, to varying degrees, the native countries of their survivor-family members as home as well. Shedding light on these descendants of survivors, Peter Somerville posits that individuals not uncommonly have a sense of home without having any experience or memory of it.[4] For those living outside the countries of their survivor-family members' births, their notions of their late families' homes and homelands are frequently not based on personal experience or memory. Rather, how they conceive of their deceased families' homes and homelands is largely a product of cognitive, affective, and imaginative investments in the lands of their forbearers.

However, by virtue of being related to survivors, members of the second and third generations have knotty attachments to the places of their survivor-family members' births. Susan Jacobowitz discusses the loss of "home" and its consequences for the second generation, explaining how pining for a world that no longer exists, in tandem with not feeling a defined sense of belonging, is a common post-refugee experience.[5] Describing the children of refugee survivors specifically, Merilyn Moos further notes how the second generation experienced an "inner sense of displacement," despite how they never lived in the original sites of displacement.[6] This post-refugee experience and its accompanying inner sense of displacement complicate the relationships that descendants of survivors have to the places of their families' births that are different from their own. Although they feel connected to the lands where their survivor-family members once lived, those lands are, at the same time, places they recognize as sites of persecution, disruption, and dislocation. The countries of survivors' births overwhelmingly turned against Jews before, during, and even after the Shoah and, in many cases, effectively forced them to emigrate post-1945. As a result, their positive associations with these countries are concomitantly colored by their negative associations, rendering these places affective sites of both meaningful and thorny legacies. Yet, as second- and third-generation authors suggest, though these places are of varied associations, the descendants of survivors nonetheless identify with, travel to, and even long for the countries of their families' origins. Indeed, although never having stepped foot in the lands of their forbearers, many deeply identify with these countries, oftentimes articulating how they feel a "homesickness" or "nostalgia" for these places.

Several literary critics and cultural theorists have discussed the descendants of Holocaust survivors and what has been described as their "nostalgia" for life before the Shoah. Most notable among this group of scholars are Sara Horowitz, Eva Hoffman, and Hirsch. Horowitz, in "Nostalgia and the Holocaust," offers cursory observations of children of survivors' "nostalgia" for pre-Shoah life, but she largely examines those who seemingly (and enigmatically) adopt "nostalgic" attachments for life *during* the Holocaust. As daughters of survivors themselves, Hoffman and Hirsch each provide accounts of their own "nostalgic" affections for their families' homeland (Ukraine) from before the Holocaust. Though not born in the country of their parents' births, both Hoffman and Hirsch describe pining for Ukraine with a measure of "nostalgia," as if they themselves had once lived there. I place "nostalgic" and "nostalgia" in scare quotes to draw attention to this puzzling phenomenon of seemingly inherited nostalgia. It is puzzling because one cannot, definitionally, feel nostalgia for that which one has not lost. Horowitz explains, "The word *nostalgia* derives from the Greek *nostos*, meaning to return home, and *algos*, meaning pain or longing. Nostalgia implies a temporal or spatial exile (or both simultaneously), and thus a longing for the past and for home, and a desire to return home in the future."[7] This conception of nostalgia is indeed applicable when discussing *survivors'* longing for life before the Holocaust; however, it cannot be applied to the descendants of survivors because, simply put, subsequent generations were not alive before the Shoah. Although Hoffman and Hirsch experience a profound longing for and attachment to the time and place of their families' pre-Shoah lives, neither Hirsch nor Hoffman were alive before the Holocaust, and neither ever lived in their parents' birthplace. Hirsch highlights this perplexity when she explains that her fantasy to "return" to where her family lived before the Shoah "was not exactly a nostalgic longing for a lost or abandoned Heimat.... [H]ow could a place I had never touched, and which my parents left under extreme duress, really be 'home'? Nor was it a yearning to recall some better past time in that city, for I had experienced no actual time there at all."[8] The questions, then, remain: What precisely is this almost-form of nostalgia, and what can be said about it?

With a focus on Foer's *Everything Is Illuminated*, I propose a new term to respond to the above questions and to name the subject at hand: *postnostalgia*. Postnostalgia, with respect to the descendants of Holocaust survivors as represented in their fictional and nonfictional writings, names the imaginative responses of children and grandchildren of survivors to their postmemories (or, more accurately for the third generation, their "post-postmemories," to borrow Christoph Ribbat's helpful phrase[9]). Postnostalgia, however, does not respond to failures, in conception or application, of the *theory* of (post-)postmemory nor is it an analogue or an improvement of its predecessor term. Rather, postnostalgia in second- and third-generation literature is a response to the *experience* of (post-)postmemory, an adaptive redirection of descendants' troubled relationships to the past, that which does not focus on death and destruction but on life and livelihood. Though this chapter stems from and centers on, for the purpose of specificity, *Everything Is Illuminated* as an illustrative exploration of postnostalgia, postnostalgia finds expression in a number of other literary texts written by the descendants of survivors. Melvin J. Bukiet's *Stories of an Imaginary Childhood* (1992), Anne Karpf's *The War After* (1996), Judith Kalman's *The County of Birches* (1998), and Erin Einhorn's *The Pages in Between* (2008) all give voice to postnostalgic attachments of the second generation to their families' pre-Shoah homelands. As for third-generation texts, Daniel Mendelsohn's *The Lost: A Search for Six of Six Million* (2006), Eduardo

Halfon's *The Polish Boxer* (2008), *Monastery* (2014), and *Mourning* (2018), Jérémie Dres's *We Won't See Auschwitz* (2012), and Rutu Modan's *The Property* (2013) also offer literary representations of grandchildren of survivors' postnostalgia. In truth, it bears noting that there are also some descendants who have no interest in the lands of their families' origins and that some share an emphatically anti-postnostalgic impulse (for example, in regard to Germany), but this study brackets off such individuals to focus on postnostalgic subjects. Though several scholars have briefly outlined the phenomenon of inherited "nostalgia" in the context of second-generation writing—without terming it postnostalgia, to be sure—little work has specifically examined the grandchildren of survivors' comparable attachments in third-generation writing.

As is represented in *Everything Is Illuminated*, and in the other above-mentioned texts, postnostalgia responds to and interacts with the effects of inherited traumatic knowledge of and embodied experiences from the Holocaust. As Hirsch and Leo Spitzer note, for the descendants of survivors, "negative and traumatic memories" are "nostalgia's complicating flip side."[10] As a result, in second- and third-generation writing, this postnostalgic yearning I am naming and its accompanying trips to sites of pre-Shoah life—those commonly known as *pilgrimages*—are always already inflected with malaise that stems from their inherited loss (for how could any perception of pre-Shoah life *not* be colored by loss that stems from the Holocaust?). Indeed, such pilgrimages, along with the postnostalgia that motivates them, function as forms of belated address to descendants of survivors' inherited traumas—a point which bears elucidating.

As the second generation's traumas issue forth from a moment of rupture (and thus a ruptured sense of time), they often retrospectively fantasize that what preceded the moment of rupture was a period of stasis (that was defined by a linear sense of time). For descendants of survivors represented in second- and third-generation writings, though they have imaginative access to life before the Shoah, they do not always have a concrete sense of this past that came before the moment of rupture known as the Holocaust. Unlike how they can locate a vast visual, documentary, and material archive that gives voice to the Holocaust as an historical event, they often do not have access to such an extensive archive of pre-Shoah *family* life. This is especially the case given how possessions and property belonging to their progenitors were lost, stolen, or destroyed at the hands of Nazis and thieving opportunists. As such, in the writings of descendants of survivors, pilgrimages to sites of pre-Shoah life become ways to fill in this archive, to flesh out, in figurative and literal senses, traces of pre-Shoah life; pilgrims seek to occupy, in the flesh, the places of their families' pre-Shoah lives, so as to find out more about their relatives. Thus, by animating those places, *their bodies become figurative archives of possibility*—of what could and should have been, had the Shoah never occurred—in both imaginative and bodily terms. Though it would of course be impossible in an actual sense to archive their families' pre-Shoah lives by way of their bodies (for how could one's body take corporeal stock of life that is no longer?), their bodies qua figurative archives of possibility furnish them with embodied narratives that become ways of connecting with their families. Their bodies, in situ, figuratively represent their deceased and surviving family members, as much as they re-present or re-introduce their families' presence in the place that they lived before the Shoah. By becoming figurative archives of possibility, they figure themselves into imagined histories that catalyze a greater corporeal sense of familial connection. In lieu of external archives, their bodies, however imperfectly and fictionally, take stock of imagined histories of how their relatives may well have lived before the Holocaust and how they themselves may have lived, if the Holocaust had never happened. Their bodies, in place—and in the place—of their late families' bodies, come to embody an imagined family history, that is, a narrative of pre-Shoah life, even if that history or narrative of what possibly may have been never actually came to pass. It is standing on-site that makes manifest a narrative that functions as a stand-in, a substitute history for what is missing in their imaginations, as is illustrated throughout second- and third-generation writings.

Therefore, for third-generation protagonists specifically, these trips are not about directly addressing the original wounding event—the Holocaust—not only because directly addressing the original wound would be impossible regardless (for any form of traumatic address is always indirect) but also because these third-generation witnesses are twice removed from the original trauma. Even if they were to know their grandparents' narrated stories of what happened, that "history" is always already constructed. This is in part because, by definition, the original traumatizing event was often never fully known by survivors themselves, insofar as it was, as Cathy Caruth explains, "experienced too soon, too unexpectedly, to be fully known and is therefore not available to consciousness,"[11] and what happened cannot therefore be narrated as such. Any narrative is a construction and is never able to articulate completely the original moment of violence. This is even more so the case for the third generation, for whom "the intergenerational passing on of trauma... is a historical process that produces history through the erasure of its own witness."[12] Because of the erasure of history's own witness—the covering over of what happened, leaving only an inscription or a trace of the wounding event—in tandem with how they were not traumatized firsthand (or secondhand for that matter), third-generation protagonists are in an even more precarious position to address their inherited traumas. Thus, whatever narrative they choose to give voice to their family's history, whether it is close to what "actually" happened (if that were ever possible to know in full) or if it is based in imagination (a projected, postnostalgic fantasy), does not ultimately seem to matter.

Instead, what matters is finding *a* narrative, *a* way of contextualizing and making sense of a past that belatedly ruptured their lives, along with a past that preceded that period of rupture.[13] Referring to third-generation Holocaust representation broadly, Gerd Bayer explains that in comparison to the first and second generations, there is a recognizable decrease in the urgency to keep specific details in perpetual memory.[14] This decreased emphasis on factual details for the third generation is a consequence of emphasizing details that are more emotionally proximal to them. In the context of postnostalgic constructions of the past in third-generation literature, this decreased emphasis on factual details is accompanied by an increased emphasis on imagined details. What becomes important for protagonists are not necessarily "objective," "historical" facts but, instead, *useable narratives* that allow them to live "after such knowledge," to borrow a phrase from the title of one of Hoffman's insightful studies. Pilgrimages thus enable third-generation characters to figure out, in bodily and imaginative ways, what preceded the Shoah in order to better understand, albeit incompletely, what was lost in the first place. As they accept that they cannot and *will not* understand the Holocaust in toto, they seek at least to *contextualize* this trauma in imagined constructions that narrate, in their own terms, what preceded it. Indeed, for the third generation, "coming to terms" with the past is precisely that: finding terms, or language, to articulate themselves in relation to their late families and thereby address their inherited trauma—all in service of constructing an emotionally true, useable narrative, even if it is not factually accurate and even if it is in large part fictional(ized).

Postnostalgia is affectively and psychically powerful given how, despite its object of desire being ultimately unattainable, it is profoundly desired by descendants of survivors, as represented in descendants' writings. Hirsch notes that no one is ever able to know the world of their progenitors, despite how many desire to know what it looked and felt like. But in comparison to those not born to survivors, members of the second generation have "a different desire, at once more powerful and more conflicted: the need not just to feel and to know, but also to re-member, to re-build, to re-incarnate, to replace, and to repair."[15] As represented in second- and third-generation writing, this intimate desire to "re-incarnate" particular geographies that are imbued with stories of family life catalyzes imaginative entry into their families' pasts that preceded the Shoah. For these descendants of survivors—poignantly exemplified by protagonist Jonathan in *Everything Is Illuminated*—postnostalgia names a longing for life before Nazi occupation, a longing that preoccupies them with their imaginative perceptions of the lands of their forbearers; it is a yearning for family existence in an uncannily familiar geography before the Shoah,[16] for Jewish livelihood before mass trauma—that is, for life before Holocaust deracination and decimation.

The fantasy of pre-Shoah life—an enabling fiction mixed with fact that is largely a function of imagination—creates a double consciousness.[17] However, this double consciousness is further complicated for descendants of survivors represented in second- and third-generation writings. Svetlana Boym refers to a double consciousness as the main feature of the exilic experience: "a double exposure of different times and spaces, a constant bifurcation."[18] For second- and third-generation protagonists, they are subject to a double consciousness as it relates to where/when they live and where/when their families once lived. But the sites of where their families once lived are further refracted through their progenitors' pre-Shoah lives, as well as through their Holocaust experiences. As a result, protagonists in second- and third-generation writings possess multiple divided consciousnesses that hold in tension their families' exilic experiences with their families' lives before, during, and after the Holocaust.

Descendants of survivors in second- and third-generation representation long to touch and inhabit, even if just temporarily, the home(land)s to which they were denied access, as a way of "reclaiming" a greater sense of rootedness and belonging. Boym's helpful division of nostalgia into two overarching categories, restorative and reflective nostalgia, sheds light on this effort to "reclaim" a sense of home. She states, "Two kinds of nostalgia are not absolute types, but rather tendencies, ways of giving shape and meaning to longing. Restorative nostalgia puts emphasis on *nostos* and proposes to rebuild the lost home and patch up the memory gaps. Reflective nostalgia dwells in *algia*, in longing and loss, the imperfect process of remembrance."[19] This dual grouping of nostalgic tendencies elucidates the multiple ways that nostalgia operates. However, when applying Boym's formulation to the study of postnostalgia, it bears noting that the nostalgic tendencies she identifies are not necessarily mutually exclusive for second- and third-generation protagonists. Many of their postnostalgic attachments parallel a combination of both nostalgic tendencies, though of course at a generational remove (or two). Boym suggests that "restorative nostalgia has no use for the signs of historical time—patina, ruins, cracks, imperfections,"[20] but for postnostalgic descendants of survivors, "the signs of historical time" are not to be avoided nor are they understood as void of utility. Rather, such signs of historical time are perceived as authenticating markers of historicity and authenticity, indexically operating as confirmation of the reality of a world that once was but is no longer. Many protagonists thus search for the "original image"—or more accurately what they *imagine* to be the original image—of home(land)s that have ceased to exist and for signs that serve to confirm the facticity of those places.[21] In locating this pastness by visiting sites of pre-Shoah life on pilgrimages, there is a perceived authentication of the reality of their families' lives before the Holocaust that enables them, imaginatively and of course imperfectly, to "re-enter," to "return," and to "re-establish" that which was lost. Postnostalgia, therefore, not only names the desire to "re-create" imaginatively the lost world of pre-Shoah family life by spatializing time and temporalizing space on their visits to the native lands of their families (which is in accordance with restorative nostalgia). But postnostalgia also seeks out, employs, and even cherishes the "shattered fragments of [post]memory" (in line with reflective nostalgia).[22] As such, in the writings of descendants of survivors, many hold fast to (largely romanticized) fantasies of their families' pre-Shoah worlds.

I prefer the term postnostalgia to what has been named "ambivalent nostalgia" by Hirsch and Spitzer,[23] "inherited attachment" by Janet Jacobs,[24] and simply "nostalgia" by Horowitz and others. It stands to reason that postnostalgia cannot be synonymized with "nostalgia" or "ambivalent nostalgia" because what is being named is, indeed, not nostalgia; postnostalgia functions comparably to nostalgia but is qualitatively different given the generational, geographical, and cognitive distance between the time and place of pre-Shoah life and descendants' post-1945 lives. Contra Jacobs's term *inherited attachment*, postnostalgia, though seemingly inherited from survivors, is not actually something that can be inherited—just like, say, memory, in experiential or biological terms, cannot be inherited *in sich*. Postnostalgia is, rather, that which is learned and smells, feels, looks, sounds, and functions like nostalgia for a place and time in which descendants have never lived but long for as if they have—similar to how postmemory is that which smells, feels, looks, sounds, and functions like memory but is not memory as such. The term postnostalgia thus serves as an intervention into the limited lexicon of naming survivors' descendants' so-called nostalgic longings for times and places that preceded their births.

Second-Generation Postnostalgia

A pressing question for many children of survivors, one which seemingly assumes greater import as they mature and age, is the question of family origins. These origin stories of course vary, depending on the individual family, and while some perceive the Holocaust as the setting of where their families began, others hold fast to expanded family histories that include life before the Shoah. For instance, Hoffman in her childhood identifies the Holocaust as the place/time of her family's genesis, whereas Hirsch discusses how she locates her family's pre-Shoah life as the setting of where her family originated. This is not to say that Hoffman did not eventually explore her family's pre-Shoah history later in life—for, in fact, she did. However, this *is* to say that Hoffman's identification of the Holocaust qua site of family origin distinguishes her postnostalgic relationship to Ukraine from Hirsch's postnostalgic attachment to the country. Those who, like Hirsch, try to find their families' pre-Shoah lives seek out this "time before" in order not to define their families—and thus themselves—in such death-dealing terms. Instead of focusing on catastrophe, they seek to discover a longer family narrative that includes pre-Shoah life. Such "discoveries," though largely imaginative, interact with and, in some cases, allow them to address, even in part, their postmemories. These individuals are able to find genealogical continuity in spite of the breach in their families' histories that directly resulted because of the Holocaust.

For many in the second generation, questions of origins correlate to how their parents perceived their lives before, during, and after the Holocaust. Helen Epstein's mother saw her time in the concentration camps as "the center of rather than the interruption in her life."[25] Similarly, Elie Wiesel, perhaps the best-known Holocaust survivor and a father himself, famously pronounced: "In the beginning there was the Holocaust."[26] Such perceptions of the Holocaust paralleled and catalyzed how many survivors' children came to perceive the Shoah: the time/place where their families-as-they-know-them began. Echoing Wiesel's sentiment, Hoffman explains her childhood theory of origins, stating, "In the beginning was the war,"[27] which Bukiet articulates this way: "In the beginning was Auschwitz."[28] As is evident, these children of survivors define their genesis, in the words of Jessica Lang, "as a moment of loss."[29] Indeed, it is common for the Holocaust to be understood as the story of origins for members of the second generation, for those who would not have come into existence had it not been for the Shoah.[30] Of course, these individuals do not disavow their families' longer genealogies, but they often do not know much, if anything, about their family members who came before and were subsequently murdered, especially because of the loss of family archives and stories. Serving as a generative example, Hoffman offers a detailed discussion of how the Holocaust became "achingly, the moment of conception, that from which all things emerge."[31] Hoffman ruminates on why her parents remained silent about their prewar lives, positing that they may have said so little because the Holocaust overwhelmed and erased all that came before or because to remember their pre-Shoah lives would have made their loss all the more piercing. She notes that in her family, the cut from the past was almost complete; other than one photo of her mother's sister, no documentation of her family from before the Holocaust remained. She continues: "There was nothing to help me imagine time expanding backward. The cut reinforced the conviction that the war, the Holocaust, was the dark root from which the world sprang."[32] The Holocaust was for Hoffman the established measure against which she understood herself and was the very source of her being.[33] As a result, she saw the Shoah as her "true origin" that created her "ex nihilo."[34] As was the case for Hoffman, the Holocaust became the starting point for many children of survivors' lives, a beginning born of death and destruction.

Others, in contrast, situate their families' origins earlier, from before the Shoah, in significantly more positive terms. Hirsch describes the city where her parents lived prior to the Holocaust, Czernowitz, as having a distant, legendary, and mythic aura,[35] identifying the city as the primordial site of origin.[36] In comparison to what took place during the Shoah, the time before the catastrophe is commonly understood by children of survivors as distinctly paradisaical.[37] Many, like Hirsch, dwell upon the fact that before the Holocaust, there was another, happier world, one yet untainted by the catastrophe that followed.[38] Hirsch—who was born and grew up in Romania in the 1950s and moved to the United States in 1961—notes how the scenes of her parents' lives in Czernowitz before the Holocaust were "in many ways more real" to her than her own childhood.[39] She posits how, in her youth, pre-Shoah Czernowitz shaped her profoundly, despite never having stepped foot in the city. She explains how her yearning to visit Czernowitz intensified over the years,[40] conceptualizing her profound longing for the Ukrainian city as "nostalgic yearning combined with negative and traumatic memories—pleasure and affection layered with bitterness, anger, and aversion."[41] She acknowledges that her conception of pre-Shoah Czernowitz is only a projection of her personal desires and needs, but that projection, though impossible to make manifest, nonetheless holds great affective and psychic sway in her life.[42]

To be sure, the postnostalgic impulse finds expression in a number of second-generation literary works, like those noted above, but also in many non-literary writings by children of survivors. From Epstein's *Children of the Holocaust* (1979) to Aaron Hass's *In the Shadow of the Holocaust* (1990), there have been many children of survivors who have written about such imaginative constructions and musings of pre-Shoah life in the fields of journalism, psychology, and beyond. One of the second-generation interviewees in *Children of the Holocaust* describes his desire to reanimate his family's presence that was removed violently from Poland because of the Holocaust and details his reason for wanting to return to the place of his family's pre-Shoah life: "I just wanted to establish some sort of contact with my past. I wanted to stand in the place where all the lost people I never knew had lived. By standing there, by being among the people they had lived with, I thought I could come as close as possible. Otherwise, they would be just phantoms, names my parents mentioned."[43] Such a desire to stand where his family had lived, to retroactively "flesh out" Jewish life where Jewish life once found its home, is not a desire to *replace* Jewish life where it was decimated. Instead, his desire to stand where his relatives once lived is a longing, as it were, to *re-place* or re-situate Jewish life where it was once situated. As Hirsch puts it, "It is an act, a performance that briefly, fleetingly, re-placed history in a landscape that had eradicated it."[44] In other words, he seeks to put himself in the same geography that his relatives once occupied and thus re-establish, through his own body, his family's presence in the place from which they were so violently destroyed and displaced.

Hass and other children of survivors also offer insight into how children of survivors fantasize about how their lives may have been, had history run a different course. Hass states: "Through a series of circumstances beyond my control, my life was displaced from where it should have taken place, from where, I believed, I would have led a far more contented existence."[45] His statement—in line with the sentiment of Epstein's interviewee—points to a deep attachment to a place that could have been his and events that "should have taken place" but did not. Such is, of course, a direct result of profound interruption and forced exilic dislocation. Drawing upon Hass's work, Erica T. Lehrer describes this backward-facing musing as "subjunctive memory work."[46] Others like Hirsch, Spitzer, and Hoffman give voice to such subjunctive memory work in their studies, too. Hirsch and Spitzer quote a travel companion of theirs who pondered aloud, "What if the Holocaust had not happened? What would my life have been like?"[47] and then ask if this question preoccupies all survivors and their offspring.[48] They describe this question as "the fantasy of a 'what if . . . ,'"[49] which Hoffman, in her adulthood, describes as the urge to ask "about what might have happened if . . ."[50] These sorts of inevitable questions in part motivate postnostalgia, inasmuch as postnostlgia, in turn, motivates such questions.

Such subjunctive memory work, where the "what if" reigns supreme, can be seen perhaps most dramatically in Hirsch and Spitzer's *Ghosts of Home* (2010). Throughout their work, Hirsch and Spitzer refer to several trips they made to Czernowitz with friends. They recount how one such friend wanted to find and enter the homes where their parents and grandparents had once lived, which promised to soften the discrepancy between the need for a sense of home and the reality of displacement.[51] This friend, once inside her family's old home, was drawn to the tile stove, the only feature of the home to survive after her family was removed. Hirsch explains that the tile stove "not only offered the most direct palpable connection to the familial past[;] it also functioned, once again, as a synecdoche of home. It could effect what she most wanted: her reanimation of this alien place with the spirits of long ago—her father as a child, her uncle as a young man."[52] However, unlike their friend, many children of survivors did not have access to the physical spaces that would and should have been the setting of their families' domestic lives.

Those who did not have such access had to rely heavily on their imaginations. Such members of the second generation, as Golan Moskowitz notes, fanaticized about their families' origins, creating "alternative fictions when the dominant fiction [did] not have room or resources for a particular experience or story of origins."[53] Moskowitz explains further that such fantasy was typically a result of sustained and direct exposure to traumatized parents with mysterious anxieties, whereas for the third generation, fantasy is the result of the incomplete or idealized nature of Holocaust stories told to them.[54] Many within the second generation, like those in the third generation, also fantasized about survivors' experiences because they had only partial details or heard heroic stories about and from their progenitors. For both generations, they drew upon their imaginations to craft narratives about their families' lives before the Holocaust while also visiting sites of pre-Shoah life to flesh out their imagined narratives. But as the third generation was and is often left with fewer clues and less insight into survivors' lives in comparison to the second generation, their task to piece together their families' pre-Shoah lives has proven in many ways even more precarious.

Everything Is Illuminated

Born in 1977, Jonathan Safran Foer is an American novelist, living in New York City as of this writing, on faculty at New York University in the creative writing program. Foer is the author of the novels *Extremely Loud & Incredibly Close* (2005) and *Here I Am* (2016), in addition to the nonfictional works *Eating Animals* (2009) and *We Are the Weather: Saving the Planet Begins at Breakfast* (2019). But Foer, a member of the third generation, first rose to prominence because of his debut novel, *Everything Is Illuminated*, a story about a grandchild of survivors that was based on his senior thesis at Princeton University. For *Everything Is Illuminated*, he received the National Jewish Book Award in 2001 and a Guardian First Book Award in 2002, and he was the co-winner of the PEN/Robert W. Bingham Prize in 2004. A *New York Times* bestseller, *Everything Is Illuminated* was turned into a film of the same name directed by Liev Schreiber in 2005.[55] The novel serves as a representative document in postnostalgia, presenting how such almost-nostalgia operates and how it motivates third-generation pilgrimages to sites of pre-Shoah family life.

Based on Foer's 1999 trip to Ukraine to find out more about his grandfather's life before the Holocaust,[56] *Everything Is Illuminated* centers on protagonist Jonathan's search to uncover his family's past in Ukraine, specifically his quest to find Trachimbrod,[57] the shtetl where his grandfather Safran lived before the Shoah. He uses this trip as the foundation for his intricate story of the shtetl, a story which functions as a means of filling in the epistemic and affective gaps about his family's history in Ukraine. The story he constructs, the lore he creates, is replete with townspeople, town festivals, traditions, and holidays, all of which he compiles as fodder for the manuscript he is writing. At the center of Jonathan's imaginatively constructed narrative is a baby, his "great-great-great-great-great-grandmother" Brod, who is adopted by a man named Yankel.[58] The majority of Jonathan's manuscript is set before the Holocaust, both in the time of Brod/Yankel and then in the years of Safran's life leading up to the Holocaust. Despite the moments throughout Foer's narrative that foreshadow the Holocaust, the central focus of *Everything Is Illuminated* is on life in Trachimbrod before the Shoah.

Everything is Illuminated is in line with many other third-generation novels, which commonly include protracted narratives that extend back to times prior to the Shoah and that explore aspects of their families' daily lives before the Holocaust.[59] Although the specter of the Holocaust is certainly present, *Everything Is Illuminated* and other third-generation narratives like, for instance, Dres's *We Won't See Auschwitz* do not inevitably centralize the Holocaust as their primary focus. As the title of *We Won't See Auschwitz* gestures, rather than "returning" to the physical site that is metonymic of Holocaust trauma (Auschwitz), the protagonists in Dres's work—akin to Jonathan in *Everything Is Illuminated*—circuitously seek to address their difficult family legacy by "returning" to sites of family life *before* the Holocaust. Despite how a number of third-generation texts include "narrative journeys, both imagined and real—both physical and psychic—back to the point of traumatic origin,"[60] such "return" journeys to sites of Holocaust trauma (e.g., sites of former concentration camps or ghettos) are uncommonly the primary focus of the larger narrative. But unlike the third-generation protagonists who *do* make visits to sites of trauma, like death camps and other sites of atrocity, protagonist Jonathan attempts, though of course is not always entirely able, to concentrate on family and Jewish life, not on Holocaust death. As Jonathan is compelled to "return" to the site of his family's pre-Shoah family life, he serves as a representative third-generation protagonist who searches to secure "a sense of familial, cultural, and ethnic belonging."[61]

Jonathan's postnostalgia prompts him to come to terms with his post-postmemories, especially as he tries to recover a sense of "home" in Trachimbrod. His "return" journey in *Everything Is Illuminated* is an adaptive, bodily, and imaginative response to the Holocaust's traumatic rupture in his family narrative, that is, a retroactive attempt to repair the breach between life before the Shoah and life after. Elaine Safer describes the novel's depiction of Trachimbrod as "Edenic," which illustrates how postmemory can prompt the fabrication of scenes and images that one wishes were real even though one knows they are not.[62] Jonathan's paradisaic fabulation of Trachimbrod speaks to his (idealized) desire for a sense of completeness or wholeness. But what motivates and informs his imaginative re-telling of Trachimbrod's history is his pilgrimage to the site of the former shtetl.[63] He states: "I want to see Trachimbrod.... To see what it's like, how my grandfather grew up, where I would be now if it weren't for the war."[64] However, as Alex, his Ukrainian tour guide and translator, explains when they arrive in the place where the shtetl once stood, it seems as if they "were in the wrong country, or the wrong century, or as if Trachimbrod had disappeared, and so had the memory of it."[65] Jonathan's search, to which Alex's words unwittingly point, is an impossible task. The Trachimbrod he seeks to find is forever gone. As the shtetl and all but two of its inhabitants were murdered, Jonathan's search for the place of his family's birth, no matter how many clues or archival documents he secures, could never materialize that which he seeks. Yet, this is the very task that nonetheless underlies the postnostalgic impulse, and it is this postnostalgic impulse that motivates the plot of *Everything Is Illuminated*.

Though the vast majority of the novel is an imaginative construction of life before the Holocaust, there are nonetheless several moments that foreshadow the catastrophe that awaits Trachimbrod at the hands of the Nazis. The peculiar image of "the feet of the dangling men ... caked in shit"[66] in the synagogue early in the novel portends the not uncommon occurrence of Jewish victims having lost their bowels after being hung by Nazis. So, too, does the description of baby Brod qua dis/assemblage of infant limbs anticipate the imminent destruction of innocent life: "It was through this hole that the women of the shtetl took turns viewing [baby Brod].... The hole wasn't even large enough to show all of the baby at once, and they had to piece together mental collages of her from each of the fragmented views—the fingers connected to the palm, which was attached to the wrist, which was at the end of the arm, which fit into the shoulder socket."[67] Jonathan describes Brod in terms of fragmented body parts, as dis/jointed anatomy; the baby's human form is divided into limbs, viewed not as a whole body by the shtetl women because of the hole's limited purview. However, the women's inability to view the baby's full body operates on a metaphorical level as well. The lack of baby Brod's corporeal wholeness retrospectively prefigures not only how Nazis saw Jews, in the German, as *figuren* or *stücken*—that is, as pieces or worthless things—but the divided-up baby body further adumbrates, in hindsight, the tangled masses of bodies of innocent Jewish Holocaust victims. These foreboding images—in tandem with both how Yankel puts baby Brod in the oven (reminiscent of crematoria), so she can sleep, and how her "body was tattooed with the newsprint" after lying on newspapers (presaging concentration camp tattoos)[68]—point to the destruction of Trachimbrod and its Jewish inhabitants that is to come. The inclusion of these images supports the idea that, in retrospect, the "idealized prewar past is seen as already containing the seeds of the catastrophe. Additionally, such idealized remembrances are projected onto the same physical spaces as genocidal violence, so that one sort of memory is invariably enfolded in the other."[69] Indeed, as protagonist Jonathan writes these scenes, his backward "view" of Trachimbrod—that is, his imaginative construction of the town—is, in part, grown from "the seeds of the catastrophe" and is inflected with Holocaust malaise. This is an inevitable consequence of growing up with family stories from the Shoah that in turn haunt those who hear them. However, though these foreshadows of the Holocaust are peppered throughout the text, they are far and few between. More so at the heart of the novel is Jonathan's search for pre-Shoah life, which is motivated by his postnostalgia.

The image of Jonathan digging up dirt when he arrives in Trachimbrod is both symbolic and symptomatic of his postnostalgia, serving as a guiding metaphor for his attempt to excavate his family's pre-Shoah past that he seeks to find. Of course, keeping soil from sites of particular importance is not necessarily an uncommon practice on such pilgrimages, but this image of Jonathan filling Ziploc bags with soil assumes additional valences of metaphorical significance in the context of the novel. Jonathan digging up soil in the place from which his family originates parallels his desire to unearth, so to speak, his family's past. Alex refers to how Jonathan *"made bags of dirt,"* explaining that the dirt is for his grandmother, should he eventually decide to inform her of his trip to Ukraine.[70] But in addition to how his trip is an effort to dig up his family's past, to disinter potential clues on-site in Trachimbrod, Jonathan's digging can further be understood as an effort, figuratively speaking, to carve out his place in the place that would have been his home, if the Holocaust had never happened. And that he then keeps the soil represents his desire to bring Trachimbrod back to the United States with him. Jonathan's somewhat sentimental—or, à la Boym, *romantic*—act of digging and collecting dirt thus functions as a symbol for how he tries to exhume the past but also as metaphors for marking his would-be place in his family's home(land) and for keeping Trachimbrod with him after he leaves. As his pilgrimage to Trachimbrod is fed by his postnostalgic romance with the shtetl, his postnostalgic romance, along with his postnostalgic fabrication of the town, is fed by his pilgrimage.

Jonathan's manuscript contains the imagined accounts of several of his family members that operate as narrative projections of himself and speak to his postnostalgia. Offering insight into Jonathan's projection of himself into the past, Alex describes how both he and Jonathan embody the characters of his manuscript. Penning his letter from Ukraine to Jonathan in the United States, Alex writes: "*Do you know that I am the Gypsy girl and you are Safran, and that I am Kolker and you are Brod, and that I am your grandmother and you are Grandfather?*"[71] Alex's statement, in part, suggests that Jonathan, as it were, *is* Brod and Safran. Otherwise put, Brod and Safran are Jonathan's imaginative constructs and egoistic projections, those in and through whom he longs to see himself. Since he cannot see himself through his family members from his limited backward-looking perspective, he comes, rather, to see *them* through *himself*. Jonathan, by writing himself into the characters of Brod and Safran, retroactively places himself in his family's imagined history, which thereby furnishes him with a more personal "familial" framework for self-understanding.

Jonathan's depiction of Brod and Yankel's relationship—idealized, yet ultimately impossible to know—represents his relationship to his family's pre-Shoah past: both romantic and fabricated. Although Alex later critiques Jonathan for not making the story idealistic enough,[72] Jonathan's vision of Brod and Yankel finds expression in paradisiac terms as he describes the father and daughter's home as a "sanctuary from Trachimbrod, a habitat completely unlike the rest of the world. No hateful words were ever spoken, and no hands raised. More than that, no angry words were ever spoken, and nothing was denied. But more than that, no unloving words were ever spoken, and everything was held up as another small piece of proof that it can be this way, it doesn't have to be that way; if there is no love in the world, we will make a new world."[73] Jonathan styles Yankel and Brod's home as a hate-less, anger-less, and affirming "new world" that functions as a "sanctuary"—a romanticized, fantastical construction of his family. Yet, Jonathan tempers his conception of this haven of a home by also explaining that Brod "didn't love Yankel, not in the simple and impossible sense of the word. In reality she hardly knew him. And he hardly knew her. They knew intimately the aspects of themselves in the other, but never the other."[74] Paralleling Brod's relationship to Yankel, Jonathan's relationship to his bygone family is defined by a subject-less love, that is, a love that has no actual subject or subjects. And yet, Jonathan's manuscript nonetheless bespeaks his love for his family he "hardly knew"—or, more accurately, never knew. Like Brod and Yankel who perceive themselves in and through each other, Jonathan projects himself into the past and onto the family members he imagines and loves. As Brod and Yankel recognize the intimate aspects of themselves in each other, so too does Jonathan find intimate aspects of himself in the fabricated person(a)s of his family. Similar to Jonathan, Brod and Yankel both intentionally create and believe "fictions necessary for life".[75] "Like Yankel, [Brod] repeats things until they are true, or until she can't tell whether they are true or not. She has become an expert at confusing *what is* with *what was* with *what should be* with *what could be*."[76] The implied parallel here is not necessarily that Jonathan is incapable of telling what is accurate and what is not regarding Trachimbrod's history. Rather, as is symptomatic of many descendants of survivors, his imaginative recreation of pre-Shoah life blurs fact (based on his archival research) with fiction ("*what was* with *what should be* with *what could be*"); although not wholly factual, that is, not *factually true*, his postnostalgic representation of Trachimbrod is nonetheless *emotionally true*, in light of how it gives voice to his desire to flesh out his family's past.

Including not only his (imagined) family members, Jonathan's manuscript is, moreover, populated with (imagined) townspeople who, together, operate as additional narrative projections of his desire to find continuity between himself and Trachimbrod's pre-Shoah past. His desire to locate a document that he invents, *The Book of Antecedents* (akin to *yizker bikher* or memorial books), makes manifest his longing to locate Trachimbrod's pre-Shoah history. In his imagined history of the shtetl, *The Book of Antecedents* started out as a record of major events like battles, famines, and the beginnings and ends of political regimes. However, it was not long before smaller events were included and described in detail like festivals, important marriages, and deaths. These new inclusions necessitated that the rather small book eventually be replaced with a three-volume set.[77] Although he has access to some archival documents, Jonathan's primary-source documentation—and thus knowledge—of life in Trachimbrod before the Holocaust is sparse, disjointed, and incomplete. Therefore, in lieu of a fleshed-out portrait of Trachimbrod—that which would offer him a more historically situated entrance into his family's pre-Shoah past—he imaginatively constructs a detailed account of shtetl life. He explains: "Even the most delinquent students read *The Book of Antecedents* without skipping a word, for they knew that they too would one day inhabit its pages, that if they could only get hold of a future edition, they would be able to read of their mistakes (and perhaps avoid them), and the mistakes of their children (and ensure that they would not happen)."[78] His projection onto these students in Trachimbrod becomes clear: if only Jonathan could locate *any* edition of *The Book of Antecedents* (or something similar), he, too, might be able to learn from the generational wisdom to which he was denied access. Had the Holocaust never occurred, he would likely have been one of these students. His fabrication of them as serious students of *The Book of Antecedents* therefore speaks to *his* (romanticized) desire to study the text conscientiously and thereby "inhabit its pages," to indwell history postnostalgically.

Jonathan and his characters' discussion of the importance of pursuing dreams speaks to his drive to explore his postnostalgia as a means of coming to terms with his family's traumatic past. Given how the third generation's postnostalgia is largely based on dreams, projections, and fantasies, the pursuit to find their families' pre-Shoah lives is to make manifest a time and place before traumatic rupture—all in hopes of working around and, indirectly, through their inherited wounds. After their trip to Trachimbrod, Alex writes to Jonathan that many of the things about which he spoke to Alex are still significant to him like, for instance, his idea that "*if you have a good and meaningful dream you are oblongated [sic] to search for it.*"[79] Though Alex means to say *obligated*, he writes "*oblongated*," a dictional error (a function of English not being his first language) that sheds light on his postnostalgia. As the derivative of "*oblongated*" is presumably *oblong*—synonymous with *long*—his word choice indirectly gestures toward how Jonathan *longs* to search for a "*good and meaningful dream.*"

And as Alex means to say "obligated," his intended diction further makes clear his postnostalgia. "Obligated"—derived from the Latin verb *obligare*, meaning "to bind, bind up, bandage"—in this context signals a sense of Jonathan being *bound to* his quest because, in short, he is *bound up* with the past. His search, then, for pre-Shoah life is an attempt to free himself from his inherited traumas by way of returning to the site of family and Jewish life before the Holocaust. Offering further insight into postnostalgia, a townsperson in Jonathan's manuscript, before adding more entries into *The Book of Recurrent Dreams*, says: "*But first ... we must review last month's entries. We must go backward in order to go forward.*"[80] This necessity to "*review*" past dreams as a way to move forward is of great import for Jonathan, though of course one cannot "review" something one has not viewed in the first place. "Reviewing" others' past dreams—or, more accurately, reviewing *dreams of others' pasts*—motivates Jonathan to "return" to the physical sites of a pre-traumatic past. Prompted by the dreams of others' pasts, Jonathan's physical "return" is intended to create a more fleshed-out perception of the past. This in turn makes room for him to move forward and begin attempting to unbind himself from the effects of intergenerational trauma.

It ought to be emphasized that Jonathan's destination is Trachimbrod, *not* sites of Holocaust atrocity, which makes clear his desire to focus on life, not destruction. Similar to how in the preface of *We Won't See Auschwitz* where Dres describes how the story's brothers' "quest breaks free of death to remember life,"[81] Jonathan does not travel to Europe with the intention to visit former sites of execution, concentration camps, or ghettos. Rather, Jonathan, focusing on life in lieu of death, travels to Trachimbrod to find the story of his grandfather and the woman whose name he believes to be Augustine. There, he meets Lista, the only person who remains in Trachimbrod after the Holocaust. Repeatedly prodding her for details, Alex's grandfather pushes her to tell Jonathan about what happened when the Nazis invaded Trachimbrod, even though she is clearly reticent to do so. Jonathan then steps in, saying, "I don't want to hear any more," at which point Alex stops translating her words.[82] Jonathan's declarative statement speaks beyond just ending the conversation in the moment; in a greater sense, his words operate as a postnostalgic declaration, an intentional posture that concentrates on life and not death. As members of the third generation have heard about the Holocaust throughout much of their lives—and, in many cases, have been inundated with stories and the history of the Shoah—many "don't want to hear any more." This is not to say that Jonathan, and the third generation in general, seek to forget the Shoah, do away with Holocaust memorialization, or wholesale stop talking about the catastrophe that indelibly shaped their families' (and their own) lives. Rather, Jonathan desires not to focus on emotionally taxing details about gratuitous atrocity; he does not fixate on Nazi decimation of Jewish life. He seeks, instead, to move outside and beyond the (re)traumatization that comes from dwelling on the Holocaust.

Jonathan's manuscript about Trachimbrod represents a new direction in Holocaust "memory." As more and more survivors (and members of the second generation) are passing away, their memories are interpreted, interpolated, and altered by the third generation. Referring to the partial draft of Jonathan's manuscript, Alex says, "*I am certain I will love very much to read the remnants.*"[83] What Alex presumably means to say is *fragments*, not "remnants." His comment, however, is ironic because, although he does not mean to say "remnants," what Jonathan has written is indeed one of the very few documents that discusses what remains from Trachimbrod, even if what remains is largely imagined, romanticized, and idealized. As the manuscript is the product of the "remnants" of history—and the product of the memory of one of the few from Trachimbrod who remained alive after the Holocaust—it functions as an extension of that history. Jonathan's construction of pre-Shoah Trachimbrod thus combines historical, narratival, and postnostalgic *"remnants,"* a combination of the narrated fragments of his family's past and his imagination.

Conclusion

A not uncommon third-generation effort to move beyond (re)traumatization is to explore family life before the moment of traumatic rupture. Of course, these efforts to circumnavigate Holocaust traumas are not fully realizable, and the Holocaust invariably colors third-generation perceptions of pre-Shoah life, always already tinting postnostalgic longing with the seeds of catastrophe. In brief, the Holocaust will most likely always be part of the purview of many in the third generation. However, by "returning" to the place of pre-Shoah life, the aim is to expand how third-generation protagonists define themselves in relation to family life before and after the Holocaust. Not basing their self-definitions primarily on the

Holocaust, many of these protagonists integrate their imaginative constructions of pre-Shoah life into longer family narratives. This extension of family narratives offers them a greater emphasis on genealogical continuity, historical rootedness, and existential belonging—all in the name of life. In a retrospective, belated rejection of Hitler's desire for *Lebensraum*, third-generation protagonists, along with second-generation protagonists, symbolically reclaim the geographic milieus where their families once lived and from which they were expelled. As their families were forcibly evicted from their homes and were effectively pushed to emigrate after the Holocaust, pilgrimages to sites of pre-Shoah family life thus reimagine such geographies as *Lebensraum* or *living space* of their own, places that are rightfully theirs and in which they re-introduce family life through their very embodied presence.

Jonathan's postnostalgia, his "homesickness" for a time and place he never lived, is thus a desire to imaginatively implicate himself into a narrative of which he was not actually a part but of which his life is a direct result; his trip better enables him to give voice to that which he never knew. Even and especially as that voice is his own, it permits him to articulate a large lacuna in his family history that had, theretofore, eluded articulation. Such a pilgrimage is thus a form of traumatic address, particularly as it enables postnostalgic constructions of pre-Shoah life. Indeed, by "returning" to the site of his family's pre-Shoah lives, though never having been there in the first place, Jonathan seeks to satisfy his postnostalgic longing for the motherland. He is in search of an alternate, subjunctive life that could and should have been otherwise, had history run a different course. That is to say, he is in pursuit of a different existence that would have been his own but emphatically was not.

Conclusion

At Home with the Holocaust treats the phenomenon of postmemory by way of examining the second generation's domestic lives, in addition to exploring how the Shoah impacts both the children and grandchildren of survivors' perceptions of place. Examining these individuals' experiences of time and space/place, particularly within survivor-family homes, may not initially appear to be a straightforward approach to better understanding the intergenerational transmission of traumatic knowledge and embodied experience. However, as historian Stephen Kern posits, time and space—fundamental philosophical and metaphysical categories—are especially suitable frameworks for cultural study because each are "comprehensive, universal and essential."[1] Not only are time and space the dimensional (and necessary) conditions for postmemory and the transmission thereof, but as this study makes clear, the second and third generations' perceptions of these categories are also altered by inherited trauma and embodied experiences in profound ways. This study provides an in-depth analysis of survivor-family homes by tracing how time and space shape and are shaped by postmemory, as represented in second-generation literature and oral history, along with an exploration of how the notion of "home" functions for children and grandchildren of survivors alike.

An examination of the literature and oral histories of children of survivors reveals a number of interrelated themes and phenomena, including how members of the second generation's relationships to their homes reveal their relationships to themselves, their parents, and the Holocaust; how postmemorial structures and material belongings contained therein spatialize, temporalize, express, and shape postmemories; how postmemorial structures paradigmatically shape subsequent domestic spaces (along with space and place more generally); how the home, often in complex ways, stands for the self in second-generation Holocaust literature and oral history; and how notions of home(lands) are complicated for descendants of survivors. An exploration of survivor-family homes as represented and described by members of the second generation, moreover, sheds light on how survivors' memories—as expressed in their verbal and nonverbal communication—manifest, invade, and permeate their and their children's affectively charged domestic lives. Such postmemorial intensities radiate from survivors and are perceived by their children as both parties navigate time and space in their family homes. Second-generation authors and narrators give expression to this affective transmission, particularly in and through their narratives about their postmemorial structures.

But although postmemorial structures are markers of haunted pasts, they are also markers of separation from those pasts—those which symbolize a severing of continuity. They stand for new starts, New-World beginnings, ruptures from the Old World, and archival containers of that which occurred after the catastrophic years of 1933–1945. Holding within them both traumatic pasts and the severing of those pasts, postmemorial structures represent the second-generation paradox: not only are they intimately connected to and gripped by the past, but they are also emphatically distant from the Shoah. This proximity and distance—this simultaneous connection and disconnection from the Holocaust—defines many second-generation lived experiences, certainly within the home but also, no doubt, without.

Survivor-family homes are privileged sites to study postmemory, insofar as domestic spaces are sites of intimate life, defined by parent-child relationships, and externalizations of inhabitants' inner lives. As survivor-family members' inner lives and their relationships with one another took place within their domiciles, their domestic spaces became permeated with intra- and interpersonal emotions and feelings. Their homes, as such, were charged and filled with (spoken and unspoken) narratives of family life, both past and present. Some of these unspoken narratives took the form of affect transmitted, seemingly osmotically, from survivor to child. The circulation of traumatic affect in the shared space of postmemorial structures, where "physical proximity and emotional engagement are entwined,"[2] created domestic environments wherein self and other often became blurred. But whether transmitted verbally or nonverbally, survivor parents' pasts were also communicated to the second generation by and through their childhood domestic spaces. Given their deeply personal, intimate, and familial associations and resonances, postmemorial structures, along with the things contained within such homes, thus prove to be rich avenues of scholarly inquiry when examining the enduring effects of the Holocaust on subsequent generations.

At Home with the Holocaust addresses a gap in trauma and memory studies, specifically how postmemory manifested and continues to manifest spatially in domestic spaces. Although much has been written about other material modes of transmitting traumatic knowledge intergenerationally—like, for instance, through photography—there has remained a lack of scholarly attention afforded to how survivor-family homes contributed to this transmission. My project intervenes by suggesting that survivor-family homes in no small part structured children of survivors' relationships to their parents' traumas, revealing how the traumatic afterlife of the Holocaust endured in and through the homes of survivor families and how the domestic held and continues to hold great potential to postmemorially domesticate the psyches of the second generation. This project offers new insight into how domestic space was shaped by inherited trauma, as well as an examination of how domestic space shaped the transmission of traumatic knowledge and embodied experience for survivor families.

Future Directions

At Home with the Holocaust serves as an initial study into survivor-family homes that can be brought to bear on a number of related and tangential projects. From examining family homes of others who struggle with mental health issues—including and especially those who have survived instances of (mass) violence—to treating additional aspects of and belongings contained within postmemorial structures, and from exploring how individuals' particular identities can impact postmemorial structures to discussing second- and third-generation oral history, there are many themes and topics explored in this study that can be used as future avenues of analysis for other projects.

Within the context of ever-escalating instances of state-sponsored violence that result in profound geopolitical displacement, affecting not only displaced people firsthand but also subsequent generations, this study can be brought to bear on other instances of inherited traumas of children born to displaced persons and their domestic lives. As the number of displaced peoples continues to grow, especially as of recent, this project can be used to address similar issues that subsequently arise from geopolitical upheaval and manifest in displaced persons' home lives thereafter, namely that of postmemory. Pointing to how postmemory can be applied in other contexts, Marianne Hirsch herself notes how capacious her theory is; though she developed this theory in regard to the children of Holocaust survivors, she notes that "it may usefully describe other second-generation memories of cultural or collective traumatic events and experiences."[3] Hirsch offers a brief discussion about the relationship between her notion of postmemory for the descendants of Holocaust survivors and Toni Morrison's conceptualization of *rememory* for the descendants of formerly enslaved peoples,[4] which serves as a generative example for how to engage in such discussions. But in addition to postmemory, there are other resonances that descendants of Holocaust survivors share with descendants of survivors of other instances of persecution, those ravaged by different conflicts and atrocities. Elizabeth Rosner notes how she finds a number of intersections between her experience of growing up with survivors and those born to survivors of, for example, the Cambodian Killing Fields, the atomic bomb in Japan, and the Rwandan Genocide.[5] Rosner self-identifies as neither unique nor exceptional and explains that she connects with millions around the globe who are overcome by the enduring traumas of war, genocide, and displacement. The more she delves into her personal inheritance, she explains, the more she recognizes other intergenerational reverberations of violence, persecution, statelessness, and annihilation—but also resilience.[6] The commonalities (and the differences) between descendants of Holocaust survivors and descendants of other instances of mass violence would allow for a comparative study of postmemorial structures in the United States and those across the globe. Of course, the politics surrounding various atrocities (including the politics of memory) are fraught, and such discussions need to be handled with much prudence and care. Accordingly, such studies would benefit from drawing upon Michael Rothberg's *Multidirectional Memory*, which argues against establishing hierarchies of suffering.[7] Rothberg's approach to the politics of memory would serve as a helpful guide for such comparative studies.

At Home with the Holocaust also provides a theoretical guide for understanding how other cases of mental health issues—those unrelated to mass violence or genocide—find expression in domestic spaces and how children of those with mental health issues navigate their homes. This study holds the potential to analyze the function of domestic space for those who experience other, albeit nonetheless consequential, mental health issues like depression, bipolar disorder, and anxiety, and can thus be employed as a tool to aid studies on a wide range of families affected by mental health issues and how said mental health issues shape their domestic lives.

There are furthermore a number of themes and topics within second- and third-generation literature that have yet to be adequately treated, particularly as they relate to postmemorial structures. There is more research to be done on the differences and similarities between postmemorial structures in different national contexts (e.g., between those in Germany versus those in, say, Canada). This is not to mention the untapped lines of inquiry that focus on the differences and similarities between postmemorial structures in urban, suburban, and rural areas, and how these various environs impact postmemorial imaginations. Second-generation texts set in suburban regions like Victoria Redel's "My Little Pledge of Us" (1995) present different geographical landscapes, cultures, and ways of life than, for example, texts set in urban centers like Thane Rosenbaum's *The Golems of Gotham* (2002). There is a variety of inquiries possible, as they relate to the roles of these settings in shaping how descendants negotiate, enact, and come to terms with their postmemories. Moreover, studies of third-generation postmemorial structures—or what may be more accurately called *post*-postmemorial structures—would serve as extensions of *At Home with the Holocaust* and thereby expand research on descendants of survivors. Third-generation texts like Amy Kurzweil's *Flying Couch* (2016) would lend themselves well to such studies. There are several other areas of inquiry that would serve as further generative scholastic discussions, including but not limited to the ways that technological developments in the 1950s and 60s, especially the emergence of the TV, shaped postmemorial structures, as explored in Gabriella Goliger's *Song of Ascent* (2000) and Bernice Eisenstein's *I Was a Child of Holocaust Survivors* (2006); domestic hoarding, as seen in, for example, Leah Kaminsky's *The Waiting Room* (2016); and the process of packing up survivors' homes, as represented in texts like Anne Karpf's *The War After* (1996) and Lydia Flem's *The Final Reminder* (2005).

Moreover, insofar as there is a wide variety of identity politics at play within survivor families, questions and issues related to individuals' race and interracial relationships, religion and interfaith relationships, gender, and sexual orientations are ripe for exploration while holding much potential to shape how we understand postmemorial structures. Taking gender and sexual orientation as illustrative examples, scholars have much to consider when thinking about how queerness shaped and continues to shape descendants' relationships to their postmemories and thus their domestic lives. Reciprocally, there is much to examine in regard to how their postmemories and home lives have shaped their queerness. Building on the pioneering work of Golan Moskovitz in the field of queer second-generation studies,[8] future research could explore how Two-Spirit, lesbian, gay, bisexual, trans, queer, and other nonnormative (2SLGBTQ+) descendants' experiences of homophobia and transphobia, along with accompanying experiences of marginality, exclusion, suffering, and shame, map onto (or do not map onto) survivors' experiences of antisemitism, marginality, exclusion, suffering, and shame during the Holocaust. The work of Lev Raphael, Harlan Greene, Susan Knabe, Sarah Schulman, Julia Creet, Rick Landman, Lisa Kron, Wendy Oberlander, Madelaine Zadik, and Mini Horrorwitz, among others, hold many generative possibilities for such future studies. These studies could ask: How are their inherited traumas affectively complicated by their queer identities, and how does their queerness similarly complicate their inherited traumas from their survivor relatives' experiences during the Shoah? Given how Jewish marriage and having Jewish children are understood as means of stymying Hitler's goal to rid the world of all Jewish life, what are 2SLGBTQ+ descendants' relationships to marriage and childbearing, and in what ways did/do interactions with survivors "reproduce" both their personal traumas and their inherited traumas?[9] Since many survivors understood their descendants' queerness as immoral—and in some instances as (enigmatically) comparable to Nazism, as is the case in Raphael's work[10]—how are the affective constellations of shame, guilt, anxiety, anger, and fear that many 2SLGBTQ+ descendants experience compounded by survivors' Holocaust experiences in the context of postmemorial structures?

Second- and third-generation oral histories also constitute further underexplored fields of inquiry. As there has been markedly little sustained research on the oral histories of children of Holocaust survivors, with the exception of Arlene Stein's *Reluctant Witnesses* (2014), there is much work to be done in this area. One of the most generative oral-history projects is Avinoam Patt's *In Our Own Words Interview Project*, a collection of over sixty second- and third-generation oral histories conducted at University of Hartford. In this collection, there is a range of postmemorial experiences represented and much to be examined in relation to postmemorial structures, not to mention how the third-generation oral histories in this collection (and other collections) remain significantly understudied. Other such oral-history collections—for example, those in the Special Collections at the College of Charleston, the New York Public Library, and the United States Holocaust Memorial Museum—would be of additional value to the study of the second and third generations.

Conclusion

I want to close this study by discussing one particular oral history from Patt's *In Our Own Words Interview Project*, narrated by a member of the second generation named Jeff I. Jeff's oral history stands out, as it provides a second-generation account of how his father's Holocaust experiences impacted him throughout his life and, subsequently, how they impacted his own son. As Jeff talks about his father's Holocaust experiences, his own personal relationship to the Shoah, and his son's relationship to the Shoah, he connects his discussion to his domestic space. Although this portrait is not representative of all survivor families—as no single portrait can represent second-generation experiences in full—it is one that includes all three generations, revealing how the Holocaust continues to reverberate decades after 1945.[11]

When Jeff first learned as a child about his father's Holocaust experiences in the camps, he did not try to glean any more information nor did he ask his father further questions (despite describing having had the "floodgates of curiosity" open up)—until, that is, he had children of his own.[12] Jeff's oldest son became fascinated with the Holocaust and fixated on his grandfather's story, which thereby catalyzed Jeff's renewed interest in the Shoah as an adult. Jeff explains that in college his son channeled his memory of his grandfather into his artwork when he made a large clay rendering of tracks leading into an unnamed camp with an arm protruding from the ground that had his grandfather's tattooed number on it. As Jeff describes this piece of art, he becomes emotional for the first time in the oral history; up until this point, he exhibits little affect and sheds no tears. Yet, while describing his son's art installation, he breaks down crying.

But of greatest significance in this moment is his description of his son's piece of art: he describes the installation as "home."[13] Jeff's diction, albeit perhaps puzzling at first, gestures toward a sense of reconciling himself to his lack of personal interest in his father's past for so long. Indeed, Jeff states that he wishes he had kept his interest in the Holocaust for as long as his son did, but his regrets for not learning more about his father's past and for not speaking about it seem to be quelled by his son's keen fascination with and artistic response to his father's Holocaust experiences. As Jeff speaks about feeling guilty for not familiarizing himself more with his father's story, it becomes clear that his son's art installation—which Jeff now keeps in his living room—became for him a domestic memorial. Otherwise put, the artwork became a site of (post)memory that offers Jeff the ability to connect vicariously through his *son's* artistic expression of his *father's* history—a history that was denied to him as a child and as an adolescent but was revealed more fully to and through his son. In his home as an adult, Jeff no longer lives in a space of silence or censorship about the Shoah. Instead, he is better able to "remember," that is, to *re-member* or piece together a history to which he was theretofore not granted access. Thus, as he houses this installation in his living room and as he maintains this visual and material point of connection to his father's past mediated through his son, Jeff is able to give voice—and shape, as it were—to his father's experiences by way of his son's artwork. Indeed, he is able to live with this reified knowledge in the form of his son's clay sculpture. By housing this clay memorial, his domestic space takes on a greater sense of imbued belonging and connects Jeff more so to his father's past that has become, postmemorially, Jeff's. Of course, it was not solely his son's art installation that allowed him to give voice to his father's past, but it was a central catalyst for learning more about his father's story.[14] And such was the experience of many second-generation witnesses: their interest in and commitment to telling the story of their parents were piqued by having children and through their children's interest in the Holocaust.

Jeff's oral history illustrates how second-generation postmemory and third-generation post-postmemory are neither static nor linear. The traumatic reverberations of the Shoah endure in a multiplicity of ways for various survivor families, and their postmemorial structures register, archive, and keep alive familial narratives of and from the Holocaust. Akin to *The Speed of Light*'s Paula, Jeff becomes reacquainted with the Shoah as an adult, reinvigorated to keep alive the memory of his father and the millions lost at the hands of Nazis. He, like several of the protagonists of the texts examined throughout this study, essays to memorialize his family's loss and tragedy while acknowledging how the Shoah impacted him personally. In line with *The Holocaust Kid*'s Zosha, Jeff passes along the story of his family's Holocaust past to his offspring—which is in and of itself a form of memorialization. And similar to *Everything Is Illuminated*, Jeff's oral history reveals how the Holocaust still impinges upon third-generation psyches in enduring ways. These continuities—along with several dissimilarities not explored here—point to the myriad ways by which the Shoah takes up residence, so to speak, in the minds and homes of many whose families were marked and marred by the Holocaust. As Jeff's oral history and the texts examined throughout *At Home with the Holocaust* suggest, the Shoah became "domestic" for descendants of survivors. As some imaginatively lived in their progenitors' Holocaust pasts and as some were overwhelmed by said pasts, many have sought to come to terms with its enduring legacy in their lives. These attempts to come to terms with the past—whether they be through writing, speaking, art, or having children—demonstrate how the second and third generations, in the spirit of Emil Fackenheim, do not grant Hitler the posthumous victory. Instead, through the process of coming to terms with their families' Holocaust legacies—so as, at least in part, not to be domesticated by them—these descendants of survivors keep alive the memory of their families, despite Hitler's attempts to rid the world of such memory, thereby giving the second and third generations the proverbial final word, even as they find themselves at home with the Holocaust.

Appendix

I offer the following list of fiction, nonfiction, poetry, dramatic works, and films to show the sheer volume of cultural productions available to children of survivors in the years that they grew up: Anatole Litvak's *Confessions of a Nazi Spy* (1939); Charlie Chaplin's *The Great Dictator* (1940); Edward Dmytryk and Irving Reis's *Hitler's Children* (1943); Fritz Lang's *Hangmen Also Die!* (1943); Douglas Sirk's *Hitler's Madman* (1943); André De Toth's *None Shall Escape* (1944); Randall Jarrell's poetry, specifically "Protocols" (1945); Orson Wells's *The Stranger* (1946); Saul Bellow's *The Victim* (1947); Dmytryk's *Crossfire* (1947); Marie Syrkin's *Blessed Is the Match* (1947); Fred Zinnemann's *The Search* (1947); Lewis Allen's *Sealed Verdict* (1948); Irwin Shaw's *The Young Lions* (1948 [made into a film in 1958]); John Hersey's *The Wall* (1950 [made into a film in 1982]); Henry Hathaway's *The Desert Fox* (1951); Charles Olson's *The Distances* (1951); Herman Wouk's *The Caine Mutiny* (1951 [adapted into a play in 1955]); Andrew Marton's *The Devil Makes Three* (1952); Dmytryk's *The Juggler* (1953 [made into a film that same year]); Gerald Reitlinger's *The Final Solution* (1953); Leo Schwarz's *The Redeemers* (1953); David Weiss's *The Guilt Makers* (1953); Robert Wise's *The Desert Rats* (1953); Aage Bertelsen's *October '43* (1954); Flannery O'Connor's "The Displaced Person" (1954); Bernie Krigstein's "Master Race," published in *Impact Magazine* (1955); Max Nosseck's *Singing in the Dark* (1956); Bernard Malamud's "The Last Mohican" and "The Lady of the Lake" (1958); Arthur Miller's *Playing for Time* (1958); Leon Uris's *Exodus*

(1958 [made into a film in 1960]); Samuel Fuller's *Verboten!* (1959); Allen Ginsberg's *Kaddish and Other Poems* (1961); Stanley Kramer's *Judgment at Nuremberg* (1961); Uris's *Mila 18* (1961); Kurt Vonnegut's *Mother Night* (1961); Edward Lewis Wallant's *The Pawnbroker* (1961 [made into a film in 1965]); Sylvia Plath's poetry, particularly "Daddy" (1962); James Baldwin's *The Fire Next Time* (1963); Stanley Kubrick's *Dr. Strangelove or: How I Learned to Stop Worrying and Love the Bomb* (1964); Miller's *After the Fall* (1964) and *Incident at Vichy* (1964); Lore Segal's *Other People's Houses* (1964); Hugh Nissenson's *A Pile of Stones* (1965); John Kander's *Cabaret* (1966 [made into a film in 1972]); in addition to his earlier short stories, Bernard Malamud's *The Fixer* (1966); Richard Elman's *The 28th Day of Elul* (1967), *Lilo's Diary* (1968), and *The Reckoning* (1969); Chaim Potok's *The Chosen* (1967 [made into a film in 1981]); Ilona Karmel's *An Estate of Memory* (1969); Potok's *The Promise* (1969); Norma Rosen's *Touching Evil* (1969); Bellow's *Mr. Sammler's Planet* (1970); Elżbieta Ettinger's *Kindergarten* (1970); Uris's *QB VII* (1970 [made into an ABC miniseries in 1974]); Hal Ashby's *Harold and Maude* (1971); Wouk's *The Winds of War* (1971); Potok's *My Name is Asher Lev* (1972); Isaac Bashevis Singer's *Enemies, A Love Story* (first published in English in 1972); John Waters's *Pink Flamingos* (1972); Arthur A. Cohen's *In the Days of Simon Stern* (1973); Susan Fromberg Schaeffer's *Anya* (1974); James F. Collier's *The Hiding Place* (1975); Arthur Hiller's *The Man in the Glass Booth* (1975); Nissenson's *My Own Ground* (1976); Cynthia Ozick's *Bloodshed* (1976); Stuart Rosenberg's *Voyage of the Damned* (1976); John Schlesinger's *Marathon Man* (1976); William Heyen's *The Swastika Poems* (1977); Wouk's *War and Remembrance* (1978); Peter Collinson's *The House on Garibaldi Street* (1979); Leslie Epstein's *King of the Jews* (1979); Philip Roth's *The Ghost Writer* (1979); Martin Sherman's *Bent* (1979 [made into a film in 1997]); and William Styron's *Sophie's Choice* (1979 [made into a film in 1982]).

Acknowledgments

The task of acknowledging all those who helped, directly or indirectly, to shape this project—along with thanking them properly—is both daunting and admittedly impossible. However, in the following meager paragraphs, I endeavor to recognize and pay tribute to those who have been of scholarly, intellectual, and/or emotional assistance throughout the years leading up to and during the writing of this book.

First and foremost, I want to dedicate this project to my dad, Keith Wilson, whom I had for the first sixteen years of my life. My dad instilled in me an intellectual curiosity that he cultivated for the years I had him, which has persisted in me and for which I owe my endurance in pursuing this project. Dad, thank you for being so excellent; thank you for being so good; thank you for all of the love, support, and guidance that still keeps me going. I love you immeasurably; I miss you thoroughly; and this one—like all my projects—goes out to you.

I want to thank my siblings, Josh, Zack, Quinn, and Ceilidh. I am still realizing how profoundly you've each shaped me. Your indefatigable support and care have proven to be life-giving. My relationships with each of you are some of the most meaningful parts of my life, and I sincerely do not know where I would be without you.

I also want to thank my extended family and friends, who have supported me over the past several years. I specifically want to thank Monika Wahba: thank you for always being in my corner.

I, of course, want to say "thank you" to my partner, Mateus. Mateus, you kind and gentle man, you have made me a better human. I love you.

I am also indebted to Nancy Janovicek, along with the Department of History and the Faculty of Arts at University of Calgary. I thank you for your incredible support over the past few years—this book would sincerely not have been possible without you.

Additionally, I'd like to thank my former colleagues at the various institutions where I have taught. Specifically, I want to thank Deborah Tihanyi, Robert Irish, and Emily Moore from University of Toronto; Jan Harris, Sonya Compton Green, Stacia Moroski-Rigney, Kimberly Capps Reed, Kate Sealy, and Jill Jerkins from Lipscomb University; and Celeste Orr, Rachel Harvey, Lindsey McRae-Graine, Ashlee Joyce, and Jacob Keszei from my time at McMaster University.

I would be remiss not to mention all the folx I have met over the past several years while conducting research for this project. I specifically want to name Sebastian Huebel, Alexandra Birch, Amber Nickell, Meghan Riley, Annamaria Orla-Bukowska, and Maciek Zabierowski from the Auschwitz Jewish Center Fellows Program; Jackie Teale from the Bergen-Belsen International Summer School; Elysa McConnell from the Holocaust Educational Foundation of Northwestern University's Summer Institute on the Holocaust and Jewish Civilization; Cathy Caruth and Sabrina Bouarour from the School of Criticism and Theory at Cornell University; Harlan Greene, Dale Rosengarten, and Alyssa Neely from the College of Charleston; Gila Naveh and Holli Levitsky from the Jewish American and Holocaust Literature Symposium; Avi Patt of New York University; Gary P. Zola and Dana Herman from The Jacob Rader Marcus Center of the Jewish American Archives; and Josh Burford and Maigen Sullivan from the Invisible Histories Project, among many others.

Furthermore, I want to thank both Christopher Rios-Sueverkruebbe and Carah Naseem of Rutgers University Press. I appreciate your support, guidance, and expertise immensely, and I am indebted to you for bringing this project to life.

I also want to thank the academic journals that have granted me permission to use versions of the articles that I have previously published. I want to thank *Modern Language Studies* (University of Buffalo), *Journal of Jewish Identities* (Johns Hopkins University Press), and *Studies in American Jewish Literature* (Penn State University Press) for allowing me to adapt the articles I published with them for *At Home with the Holocaust*.

I want to acknowledge all the funding sources that have made this project possible, those which enabled me to travel across Europe and North America to conduct research for this project. I not only want to thank Florida Atlantic University, Vanderbilt University, and McMaster University for their generous support but also want to recognize the other sources of funding that made this project possible, including the Honor Society of Phi Kappa Phi; the American Academy of Jewish Research; the Jacob Rader Marcus Center of the Jewish American Archives; the Northeast Modern Language Association; the Feinstein Center of Temple University; Sigma Tau Delta International English Honor Society; the European Holocaust Research Infrastructure; the College of Charleston; the New York Public Library; the Southern Jewish Historical Society; the Maurice Greenberg Center for Judaic Studies at University of Hartford; the Auschwitz Jewish Center; and the Friends of Simon Wiesenthal Center for Holocaust Studies.

Last but certainly not least, I want to thank the folks who helped shape this project in various ways and who assisted with providing immensely helpful feedback. I want to thank Jay Geller, Adam Meyer, and Victor Judge from Vanderbilt University—you all, in your own way, helped me conceive of this project. I am beyond grateful to have worked with each of you.

Victoria Aarons, I want to thank you for your extensive feedback. From the first day I met you, you made me feel like I was and am "part of the group." As a young scholar, it can sometimes be tough to break into an established scholarly community, but when we were first introduced on the campus of Claremont McKenna College, you made me feel accepted, heard, and welcomed. The commentary you provided for this project, among other projects, has been extensive, thorough, and challenging in the best way possible—without your constructive criticism and suggestions, this project would not be where it is today. Thank you also for being one of my mentors and a deeply kind human—I appreciate you greatly and think so very highly of you as both a scholar and a person.

Andrew Furman, thank you so much for your sustained support since we first connected. Your feedback has always been detailed, rigorous, and genuinely thought provoking. You have been so generous with your time and consideration, and you have been nothing but kind to me. It has been a sincere honor working with you.

Eric Berlatsky, I am so wildly grateful for your support, kindness, guidance, and presence. Your sense of humor and keen insight have made working with you so fun and an honest thrill. Thank you for making me a better scholar. You have helped shape my mind, which is a gift for which I cannot repay you, but I want you to know that I wholeheartedly appreciate all that you've done for me over the past several years.

Alan L. Berger: this is possibly the easiest but also the hardest "thank you" in these acknowledgements. You are, very sincerely, one of the most important people in my life. Your unrelenting support, your belief in me, your never-ending jokes, your genuine care, and your commitment to make the world a better place have made me intensely grateful to have worked with you. You are a good man. When I was at my lowest when I was still in Florida, you took it upon yourself to buy me lunch, pulled out a box of tissues, and gave me the time and space to talk—and you listened. When I approached you about coediting a volume together, you very graciously agreed to collaborate. I always look forward to our many FaceTime chats; I consistently feel lighter, with a smile on my face, after we chat. I mean it when I say that I truly do not think that I could have asked for a better-suited PhD supervisor than you. And for all this, I say with unending gratitude and so much admiration: thank you.

Notes

Preface

1 Lucas Wilson, "Unlearning Evangelicalism: What a Poor Education Taught Me," in *Becoming: Transformative Storytelling for Education's Future*, ed. Laura Colket, Tracy Penny Light, and M. Adam Carswell (New York: DIO Press, 2021), 27–34.
2 Lucas Wilson, "Dismantling Christian Readings of Jewish American Literature in the Christian College: A. M. Klein's *The Second Scroll*," in *Teaching Jewish American Literature*, ed. Roberta Rosenberg and Rachel Rubenstein (New York: Modern Language Association of America, 2020), 58–62.

Introduction

1 I define survivors not only as those who went through concentration camps—including death, work, and transit camps—but also as those who lived in ghettos and/or survived in hiding, along with refugees who escaped Hitler's reach and immigrated elsewhere between 1933 and 1945. See Dan Bar-On, *Fear and Hope: Three Generations of the Holocaust* (Cambridge, MA: Harvard University Press, 1995); Esther Jilovsky, *Remembering the Holocaust: Generations, Witnessing and Place* (New York: Bloomsbury Academic, 2015); Arlene Stein, *Reluctant Witnesses: Survivors, Their Children, and the Rise of Holocaust Consciousness* (Oxford: Oxford University Press, 2014); Nina Fischer, *Memory Work: The Second Generation* (London: Palgrave, 2015). In the context of this study, the term *survivors* refers specifically to Jewish survivors, the principal targets of the Nazi regime.
2 Deborah E. Lipstadt, *Holocaust: An American Understanding* (New Brunswick, NJ: Rutgers University Press, 2016). See also Hasia Diner, "Post-World-War-II American Jewry and the Confrontation with Catastrophe," *American Jewish History* 91, no. 3–4 (2003): 439–67.
3 See, for instance, Peter Novick, *The Holocaust in American Life* (Boston: Mariner Books, 2000).

4 Diner, "Post-World-War-II American Jewry," 446.
5 Lipstadt, *Holocaust*, 10.
6 Although some of the younger members of the second generation grew up in the 1980s, a substantial number were born soon after liberation and were thus already in their thirties and out of their parents' homes by the 1980s. As such, I concentrate my discussion on this thirty-five-year time span, in order to flesh out the cultural environment that shaped the children of survivors.
7 For instance, picture magazines like *Time-Life* published a series of issues that depicted concentration camps in both text and photos. See Dora Apel, *Memory Effects: The Holocaust and the Art of Secondary Witnessing* (New Brunswick, NJ: Rutgers University Press, 2002), 15.
8 Other shows included *The Defenders*, *Sam Benedict*, *Dragnet*, and *This Is Your Life*. These were in addition to radio shows like *Faith in Our Time* (broadcasted by the Mutual Broadcasting System) and *The Eternal Light* (broadcasted on the NBC Radio Network) that discussed the Holocaust. But the most popular and impactful (even if sensationalized) was the 1978 miniseries *Holocaust*. See Diner, "Post-World-War-II American Jewry," 448, 456; Lipstadt, *Holocaust*, 93.
9 Holocaust survivors constitute a wide-ranging group of individuals. Survivors were displaced from all over Europe, North Africa, and Asia. Some came from shtetls and others from Christian-dominant communities. Some were religiously observant, whereas others were secular. Some were well-educated; others never went to high school. As for their experiences during the Shoah, survivors were affected in a multiplicity of ways, and there was no uniform experience of survival. Some endured the horrors of the Shoah as children, some as adolescents, and others as adults. Whether they lived through camps, ghettos, and/or periods of hiding—and/or if they fled—survivors were directly implicated in the Holocaust sometimes for several years and sometimes for less than one.
10 Such heterogeneity was a result of numerous factors. Though many were born soon after the Holocaust, there is an age range within the second generation of approximately twenty years. See Fischer, *Memory Work*, 13. The second generation is further varied in regard to where its members were born; some were born in displaced persons camps, and others were born elsewhere, predominantly in the United States, Israel, Canada, and Australia. Some stayed in Europe permanently; some stayed for several years and then emigrated; and some never stepped foot in the place of their parents' births. There are also a number of identity-based variables that further diversify the second generation, including sexual orientations, gender identities, racial makeups, socioeconomic statuses, vocations, and religious and political beliefs. This is not to mention how family configurations and dynamics further individuate members of this community. As a result of this heterogeneity, these individuals have highly mediated relationships to the Holocaust, and how they relate to and deal with the legacy of the Holocaust is emphatically personal.
11 Janice F. Bistritz, "Transgenerational Pathologies in Families of Holocaust Survivors," in *The Psychological Perspectives of the Holocaust and of Its Aftermath*, ed. Randolph L. Braham (New York: Columbia University Press, 1988), 130.
12 Bistritz, "Transgenerational Pathologies," 130, 131, 133.
13 See, for instance, Dov Shmotkin et al., "Resilience and Vulnerability among Aging Holocaust Survivors and Their Families: An Intergenerational Overview," *Journal of Intergenerational Relationships* 9 (2011): 7–21.

14 Marianne Hirsch, *Family Frames: Photography, Narrative, and Postmemory* (Cambridge, MA: Harvard University Press, 1997), 22.
15 Marianne Hirsch, *The Generation of Postmemory: Writing and Visual Culture after the Holocaust* (New York: Columbia University Press, 2012), 31.
16 In truth, some of these characteristics of children of survivors were not completely a function of survivors' Holocaust experiences. Some were a result of other compounding processes and dynamics like emigration and immigration, pre-Shoah family structures, their individual personalities, their lives before the Holocaust, whether one lived in a shtetl or in a city, their country of origin, and so on. As a result, assessing the extent to which the Holocaust affected survivors' parenting is not always simple or neat. These other factors complicate such assessments and need to be considered when ascertaining the Shoah's role in how they raised their children. Yet, these complicating factors, which may or may not be related specifically to the Holocaust, speak more broadly to families' ruptured lives, to a "life before" that is no longer and is thus forever lost. Such additional factors, though not necessarily traumatic, in some ways amplify the second generation's difficult relationship to the Holocaust.
17 Helen Epstein, *Children of the Holocaust: Conversations with Sons and Daughters of Survivors* (New York: Penguin, 1988), 220.
18 Martin S. Bergmann and Milton E. Jucovy, *Generations of the Holocaust* (New York: Columbia University Press, 1982), 312; emphasis added.
19 Rachel Yehuda et al., "Low Cortisol and Risk for PTSD in Adult Offspring of Holocaust Survivors," *American Journal of Psychiatry* 157, no. 8 (2000): 1252. See also Shmotkin et al., "Resilience and Vulnerability," 10; Rachel Yehuda and Linda M. Bierer, "The Relevance of Epigenetics to PTSD: Implications for the DSM-V," *Journal of Traumatic Stress* 22 (2009): 427–34.
20 Hirsch, *The Generation of Postmemory*, 6.
21 As Jeff E. Malpas notes, "It is something of a truism to say that that which is closest and most familiar to us is often that which is most easily overlooked and forgotten." See Jeff E. Malpas, *Place and Experience: A Philosophical Topography* (Cambridge: Cambridge University Press, 1999), 19.
22 Janet Jacobs, "The Cross-Generational Transmission of Trauma: Ritual and Emotion among Survivors of the Holocaust," *Journal of Contemporary Ethnography* 40, no. 3 (2011): 345.
23 Jacobs, "The Cross-Generational Transmission of Trauma," 345.
24 Fischer, *Memory Work*, 25.
25 Hirsch, *The Generation of Postmemory*, 6; emphasis in the original.
26 Gaston Bachelard, *The Poetics of Space*, trans. Maria Jolas (Boston: Beacon Press, 1994).
27 James Krasner, *Home Bodies: Tactile Experience in Domestic Space* (Columbus: The Ohio State University Press, 2010), 16.
28 Krasner, *Home Bodies*, 191.
29 Bettina Hofmann and Ursula Reuter, eds., *Translated Memories: Transgenerational Perspectives on the Holocaust* (Lanham, MD: Lexington Books, 2020), 7–8.
30 Fischer, *Memory Work*, 18.
31 Fischer, *Memory Work*, 19.
32 For the children of survivors, though the task of finding their parents' complete stories from the Holocaust and representing them is ultimately impossible, the

commitment to locate such narratives and give voice to them is persistent. As such, regardless of how second-generation literature does not (and cannot) depict "the real" in full, its ethical concern to enter some semblance of referential discourse—of representing both survivors' Holocaust experiences and the experiences of growing up with them—undergirds and motivates much of the canon.

33 Holocaust literature has a number of defining characteristics. These characteristics include the aesthetic issue of reconciling normalcy with the horrific; the eclipsing of life by death; the destruction of childhood innocence; the desecration of the body and material reality; the breakdown of rationality; and the disturbance of chronological time. See Lawrence Langer, *The Holocaust and the Literary Imagination* (New Haven, CT: Yale University Press, 1975), xii, 251, 252. Many of these characteristics also find expression, to varying degrees, in the literature of children of survivors. The blurring of daily life and imagined violence, along with the confusion of past and present, pervades second-generation literature. Second-generation Holocaust literature, because of its many continuities with the literature written by survivors, can and should be understood as part of the Holocaust literary canon. See Andrew Furman, *Contemporary Jewish American Writers and the Multicultural Dilemma: The Return of the Exiled* (Syracuse, NY: Syracuse University Press, 2000), 63.

34 Cathy Caruth, *Unclaimed Experience: Trauma, Narrative, and History* (Baltimore: Johns Hopkins University Press, 1996), 91.

35 Cathy Caruth, *Literature and the Ashes of History* (Baltimore: Johns Hopkins University Press, 2013), 5.

36 Dori Laub, "An Event without a Witness: Truth, Testimony and Survival," in *Testimony: Crises of Witnessing in Literature, Psychoanalysis, and History*, ed. Shoshana Felman and Dori Laub (New York: Routledge, 1991), 69.

37 Roger Luckhurst, *The Trauma Question* (New York: Routledge, 2008), 9.

38 Dori Laub, "Bearing Witness or the Vicissitudes of Listening," in *Testimony: Crises of Witnessing in Literature, Psychoanalysis, and History*, ed. Shoshana Felman and Dori Laub (New York: Routledge, 1991), 58.

39 Fischer, *Memory Work*, 24. See also Marianne Hirsch and Leo Spitzer, *Ghosts of Home: The Afterlife of Czernowitz in Jewish Memory* (Berkeley: University of California Press, 2010), xix.

Chapter 1 Postmemorial Structures

1 Thane Rosenbaum, "Cattle Car Complex," in *Elijah Visible* (New York: St. Martin's Press, 1996), 5; emphasis added.

2 Rosenbaum, "Cattle Car Complex," 5.

3 Shelley Mallett, "Understanding Home: A Critical Review of the Literature," *The Sociological Review* 52, no. 1 (2004): 71.

4 Mallett, "Understanding Home," 71.

5 Mallett, "Understanding Home," 63, 81–82.

6 Mallett, "Understanding Home," 84.

7 Mihaly Csikszentmihalyi and Eugene Rochberg-Halton, *The Meaning of Things: Domestic Symbols and the Self* (Cambridge: Cambridge University Press, 1981), 123. See also Carole Després, "The Meaning of Home: Literature Review and Directions for Future Research and Theoretical Development," *Journal of Architectural*

and *Planning Research* 8, no. 2 (1991): 98, 100; Mallett, "Understanding Home," 71, 81–82, 84; Yi-Fu Tuan, *Space and Place: The Perspective of Experience* (Minneapolis: University of Minnesota Press, 2011), 164; Dale Pattison, "Writing Home: Domestic Space, Narrative Production, and the Homeland in Roth's *American Pastoral*," *Twentieth Century Literature* 60, no. 2 (2014): 224.
8 Bachelard, *The Poetics of Space*. See also Kris Pint, "Bachelard's House Revisited: Toward a New Poetics of Space," *Interiors* 4, no. 2 (2013): 111. See also Tuan, *Space and Place*, 164.
9 Després, "The Meaning of Home," 98, 100.
10 Després, "The Meaning of Home," 100.
11 Csikszentmihalyi and Rochberg-Halton, *The Meaning of Things*, 104.
12 For example, the protagonist in second-generation writer Thomas Friedmann's *Damaged Goods* himself notes that "houses were important for American writers." See Thomas Friedmann, *Damaged Goods* (Sag Harbor, NY: The Permanent Press, 1984), 187.
13 Narratives that fit into the first category—of *representations of the home as a positive and crucial institution*—largely fall into three subcategories: children's literature, domestic fiction, and Christian fiction.
14 This second category—*ambivalent representations of the home*—might arguably be the largest of all four proposed categories, in light of how most narratives that are primarily situated in domestic spaces are in some way ambivalent about the role and space of the home. Though many texts paint the home as a space of safety and/or refuge, such positive associations are often complicated by other social, political, material, psychological, and/or spiritual factors.
15 The third category—*narrative hauntings of the home*—includes a wide range of texts throughout the nineteenth, twentieth, and twenty-first centuries. Whether they be in horror, Gothic, or science-fiction narratives—or otherwise—narrative hauntings find expression in a number of literary traditions and genres. The symbolism behind such hauntings is varied, depending on the text, and includes a variety of purposes (e.g., to represent unresolved traumas, to metaphorize undesirable histories that invade the present, and so on). In texts within this category, the trope of the home qua shelter is subverted, in order to give voice to undesirable pasts that are not easily forgotten and/or resolved.
16 The fourth category—*narrative flights from (and, in some cases, returns to) the home*—constitutes another common trope in U.S. literatures. In some cases, protagonists' departures from the home take place early in the text, so that the majority of the narrative is set outside of the home. However, departures mark catalytic moments in such narratives and oftentimes frame the protagonists' journeys in contrast to such conceptions of home. Sometimes, these departures from the home are the vehicles by which characters come to "find" themselves, especially (and ironically?) as they are without their familiar environs and communities. Narratives in this category reveal how foundational the home is in how individuals define and understand themselves, such that the home is consistently the paradigmatic point of comparison to all other spaces and places.
17 Bachelard, *The Poetics of Space*, 38.
18 Bachelard, *The Poetics of Space*, 8.
19 Bachelard, *The Poetics of Space*, xxxv; emphasis in the original.
20 Bachelard, *The Poetics of Space*, xxxvi.

21. Mary Douglas, "The Idea of Home: A Kind of Space," *Social Research* 58, no. 1 (1991): 288.
22. Although shtetl life was by no means uniformly negative, there are a number of literary and historical accounts that give voice to the antisemitic attacks of surrounding Christian communities that defined shtetl life. Such accounts point to how domestic life for many who lived in shtetls was shaped by feelings of threat and unsafety. Such shtetl experiences eventually complicated the affective environment of postmemorial structures, insofar as the traumas stemming from the shtetl compounded survivors' Holocaust traumas. For these survivor families, shtetl life was yet another reason why the domestic was emotionally and affectively fraught.
23. See, for instance, Asher Z. Milbauer, "Teaching to Remember," in *Second-Generation Voices: Reflections by Children of Holocaust Survivors and Perpetrators*, ed. Alan L. Berger and Naomi Berger (Syracuse, NY: Syracuse University Press, 2001).
24. Bachelard, *The Poetics of Space*, xxxvi.
25. Jacques Derrida, *Archive Fever: A Freudian Impression*, trans. Eric Prenowitz (Chicago: University of Chicago Press, 1998), 2.
26. Jessica Lang, *Textual Silence: Unreadability and the Holocaust* (New Brunswick, NJ: Rutgers University Press, 2017), 85.
27. Jacobs, "The Cross-Generational Transmission of Trauma," 343.
28. Yael Danieli, "The Heterogeneity of Postwar Adaptation in Families of Holocaust Survivors," in *The Psychological Perspectives of the Holocaust and of Its Aftermath*, ed. Randolph L. Braham (New York: Columbia University Press, 1988), 112.
29. Robyn Fivush, "Remembering and Reminiscing: How Individual Lives Are Constructed in Family Narratives," *Memory Studies* 1, no. 1 (2008): 51.
30. Fivush, "Remembering and Reminiscing," 47.
31. Anne Karpf, *The War After: Living with the Holocaust* (London: William Heinemann, 1996), 5.
32. Karpf, *The War After*, 96; emphasis added.
33. Eva Hoffman, *After Such Knowledge: Memory, History, and the Legacy of the Holocaust* (New York: PublicAffairs, 2004), 12.
34. Danieli, "The Heterogeneity of Postwar Adaptation in Families of Holocaust Survivors," 111, 112. See also Stein, *Reluctant Witnesses*, 4.
35. Alan L. Berger, *Children of Job: American Second-Generation Witnesses to the Holocaust* (Albany: State University of New York Press, 1997), 142.
36. Bar-On, *Fear and Hope*, 20. See also Merilyn Moos, *Breaking the Silence: Voices of the British Children of Refugees from Nazism* (Lanham, MD: Rowman and Littlefield, 2015), 73.
37. See, for instance, Bernice Eisenstein, *I Was a Child of Holocaust Survivors* (Toronto: McClelland and Stewart, 2006), 30.
38. Karpf, *The War After*, 96.
39. Claire Nouvet, "The Inarticulate Affect: Lyotard and Psychoanalytic Testimony," *Discourse* 25, no. 1–2 (2018): 233.
40. Naomi Berger, "Coming Full Circle," in *Second Generation Voices: Reflections by Children of Holocaust Survivors and Perpetrators*, ed. Alan L. Berger and Naomi Berger (Syracuse, NY: Syracuse University Press, 2001), 96.
41. Karpf, *The War After*, 4.
42. Epstein, *Children of the Holocaust*, 64.

43 Epstein, *Children of the Holocaust*, 180. Another of Epstein's interviewees also describes the affective environment of the home, saying, "I remember hearing things in the air. Tensions. I was always expecting some kind of explosion" (38). See also Miriam Parker, "Holocaust Survivors Give Legacy to the World," *The American Israelite*, May 1984, 4.
44 Hoffman, *After Such Knowledge*, 33; Jacobs, "The Cross-Generational Transmission of Trauma," 343.
45 Epstein, *Children of the Holocaust*, 137, 193.
46 Sigmund Freud, *Beyond the Pleasure Principle*, trans. James Strachey (New York: W. W. Norton, 1961), 28–33.
47 Teresa Brennan, *The Transmission of Affect* (Ithaca, NY: Cornell University Press, 2004), 1.
48 Karpf, *The War After*, 105.
49 Hoffman, *After Such Knowledge*, 54. See also Dominick LaCapra, *History and Memory after Auschwitz* (Ithaca, NY: Cornell University Press, 2004), 155.
50 Luckhurst, *The Trauma Question*, 3. See also Caruth, *Unclaimed Experience*, 59.
51 Aaron Hass, *The Aftermath: Living with the Holocaust* (Cambridge: Cambridge University Press, 1995), 127. See also Leah Kaminsky, *The Waiting Room: A Novel* (New York: Harper Perennial, 2016), 29; Karpf, *The War After*, 9.
52 See also Victor J. Seidler, *Shadows of the Shoah: Jewish Identity and Belonging* (Oxford: Berg, 2000), 75.
53 Rosenbaum, "Cattle Car Complex," 4.
54 There are several literary examples of similar anxieties surrounding the breaching of domestic boundaries, including, for instance, Sonia Pilcer's *The Holocaust Kid* (2001), wherein the protagonist describes a recurrent dream about the locks on her apartment being forced and a man entering with a knife. See Sonia Pilcer, *The Holocaust Kid* (New York: Persea Books, 2001), 97.
55 Art Spiegelman, *Maus II: A Survivor's Tale: And Here My Troubles Began* (New York: Knopf, 1992), 16.
56 Pilcer, *The Holocaust Kid*, 35.
57 Hirsch and Spitzer, *Ghosts of Home*, 31; Fischer, *Memory Work*, 31.
58 Oren B. Stier, *Holocaust Icons: Symbolizing the Shoah in History and Memory* (New Brunswick, NJ: Rutgers University Press, 2015), 35.
59 Victoria Aarons, "Found Objects: The Legacy of Third-Generation Holocaust Memory," in *Translated Memories: Transgenerational Perspectives on the Holocaust*, ed. Bettina Hofmann and Ursula Reuter (Lanham, MD: Lexington Books, 2020), 233, 236.
60 Stein, *Reluctant Witnesses*, 139.
61 Hirsch, *The Generation of Postmemory*, 6.
62 Bruno Latour defines *mediators* as items that served to "transform, distort, and modify the meaning . . . they are supposed to carry." See Bruno Latour, *Reassembling the Social: An Introduction to Actor-Network-Theory* (New York: Oxford University Press, 2005), 39.
63 Bill Brown, "Thing Theory," *Critical Inquiry* 28, no. 1 (2001): 7.
64 Bill Brown, *A Sense of Things: The Object Matter of American Literature* (Chicago: University of Chicago Press, 2003), 4.
65 My article on this topic, specifically as it relates to clothing, fleshes this discussion out further. See Lucas F. W. Wilson, "Inherited Traumatic Threads: Postmemory

and the Dis/function of Hand-Me-Downs in Bernice Eisenstein's *I Was the Child of Holocaust Survivors*," *Canadian Jewish Studies* 32 (2021): 86–98.
66. Stier, *Holocaust Icons*, 36.
67. Terrance Des Pres, *The Survivor: An Anatomy of Life in the Death Camps* (New York: Oxford University Press, 1976). Des Pres defines excremental assault as an attack against inmates' cleanliness (and thus dignity) by way of filth, dirt, and feces (57).
68. Aarons, "Found Objects," 231–250.
69. Fisher, *Memory Work*.
70. Fischer, *Memory Work*, 29.
71. Aarons, "Found Objects," 246. See also Berger, *Children of Job*, 147.
72. Hirsch, *Family Frames*; Marianne Hirsch, "Family Pictures: *Maus*, Mourning, and Post-Memory," *Discourse* 15, no. 2 (1992–1993); Marianne Hirsch, "Objects of Return," in *After Testimony: The Ethics and Aesthetics of Holocaust Narrative for the Future*, ed. Jakob Lothe, Susan R. Suleiman, and James Phelan (Columbus: The Ohio State University Press, 2012); Marianne Hirsch, "Surviving Images: Holocaust Photographs and the Work of Postmemory," *The Yale Journal of Criticism* 14, no. 1 (2001): 5–37; Hirsch, *The Generation of Postmemory*; Hirsch and Spitzer, *Ghosts of Home*.

Chapter 2 "Remember, my house it's also your house too"

1. This chapter is an expanded version of an article I previously published. See Lucas F. W. Wilson, "'Remember, my house it's also your house too': Survivor-Family Homes as Postmemorial Structures in Art Spiegelman's *Maus*," *Modern Language Studies* 52, no. 2 (2023): 10–33. I want to thank *Modern Language Studies* for the permission to print an adapted version of my article in *At Home with the Holocaust*.
2. Philip Smith, *Reading Art Spiegelman* (New York: Routledge, 2016), 2.
3. Spiegelman's work has been understood as defying easy or traditional categorization in terms of genre. Much has been discussed about how to define *Maus*: Does it fall under the umbrella of fiction or nonfiction? LaCapra succinctly answers this question: "*Maus* is not made up, although it is obviously made or shaped." LaCapra, *History and Memory after Auschwitz*, 146.
4. There is much discussion about to what extent we can read the drawn character Artie as representative of Art Spiegelman qua author. Michael Rotenberg-Schwartz states that "Art the author is not the same as Artie the character in *Maus*," and, in line with Rotenberg-Schwartz, Eric Berlatsky refers to Artie as "Spiegelman's textual surrogate." See Michael Rotenberg-Schwartz, "Looking at/in *Maus*: A Survey of Critical Approaches," in *Critical Insights: Holocaust Literature*, ed. Dorian Stuber (New York: Salem Press, 2016), 79; Eric L. Berlatsky, *The Real, the True, and the Told: Postmodern Historical Narrative and the Ethics of Representation* (Columbus: The Ohio State University Press, 2011), 145. Smith argues, "It would be entirely incorrect to suggest that Maus is purely a work of fiction, and yet it is epistemologically naïve and perhaps both ethically and politically dangerous to read the characters of Artie and Vladek as transparent and complete representations of historical personages." See Smith, *Reading Art Spiegelman*, 61. With this in mind, it is not my goal to figure out what is factually accurate and

what is not about Artie. With little interest in such a discussion, I, instead, explore how the text presents Artie's childhood and adulthood homes, in order to better understand how survivor parents' Holocaust traumas and losses are made manifest and are transferred within their postmemorial structure.

5 Eliciting much praise from academic audiences, *Maus* became the first canonical graphic narrative and a pillar of the comics medium, and Spiegelman thereby rose to prominence as a well-established author in American letters. It is not uncommon to find his work anthologized in edited collections of U.S. literatures or to find Spiegelman and his work discussed in reference works. With over 100 scholarly articles written on the text, *Maus* has served as the object of academic inquiry for decades. Having been translated into multiple languages, including French, Polish, German, Japanese, and Hebrew, *Maus* has unequivocally become an important cultural document that has been studied by numerous scholars (and students) across the world.

6 Many studies treat Spiegelman's work as the second-generation "'Ur' text," "the touchstone of the genre," and "the paradigmatic example of postmemory and the second generation." See Susan Jacobowitz, "The Holocaust at Home: Representations and Implications of Second Generation Experience" (PhD diss., Brandeis University, 2004), 53; Samantha Baskind, "A Conversation with Miriam Katin," in *The Jewish Graphic Novel: Critical Approaches,* ed. Samantha Baskind and Ranen Omer-Sherman (New Brunswick, NJ: Rutgers University Press, 2010), 240; Claire Gorrara, "Not Seeing Auschwtiz: Memory, Generation and Representations of the Holocaust in Twenty-First Century French Comics," *Journal of Modern Jewish Studies* 17, no. 1 (2018): 121. But even if studies on second-generation literature do not take *Maus* as a *central* focus, *Maus* is at minimum almost always referenced, quoted, and/or discussed.

7 Csikszentmihalyi and Rochberg-Halton, *The Meaning of Things*, 123.
8 Csikszentmihalyi and Rochberg-Halton, *The Meaning of Things*, 123.
9 Art Spiegelman and Hillary Chute, *MetaMaus* (New York: Pantheon Books, 2011), 208.
10 Art Spiegelman, *Maus I: A Survivor's Tale: My Father Bleeds History* (New York: Knopf, 1986), 6; emphasis in the original.
11 Spiegelman, *Maus I*, 52.
12 Spiegelman, *Maus II*, 44.
13 Spiegelman and Chute, *MetaMaus*, 105.
14 Spiegelman and Chute, *MetaMaus*, 106; emphasis in the original.
15 Edward A. Mason and Eva Fogelman, *Breaking the Silence: The Generation After the Holocaust* (1984; Waltham, MA: National Center for Jewish Film, 2008), DVD.
16 Spiegelman and Chute, *MetaMaus*, 12.
17 Spiegelman and Chute, *MetaMaus*, 12–13.
18 Spiegelman and Chute, *MetaMaus*, 22.
19 Spiegelman and Chute, *MetaMaus*, 14.
20 Spiegelman and Chute, *MetaMaus*, 15.
21 Spiegelman, *Maus II*, 14.
22 Daniel R. Schwarz, *Imagining the Holocaust* (New York: St. Martin's Press, 1999), 295.
23 Spiegelman, *Maus II*, 16.

24. Spiegelman, *Maus I*, 100.
25. Michael Levine, "Necessary Stains: Art Spiegelman's *Maus* and the Bleeding of History," in *Considering* Maus: *Approaches to Art Spiegelman's "Survivor's Tale" of the Holocaust*, ed. Deborah R. Geis (Tuscaloosa: University of Alabama Press, 2003), 86.
26. Art Spiegelman, "Mad Youth," in *Comix, Essays, Graphics and Scraps: From MAUS to Now,* ed. by Art Spiegelman (New York: Raw Books and Graphics, 1999), 22.
27. Spiegelman, *Maus I*, 100. For a more extended discussion, see Wilson, "Inherited Traumatic Threads," 89.
28. Spiegelman, *Maus I*, 103.
29. Spiegelman, *Maus I*, 100.
30. Hirsch, *Family Frames*, 2.
31. Hamida Bosmajian, "The Orphaned Voice in Art Spiegelman's *Maus*," in Geis, *Considering* Maus, 38.
32. Spiegelman and Chute, *MetaMaus*, 218.
33. Spiegelman and Chute, *MetaMaus*, 218.
34. Bosmajian, "The Orphaned Voice," 30.
35. Spiegelman, *Maus I*, 103.
36. Bosmajian, "The Orphaned Voice," 40.
37. Spiegelman, *Maus I*, 103.
38. Levine, "Necessary Stains," 82.
39. Spiegelman, *Maus I*, 103.
40. Levine, "Necessary Stains," 82.
41. Spiegelman, *Maus I*, 103.
42. Victoria Elmwood, "'Happy, Happy Ever After': The Transformation of Trauma between the Generations in Art Spiegelman's 'Maus: A Survivor's Tale,'" *Biography* 27, no. 4 (2004): 710–11.
43. Hillary Chute, "'The Shadow of a Past Time': History and Graphic Representation in 'Maus,'" *Twentieth Century Literature* 52, no. 2 (2006): 208.
44. Spiegelman, *Maus I*, 103; emphasis in the original.
45. Spiegelman, *Maus I*, 101.
46. Scott McCloud, *Understanding Comics* (New York: HarperPerennial, 1993), 102, 100, emphasis in original. See also Berlatsky, *The Real, the True, and the Told*, 173.
47. Spiegelman, *Maus I*, 103. Artie also accuses Vladek of murder after Vladek burns Anja's diaries. See Spiegelman, *Maus I*, 159.
48. Spiegelman, *Maus I*, 103.
49. Epstein, *Children of the Holocaust*, 28.
50. Spiegelman, *Maus I*, 102.
51. Spiegelman, *Maus I*, 101.
52. Spiegelman, *Maus I*, 103.
53. Hoffman, *After Such Knowledge*, 9.
54. Hirsch, *Family Frames*, 34.
55. LaCapra, *History and Memory after Auschwitz*, 172.
56. LaCapra, *History and Memory after Auschwitz*, 144. See also Hirsch, *Family Frames*, 35; E. Miller Budick, *The Subject of Holocaust Fiction* (Bloomington: Indiana University Press, 2015), 81; Berlatsky, *The Real, the True, and the Told*, 147; Miles Orvell, "Writing Postmemory: *Krazy Kat, Maus*, and the Contemporary

Fiction Cartoon," *American Literary History* 4, no. 1 (1992): 124. See also Barry Laga, "*Maus*, Holocaust, and History: Redrawing the Frame," *Arizona Quarterly* 57, no. 1 (2001): 80–83.
57 Sigmund Freud, *Civilizations and Its Discontents*, trans. and ed. James Strachey (New York: W. W. Norton, 1962), 13.
58 Tuan, *Space and Place*, 29.
59 Spiegelman, *Maus I*, 12.
60 Spiegelman, *Maus I*, 11.
61 James Baldwin, "Here Be Dragons," in *The Price of the Ticket: Collected Nonfiction 1948–1985*, ed. Toni Morrison (New York: St. Martin's Press, 1985), 682; emphasis in the original.
62 Spiegelman, *Maus I*, 96.
63 Bachelard, *The Poetics of Space*, 5–6.
64 Spiegelman, *Maus II*, 24.
65 Spiegelman, *Maus II*, 41.
66 Spiegelman, *Maus I*, 96.
67 Spiegelman, *Maus II*, 15; emphasis in the original.
68 Erin McGlothlin, "No Time like the Present: Narrative and Time in Art Spiegelman's 'Maus,'" *Narrative* 11, no. 2 (2003): 187; emphasis in the original.
69 Spiegelman, *Maus II*, 41.
70 McGlothlin, "No Time like the Present," 189.
71 Spiegelman, *Maus II*, 74.
72 Spiegelman, *Maus II*, 74.
73 Here, I am drawing on Aarons's analysis of Elie Wiesel's *The Gates of the Forest*. See Victoria Aarons, "The Trauma of History in *The Gates of the Forest*," in *Elie Wiesel: Jewish, Literary, and Moral Perspectives*, ed. Steven T. Katz and Alan Rosen (Bloomington: Indiana University Press, 2013), 148.

Chapter 3 Domestic(ated) (Un)fashioning

1 This chapter is an expanded version of a coauthored article I previously published. See Lucas F. W. Wilson and Alex Anderson, "'I Was a Prisoner. Jew. Whore': Inherited Sexualized Trauma in Sonia Pilcer's *The Holocaust Kid*," *Journal of Jewish Identities* 16, no. 1–2 (2023): 5–21. I want to thank the *Journal of Jewish Identities* for the permission to reprint an adapted version of my article in *At Home with the Holocaust*.
2 Pilcer received her Bachelor of Arts in English Literature from Queens College. Upon graduation, she took her first job as a writer for *Ingenue*, a young women's fashion magazine. Teaching at the Writers Voice in New York and Berkshire Community College in Massachusetts as of this writing, Pilcer is a poet, a playwright, an essayist, and a novelist. Notably, she is the author of the influential essay "2G" (1987), published in *7 Days*, wherein she coined the titular term *2G*, the now-common shorthand that stands for the "second generation." Of all her creative output, however, Pilcer is best known for her longer works. In addition to *The Holocaust Kid*, she is the author of the cult classic *Teen Angel* (1978), a novel that was later adapted for a Universal Studios screenplay (though it was never actually produced). She also penned *Little Darlings* (1980), *Maiden Rites* (1982), and *I-Land* (1987).

3. Rachel Bowlby, "Domestication," in *Deconstruction: A Reader*, ed. Martin McQuillan (New York: Routledge, 2001), 306.
4. In addition to Fischer's work, only a few studies briefly mention, describe, and/or discuss *The Holocaust Kid*. See, for example, Efraim Sicher, *The Holocaust Novel* (New York: Routledge, 2005), and Judy E. Stanger, "Children of Holocaust Survivors: A Life History Study" (PhD diss., State University of New York at Albany, 2004).
5. Hirsch, *The Generation of Postmemory*, 6.
6. Pilcer, *The Holocaust Kid*, 8; emphasis in the original.
7. Jacobowitz, "The Holocaust at Home," 39.
8. Ronit Lentin, "Re-occupying the Territories of Silence: Israeli Daughters of Shoah Survivors Between Language and Silence," in *Women and the Holocaust: Narrative and Representation*, ed. Esther Fuchs (Lanham, MD: University Press of America, 1999), 52.
9. Judith S. Kestenberg, "A Metapsychological Assessment Based on an Analysis of a Survivor's Child," in *Generations of the Holocaust*, ed. Martin S. Bergman and Milton E. Jucovy (New York: Basic Books, 1982), 141; emphasis in the original.
10. Pilcer, *The Holocaust Kid*, 161.
11. Pilcer, *The Holocaust Kid*, 29.
12. For instance, as Genia slices bread in the kitchen with Zosha, Genia tells her daughter about how the Russians gave Heniek two loaves of bread after the war, again invoking the Shoah in everyday conversation. See Pilcer, *The Holocaust Kid*, 104. Similar to how Vladek brings up the Holocaust in the opening scene of *Maus*, so too does Genia perceive quotidian tasks, like food prep, as an opportunity to discuss the Holocaust.
13. Pilcer, *The Holocaust Kid*, 29.
14. Pilcer, *The Holocaust Kid*, 54.
15. Pilcer, *The Holocaust Kid*, 58.
16. Pilcer, *The Holocaust Kid*, 37.
17. Pilcer, *The Holocaust Kid*, 28.
18. Stein, *Reluctant Witnesses*, 48.
19. Pilcer, *The Holocaust Kid*, 27.
20. Csikszentmihalyi and Rochberg-Halton, *The Meaning of Things*, 118.
21. Lawrence Sutin, "An Afterword on the 'Second Generation,'" in *Jack and Rochelle: A Holocaust Story of Love and Resistance*, ed. Lawrence Sutin (Minneapolis: Graywolf Press, 2008), 216.
22. Pilcer, *The Holocaust Kid*, 31.
23. Pilcer, *The Holocaust Kid*, 8.
24. Pilcer, *The Holocaust Kid*, 67.
25. Genia's focus on her daughter is suggestive of the experience of many children of survivors who grow up with overbearing mothers. Another literary example of a survivor mother's domestic control of her daughter is found in Gabriella Goliger's *Song of Ascent* (2000), a novel published the year prior to the publication of *The Holocaust Kid*. *Song of Ascent* depicts how survivor-mother Hannah continuously encroaches on her daughter Rachel's personal space and forcibly tries to keep Rachel by her side. Hannah's overinvestment in Rachel in many ways parallels Genia's treatment of Zosha (along with Anja's smothering of Artie in *Maus*, especially in "Hell Planet").

26 Lucas Wilson, "Jewish Heritage Collection: Oral History Interview with Evaline E. Kalisky Delson," 2019, https://lcdl.library.cofc.edu/lcdl/catalog/246432.

27 See also Hillel Klein, *Survival and Trials of Revival: Psychodynamic Studies of Holocaust Survivors and Their Families in Israel and the Diaspora* (Boston: Academic Studies Press, 2012), 155.

28 Wilson, "Jewish Heritage Collection."

29 Pilcer, *The Holocaust Kid*, 33.

30 Pilcer, *The Holocaust Kid*, 112.

31 Wilson, "Jewish Heritage Collection."

32 Wilson, "Jewish Heritage Collection."

33 Tennessee Williams, *The Glass Menagerie* (New York: New Directions, 1999), 3.

34 Pilcer, *The Holocaust Kid*, 135.

35 Douglas, "The Idea of Home," 303.

36 For further discussion of how children of survivors attempt to create spaces that are different and far from the ones in which they grew up, see Robert M. Prince, *The Legacy of the Holocaust: Psychohistorical Themes in the Second Generation* (Ann Arbor, MI: UMI Research Press, 1999), and Hadas Wiseman and Jacques P. Barber, *Echoes of the Trauma: Relational Themes and Emotions in Children of Holocaust Survivors* (Cambridge: Cambridge University Press, 2008).

37 Pilcer, *The Holocaust Kid*, 119.

38 Pilcer, *The Holocaust Kid*, 102.

39 Pilcer, *The Holocaust Kid*, 105.

40 Pilcer, *The Holocaust Kid*, 105, 117–21.

41 Stephen Kern, *The Culture of Time and Space: 1880–1918* (Cambridge, MA: Harvard University Press, 2003), 316.

42 Kern, *The Culture of Time and Space*, 91.

43 Pilcer, *The Holocaust Kid*, 9.

44 Bowlby, "Domestication," 307.

45 Pilcer, *The Holocaust Kid*, 51.

46 Sylvia Plath, "The Colossus," accessed March 16, 2022, https://www.poetryfoundation.org/poems/89119/the-colossus.

47 Plath, "The Colossus."

48 Pilcer, *The Holocaust Kid*, 103.

49 Pilcer, *The Holocaust Kid*, 110.

50 Unlike some other literary and filmic texts that erogenously sensationalize the Holocaust, *The Holocaust Kid* does not eroticize the Holocaust itself. Rebecca Scherr notes how, for example, the director of *The Night Porter*, Liliana Cavani, "transforms the memory of the camp into a 'sexy memory,' which through the depiction of eroticism and the sexualized female body, elicits a reaction of pleasure in the spectator, completely warping the historical facts of the Holocaust, in particular, the fact that the Holocaust was by no means, in any way, sexy." See Rebecca Scherr, "The Uses of Memory and Abuses of Fiction: Sexuality in Holocaust Film, Fiction, and Memoir," in *Experience and Expression: Women, the Nazis, and the Holocaust*, ed. Elizabeth R. Baer (Detroit: Wayne State University Press, 2003), 282. In sharp contradistinction, Pilcer's work does not eroticize the Shoah for the sake of some twisted titillation; rather, the eros that defines this scene is a vehicle by which Zosha expresses, explores, and responds to the sexualized trauma that, in part, undergirds her belated relationship to the Shoah.

51 *The Holocaust Kid* is one of many second-generation texts that explores sex and sexuality, with numerous other examples, including, for example, Helen Epstein's *The Long Half Lives of Love and Trauma* (2017), Leah Kaminsky's *The Waiting Room* (2015), Lev Raphael's *My Germany* (2009) and *Secret Anniversaries of the Heart* (2006), Goliger's *Song of Ascent* (2000), Lily Brett's *Just Like That* (1994), Raphael's *Dancing on Tisha B'Av* (1990), and Savyon Liebrecht's "'What Am I Speaking, Chinese?' She Said to Him" (1986).

52 Brigitte Halbmayr, "Sexualized Violence against Women during Nazi 'Racial' Persecution," in *Sexual Violence against Jewish Women during the Holocaust*, ed. Sonja M. Hedgepeth and Rochelle G. Saidel (Waltham, MA: Brandeis University Press, 2010), 30. See also Stacy Banwell, "Rassenschande, Genocide and the Reproductive Jewish Body: Examining the Use of Rape and Sexualized Violence against Jewish Women during the Holocaust?," *Journal of Modern Jewish Studies* 15, no. 2 (2016): 209.

53 Halbmayr, "Sexualized Violence against Women during Nazi 'Racial' Persecution," 30, and Sara R. Horowitz, "What We Learn, at Last: Recounting Sexuality in Women's Deferred Autobiographies and Testimonies," in *The Palgrave Handbook of Holocaust Literature and Culture*, ed. Victoria Aarons and Phyllis Lassner (Cham, Switzerland: Palgrave Macmillan, 2020), 46.

54 There are a number of instances of inherited sexualized trauma in second-generation representation. For example, second-generation protagonist Yaakov/Jason in Thomas Friedmann's *Damaged Goods* (1984) explains: "I torture myself with dreams of my mother bidden to do whore's service." See Friedmann, *Damaged Goods*, 73. Al, a child of survivors interviewed for Epstein's *Children of the Holocaust*, also notes that he feared his mother was raped during the Holocaust. See Epstein, *Children of the Holocaust*, 227. Epstein herself anecdotally explains that in a film she watched in her youth, *The Pawnbroker* (1964), "female concentration camp inmates were shown working as prostitutes, waiting naked in small rooms until the next S.S. officer returned. That image too had been forced down into my iron box and now it hung in the air between us. I had never had the courage to ask my mother whether it happened to her." See Epstein, *Children of the Holocaust*, 227.

55 Fischer, *Memory Work*, 154, 101. See also Dina Wardi, *Memorial Candles: Children of the Holocaust* (London: Routledge, 1992), 179.

56 Fischer, *Memory Work*, 110.

57 Janet Jacobs, *The Holocaust across Generations: Trauma and Its Inheritance among Descendants of Survivors* (New York: New York University Press, 2016), 23, 24.

58 Judith S. Kestenberg, "Survivor-Parents and Their Children,'" in *Generations of the Holocaust*, ed. Martin S. Bergman and Milton E. Jucovy (New York: Basic Books, 1982), 101.

59 Pilcer, *The Holocaust Kid*, 6.

60 Pilcer, *The Holocaust Kid*, 97.

61 Pilcer, *The Holocaust Kid*, 86.

62 Pilcer, *The Holocaust Kid*, 87.

63 Pilcer, *The Holocaust Kid*, 54.

64 Pilcer, *The Holocaust Kid*, 85.

65 Pilcer, *The Holocaust Kid*, 91.

66 Caruth, *Literature and the Ashes of History*, 6.

67 The text establishes an additional connection between mother and daughter by way of bodily metaphor. When Zosha is a newborn in the DP camp in Landsberg, strangers stop Genia on the street to complement Zosha's appearance. They exclaim, "What a beauty! Exquisite. The eyes... [l]ike the mother." See Pilcer, *The Holocaust Kid*, 15. Genia feels a tremendous amount of pride for her daughter's striking eyes and in the resemblance they bear to her own eyes. Genia tells baby Zosha, "No one has eyes like you, although everyone admires mine too," revealing the connection that she and her daughter share—a point that is later underscored when Genia describes Zosha as "my little blue eyes." See Pilcer, *The Holocaust Kid*, 20, 16. That Zosha's eyes are Genia's speaks to how Genia's traumatized lens is inherited by Zosha and filters her everyday perspective and experience.
68 Pilcer, *The Holocaust Kid*, 94.
69 Pilcer, *The Holocaust Kid*, 78.
70 Pilcer, *The Holocaust Kid*, 94.
71 Pilcer, *The Holocaust Kid*, 44.
72 Pilcer, *The Holocaust Kid*, 97.
73 Pilcer, *The Holocaust Kid*, 96.
74 Pilcer, *The Holocaust Kid*, 95–96.
75 Jacobs, *The Holocaust across Generations*, 38.
76 Pilcer, *The Holocaust Kid*, 96.
77 Pilcer, *The Holocaust Kid*, 88.
78 Pilcer, *The Holocaust Kid*, 73.
79 Spiegelman, *Maus II*, 24.
80 Pilcer, *The Holocaust Kid*, 109.
81 Pilcer, *The Holocaust Kid*, 109.
82 Pilcer, *The Holocaust Kid*, 138.
83 Pilcer, *The Holocaust Kid*, 147.
84 Pilcer, *The Holocaust Kid*, 150.
85 Pilcer, *The Holocaust Kid*, 147.
86 Hirsch, *The Generation of Postmemory*, 6.

Chapter 4   A Tale of Two Storeys

1 Beginning her studies at Brown University, Rosner went on to graduate from Stanford University, the MFA Program at UC Irvine, and the University of Queensland in Australia. Her short fiction and poetry have appeared in a number of literary magazines, including *Poetry*, *Poetry East*, *Another Chicago Magazine*, *Catamaran*, *The Cream City Review*, and *Southern Poetry Review*. Her essays have been published in the *New York Times Magazine*, *Elle*, *The Forward*, and numerous anthologies. Her longer works include her novel *Blue Nude* (2006), her poetry collection *Gravity* (2014), her novel *Electric City* (2014), and her nonfictional *Survivor Café: The Legacy of Trauma and the Labyrinth of Memory* (2017). For more than thirty years, she has been writing full-time while teaching part-time at the college level.
2 Elizabeth Rosner, "Bio," accessed January 15, 2022, http://elizabethrosner.com/bio/.
3 *The Speed of Light* has been translated into nine languages and is the recipient of numerous awards. It was a finalist for the prestigious Prix Femina and was selected as one of Borders Original Voices, in addition to winning the Great Lakes

Colleges New Writer's Award for Fiction, the Prix France Blue Gironde, and the Harold U. Ribalow Prize administered by *Hadassah Magazine* and judged by Elie Wiesel. See Rosner, "Bio."

4 Forced to engage in such horrific work, *Sonderkommandos* were, as Lawrence Langer opines, "driven to choose survival at the expense of their humanity, creating a kind of solipsistic animality as the supreme value." See Langer, *The Holocaust and the Literary Imagination*, 6. In truth, as Langer explains, the "choice" to work in *Sonderkommandos* (or to do any work in the camps) was no choice at all; prisoners' "choices" can more accurately be described as "choiceless choices," forced "decisions" to implicate themselves in routinely barbaric labor with the penalty of death, should they not comply. See Lawrence L. Langer, *Holocaust Testimonies* (New Haven, CT: Yale University Press, 1991), 26.

5 The homelife Jacob creates aligns with what Yael Danieli describes as the homelives of *numb families*. See Danieli, "The Heterogeneity of Postwar Adaptation," 112, 119–20.

6 Elizabeth Rosner, *The Speed of Light* (New York: Ballantine, 2003), 23.

7 Bachelard, *The Poetics of Space*, 17.

8 Katharina Koerfer, "Legacies of Survival and Perpetration in Elizabeth Rosner's Second-Generation Holocaust Fiction" (master's thesis, Technische Universität Dortmund, 2013).

9 Although some may anticipate a gendered analysis of *The Speed of Light*, given how Julian is a man and Paula is a woman, the novel does not lend itself well to an exploration of gender. Indeed, the siblings both defy and conform to gender norms, but this does not bear heavily on their postmemorial divergences. As such, I do not treat gender as a generative category of analysis in this chapter.

10 Rosner, *The Speed of Light*, 37.

11 Rosner, *The Speed of Light*, 2.

12 Friedmann, *Damaged Goods*, 218.

13 Rosner, *The Speed of Light*, 2.

14 Rosner, *The Speed of Light*, 151.

15 Louise Kaplan, *No Voice Is Ever Wholly Lost: An Exploration of the Everlasting Attachment between Parent and Child* (New York: Simon and Schuster, 1995), 219.

16 Rosner, *The Speed of Light*, 175.

17 Rosner, *The Speed of Light*, 8.

18 Rosner, *The Speed of Light*, 30.

19 Rosner, *The Speed of Light*, 35.

20 Rosner, *The Speed of Light*, 2.

21 Koerfer, "Legacies of Survival and Perpetration in Elizabeth Rosner's Second-Generation Holocaust Fiction," 21.

22 Epstein, *Children of the Holocaust*, 9.

23 Epstein, *Children of the Holocaust*, 13. See also Epstein, *Children of the Holocaust*, 11, 43, 332, 335. 43; Hoffman, *After Such Knowledge*, 193, 14, x; Lydia Flem, *The Final Reminder: How I Emptied My Parents' House* (London: Souvenir Press, 2005), 57; Vivian M. Rakoff, J. J. Sigal, and N. B. Epstein, "Children of Families of Concentration Camp Survivors," *Canada's Mental Health* 14 (1966): 25; Nirit Pisano, *Granddaughters of the Holocaust: Never Forgetting What They Didn't Experience* (Brighton, UK: Academic Studies Press, 2013), 52; Moos, *Breaking the Silence*, 245; Marita Grimwood, *Holocaust Literature of the Second Generation*

(London: Palgrave, 2007), 10; Golan Moskowitz, "Grandsons Who Remember: Intersections of Holocaust Heritage and Contemporary Male Positioning" (Master's thesis, Brandeis University, 2012), 35.
24 Rosner, *The Speed of Light*, 73.
25 Rosner, *The Speed of Light*, 46.
26 Rosner, *The Speed of Light*, 77.
27 Rosner, *The Speed of Light*, 78.
28 Rosner, *The Speed of Light*, 27.
29 Rosner, *The Speed of Light*, 57, 27.
30 Rosner, *The Speed of Light*, 60.
31 Rosner, *The Speed of Light*, 47.
32 Rosner, *The Speed of Light*, 75.
33 Karpf, *The War After*, 250.
34 Rosner, *The Speed of Light*, 8.
35 Rosner, *The Speed of Light*, 22, 86.
36 Rosner, *The Speed of Light*, 94, 202, 203, 224.
37 Rosner, *The Speed of Light*, 94.
38 Rosner, *The Speed of Light*, 56.
39 Rosner, *The Speed of Light*, 224.
40 Rosner, *The Speed of Light*, 48.
41 Rosner, *The Speed of Light*, 44.
42 Rosner, *The Speed of Light*, 6.
43 Rosner, *The Speed of Light*, 43.
44 Rosner, *The Speed of Light*, 43.
45 Krasner, *Home Bodies*, 13.
46 Rosner, *The Speed of Light*, 108.
47 Rosner, *The Speed of Light*, 2.
48 There are other postmemorial things represented in *The Speed of Light*. For further discussion of these things, see Wilson, "Inherited Traumatic Threads," 95–96.
49 Rosner, *The Speed of Light*, 213, 235.
50 Rosner, *The Speed of Light*, 38.
51 Kern, *The Culture of Time and Space*, 16.
52 Rosner, *The Speed of Light*, 77.
53 Rosner, *The Speed of Light*, 70.
54 Rosner, *The Speed of Light*, 1.
55 Rosner, *The Speed of Light*, 56.
56 Rosner, *The Speed of Light*, 38–39, 25.
57 Epstein, *Children of the Holocaust*, 92.
58 Rosner, *The Speed of Light*, 67.
59 Rosner, *The Speed of Light*, 31.
60 Rosner, *The Speed of Light*, 24.
61 Epstein, *Children of the Holocaust*, 61.
62 Prince, *The Legacy of the Holocaust*, 115.
63 Rosner, *The Speed of Light*, 44.
64 Rosner, *The Speed of Light*, 22.
65 Mary Douglas, *Purity and Danger: An Analysis of the Concepts of Pollution and Taboo* (New York: Routledge, 1966), 2.
66 Douglas, *Purity and Danger*, 36.

67 Rosner, *The Speed of Light*, 8.
68 Rosner, *The Speed of Light*, 52.
69 Csikszentmihalyi and Rochberg-Halton, *The Meaning of Things*, 74.
70 Csikszentmihalyi and Rochberg-Halton, *The Meaning of Things*, 75.
71 Rosner, *The Speed of Light*, 44–45, 51.
72 Rosner, *The Speed of Light*, 32.
73 Rosner, *The Speed of Light*, 33.
74 Brown, *A Sense of Things*, 12.
75 Rosner, *The Speed of Light*, 75.
76 Rosner, *The Speed of Light*, 2.
77 Rosner, *The Speed of Light*, 125.
78 Rosner, *The Speed of Light*, 142.
79 Rosner, *The Speed of Light*, 12.
80 Rosner, *The Speed of Light*, 12–13.
81 Rosner, *The Speed of Light*, 13.
82 Rosner, *The Speed of Light*, 22.
83 Rosner, *The Speed of Light*, 199.
84 Rosner, *The Speed of Light*, 83.
85 Rosner, *The Speed of Light*, 83.
86 Rosner, *The Speed of Light*, 119.
87 Rosner, *The Speed of Light*, 241.
88 Rosner, *The Speed of Light*, 219–20.
89 Rosner, *The Speed of Light*, 127.
90 Rosner, *The Speed of Light*, 142.
91 Rosner, *The Speed of Light*, 129.
92 Rosner, *The Speed of Light*, 144.
93 Rosner, *The Speed of Light*, 8.
94 Rosner, *The Speed of Light*, 152.
95 Rosner, *The Speed of Light*, 163.
96 Marianne Hirsh discusses the idea of the punctum in the context of photography as "that prick and shock of recognition, that unique and very personal response to the photographic detail that attracts and repels us at the same time." See Hirsh, *Family Frames*, 4.
97 Rosner, *The Speed of Light*, 184.
98 Rosner, *The Speed of Light*, 200.
99 Rosner, *The Speed of Light*, 231.
100 Rosner, *The Speed of Light*, 154.
101 Rosner, *The Speed of Light*, 219.
102 Rosner, *The Speed of Light*, 220.
103 Rosner, *The Speed of Light*, 237.

Chapter 5   Pre/Occupied Longing

1 This chapter is an expanded version of an article I previously published (used with permission from Penn State University Press). See Lucas F. W. Wilson, "Pre/Occupied Longing: Toward a Definition of Postnostalgia in Jonathan Safran Foer's *Everything Is Illuminated*," *Studies in American Jewish Literature* 42, no. 2 (2023): 121–40.

I want to thank *Studies in American Jewish Literature* for the permission to print an adapted version of my article in *At Home with the Holocaust*.
2. Hirsch, *The Generation of Postmemory*, 6.
3. Anne Buttimer, "Home, Reach, and the Sense of Place," in *The Human Experience of Space and Place*, ed. Anne Buttimer and David Seamon (New York: St. Martin's Press, 1980), 167.
4. Peter Somerville, "Homelessness and the Meaning of Home: Rooflessness and Rootlessness?," *International Journal of Urban and Regional Research* 16, no. 4 (1992): 530.
5. Jacobowitz, "The Holocaust at Home," 40.
6. Moos, *Breaking the Silence*, 319.
7. Sara R. Horowitz, "Nostalgia and the Holocaust," in *After Representation? The Holocaust, Literature, and Culture*, ed. R. Clifton Spargo and Robert M. Ehrenreich (New Brunswick, NJ: Rutgers University Press, 2010), 47.
8. Hirsch and Spitzer, *Ghosts of Home*, 11.
9. Christoph Ribbat, "Nomadic with the Truth: Holocaust Representation in Michael Chabon, James McBride, and Jonathan Safran Foer," in *Twenty-First Century Fiction: Readings, Essays, and Conversations*, ed. Christoph Ribbat (Heidelberg: Universitätsverlag Winter, 2005), 213.
10. Hirsch and Spitzer, *Ghosts of Home*, 8.
11. Caruth, *Unclaimed Experience*, 4.
12. Cathy Caruth, "Lost in Transmission: Studies of Trauma across Generations," *International Journal of Psychoanalysis* 95, no. 2 (2014): 403.
13. Howard Cooper, "The Second Generation 'Syndrome,'" *Journal of Holocaust Education* 4, no. 2 (1995): 145.
14. Gerd Bayer, "After Postmemory: Holocaust Cinema and the Third Generation," *Shofar: An Interdisciplinary Journal of Jewish Studies* 28, no. 4 (2010): 117.
15. Hirsch, *Family Frames*, 243.
16. Audrey Bardizbanian, "From Silence to Testimony: Performing Trauma and Postmemory in Jonathan Safran Foer's *Everything Is Illuminated*," *Holocaust Studies: A Journal of Culture and History* 25, no. 1–2 (2019): 46.
17. Svetlana Boym, *The Future of Nostalgia* (New York: Basic Books, 2001), xiii–xiv.
18. Boym, *The Future of Nostalgia*, 256.
19. Boym, *The Future of Nostalgia*, 41.
20. Boym, *The Future of Nostalgia*, 45.
21. Boym, *The Future of Nostalgia*, 49.
22. Boym, *The Future of Nostalgia*, 49.
23. Hirsch and Spitzer, *Ghosts of Home*, 19.
24. Jacobs, *The Holocaust across Generations*, 102.
25. Helen Epstein, *Where She Came From: A Daughter's Search for Her Mother's History* (Teaneck, NJ: Holmes and Meier, 2005), 234.
26. Wiesel qtd. in Langer, *The Holocaust and the Literary Imagination*, 202.
27. Hoffman, *After Such Knowledge*, 3.
28. Melvin J. Bukiet, introduction to *Nothing Makes You Free: Writings by Descendants of Jewish Holocaust Survivors*, ed. Melvin J. Bukiet (New York: W. W. Norton, 2002), 13.
29. Lang, *Textual Silence*, 86.

30 Horowitz, "Nostalgia and the Holocaust," 52.
31 Victoria Aarons, *Holocaust Graphic Narratives: Generation, Trauma and Memory* (New Brunswick, NJ: Rutgers University Press, 2020), 99.
32 Hoffman, *After Such Knowledge*, 13. See also Seidler, *Shadows of the Shoah*, 23.
33 Horowitz, "Nostalgia and the Holocaust," 42.
34 Eva Hoffman, *Lost in Translation: A Life in a New Language* (New York: Penguin Books, 1990), 23.
35 Hirsch and Spitzer, *Ghosts of Home*, 10, 12, 4.
36 Hirsch and Spitzer, *Ghosts of Home*, 9; Hirsch, *Family Frames*, 226.
37 Horowitz, "Nostalgia and the Holocaust," 50.
38 Hirsch, *The Generation of Postmemory*, 51.
39 Hirsch, *Family Frames*, 226.
40 Hirsch and Spitzer, *Ghosts of Home*, 9.
41 Hirsch and Spitzer, *Ghosts of Home*, 9.
42 Hirsch and Spitzer, *Ghosts of Home*, xv; Hirsch, *Family Frames*, 243.
43 Epstein, *Children of the Holocaust*, 29–30.
44 Hirsch and Spitzer, *Ghosts of Home*, 230.
45 Aaron Hass, *In the Shadow of the Holocaust: The Second Generation* (Ithaca, NY: Cornell University Press, 1990), 2.
46 Erica T. Lehrer, *Jewish Poland Revisited: Heritage Tourism in Unquiet Places* (Bloomington, IN: Indiana UP, 2013), 102.
47 Hirsch and Spitzer, *Ghosts of Home*, 290.
48 Hirsch and Spitzer, *Ghosts of Home*, 291.
49 Hirsch and Spitzer, *Ghosts of Home*, 298.
50 Hoffman, *After Such Knowledge*, 205.
51 Hirsch and Spitzer, *Ghosts of Home*, 296–97.
52 Hirsch and Spitzer, *Ghosts of Home*, 298.
53 Moskowitz, "Grandsons Who Remember," 97.
54 Moskowitz, "Grandsons Who Remember," 97.
55 Victoria Aarons and Alan L. Berger, *Third-Generation Holocaust Representation: Trauma, History, and Memory* (Evanston, IL: Northwestern University Press, 2017), 139.
56 Aarons and Berger, *Third-Generation Holocaust Representation*, 139.
57 I discuss Jonathan's quest to Trachimbrod as that which is motivated by his postnostalgia and that which in turn feeds his postnostalgia; however, others have examined his quest in the context of heritage tourism. See Jenni Adams, *Magic Realism in Holocaust Literature: Troping the Traumatic Real* (London: Palgrave Macmillan, 2011), 34–35. See also Bardizbanian, "From Silence to Testimony," 46, 47; Katrin Amian, *Rethinking Postmodernism(s): Charles S. Peirce and the Pragmatist Negotiations of Thomas Pynchon, Toni Morrison, and Jonathan Safran Foer* (Amsterdam: Rodopi, 2008), 163. Though the parodying of such "commercial and ideological forces" to which Jenni Adams points certainly informs the novel's representation of Jonathan's quest, his trip to Trachimbrod can also be understood as a portrait of a third-generation traveler who takes seriously (and should be taken seriously in) his search for his family's past. See Adams, *Magic Realism in Holocaust Literature*, 34–35. As such, I focus on his search for the past (and his fabulation of the past) in this study.

58 Jonathan Safran Foer, *Everything Is Illuminated: A Novel* (New York: Penguin Books, 2003), 16, 22.
59 Lang, *Textual Silence*, 94.
60 Aarons and Berger, *Third-Generation Holocaust Representation*, 7–8.
61 Lang, *Textual Silence*, 83.
62 Elaine Safer, "Illuminating the Ineffable: Jonathan Safran Foer's Novels," *Studies in American Jewish Literature* 25 (2006): 128.
63 Safer, "Illuminating the Ineffable," 113.
64 Foer, *Everything Is Illuminated*, 59.
65 Foer, *Everything Is Illuminated*, 115.
66 Foer, *Everything Is Illuminated*, 20.
67 Foer, *Everything Is Illuminated*, 20.
68 Foer, *Everything Is Illuminated*, 43.
69 Horowitz, "Nostalgia and the Holocaust," 49.
70 Foer, *Everything Is Illuminated*, 102, 187.
71 Foer, *Everything Is Illuminated*, 214.
72 Foer, *Everything Is Illuminated*, 179.
73 Foer, *Everything Is Illuminated*, 89.
74 Foer, *Everything Is Illuminated*, 82.
75 Foer, *Everything Is Illuminated*, 83.
76 Foer, *Everything Is Illuminated*, 87.
77 Foer, *Everything Is Illuminated*, 196.
78 Foer, *Everything Is Illuminated*, 196.
79 Foer, *Everything Is Illuminated*, 52.
80 Foer, *Everything Is Illuminated*, 37.
81 Jérémie Dres, *We Won't See Auschwitz*, trans. Edward Gauvin (London: SelfMadeHero, 2012), v.
82 Foer, *Everything Is Illuminated*, 186.
83 Foer, *Everything Is Illuminated*, 25.

Conclusion

1 Kern, *The Culture of Time and Space*, 2.
2 Krasner, *Home Bodies*, 28.
3 Hirsch, *Family Frames*, 22. See also Hirsch, *The Generation of Postmemory*, 18.
4 Hirsch, *The Generation of Postmemory*, 82–91.
5 Elizabeth Rosner, *Survivor Café: The Legacy of Trauma and the Labyrinth of Memory* (Berkeley, CA: Counterpoint, 2017), 4–5.
6 Rosner, *Survivor Café*, 10.
7 Michael Rothberg, *Multidirectional Memory: Remembering the Holocaust in the Age of Decolonization* (Redwood City, CA: Stanford University Press, 2009), 3.
8 Golan Moskowitz, "Claustrophobic in the Gaps of Others: Affective Investments from the Queer Margins," in *The Palgrave Handbook of Holocaust Literature and Culture*, ed. Victoria Aarons and Phyllis Lassner (Cham, Switzerland: Palgrave Macmillan, 2020), 553–73; Golan Moskowitz, "Like Daughter, Like Grandson: Queering Post-Traumatic Memory," *Memory Studies* 16, no. 4 (2021): 1–25; Golan

Moskovitz, *Wild Visionary: Maurice Sendak in Queer Jewish Context* (Redwood City, CA: Stanford University Press, 2020).

9. Jacob Evoy addresses similar questions when he discusses LGBTQ+ descendants of survivors in his important work. See Jacob Evoy, "LGBTQ Children of Holocaust Survivors," *Perspectives: The Magazine of the Association for Jewish Studies*, Spring 2019, 71–72.
10. See, for instance, Lev Raphael, "Caravans," in *Dancing on Tisha B'Av* (New York: St. Martin's Press, 1990), 69–82.
11. Avinoam Patt and Jeff I., "In Our Own Words Interview Project," University of Hartford, Greenberg Center Special Collections, November 25, 2013.
12. Patt and I., "In Our Own Words Interview Project."
13. Patt and I., "In Our Own Words Interview Project"
14. Patt and I., "In Our Own Words Interview Project."

Bibliography

Aarons, Victoria. "Found Objects: The Legacy of Third-Generation Holocaust Memory." In *Translated Memories: Transgenerational Perspectives on the Holocaust*, edited by Bettina Hofmann and Ursula Reuter, 231–50. Lanham, MD: Lexington Books, 2020.

———. *Holocaust Graphic Narratives: Generation, Trauma and Memory*. New Brunswick, NJ: Rutgers University Press, 2020.

———. "The Trauma of History in *The Gates of the Forest*." In *Elie Wiesel: Jewish, Literary, and Moral Perspectives*, edited by Steven T. Katz and Alan Rosen, 146–59. Bloomington: Indiana University Press, 2013.

Aarons, Victoria, and Alan L. Berger. *Third-Generation Holocaust Representation: Trauma, History, and Memory*. Evanston, IL: Northwestern University Press, 2017.

Adams, Jenni. *Magic Realism in Holocaust Literature: Troping the Traumatic Real*. London: Palgrave Macmillan, 2011.

Amian, Katrin. *Rethinking Postmodernism(s): Charles S. Peirce and the Pragmatist Negotiations of Thomas Pynchon, Toni Morrison, and Jonathan Safran Foer*. Amsterdam: Rodopi, 2008.

Apel, Dora. *Memory Effects: The Holocaust and the Art of Secondary Witnessing*. New Brunswick, NJ: Rutgers University Press, 2002.

Bachelard, Gaston. *The Poetics of Space*. Translated by Maria Jolas. Boston: Beacon Press, 1994.

Baldwin, James. "Here Be Dragons." In *The Price of the Ticket: Collected Nonfiction 1948–1985*, edited by Toni Morrison, 677–90. New York: St. Martin's Press, 1985.

Banwell, Stacy. "Rassenschande, Genocide and the Reproductive Jewish Body: Examining the Use of Rape and Sexualized Violence against Jewish Women during the Holocaust?" *Journal of Modern Jewish Studies* 15, no. 2 (2016): 208–27.

Bardizbanian, Audrey. "From Silence to Testimony: Performing Trauma and Postmemory in Jonathan Safran Foer's *Everything Is Illuminated*." *Holocaust Studies: A Journal of Culture and History* 25, no. 1–2 (2019): 43–58.

Bar-On, Dan. *Fear and Hope: Three Generations of the Holocaust*. Cambridge, MA: Harvard University Press, 1995.
Baskind, Samantha. "A Conversation with Miriam Katin." In *The Jewish Graphic Novel: Critical Approaches*, edited by Samantha Baskind and Ranen Omer-Sherman, 237–43. New Brunswick, NJ: Rutgers University Press, 2010.
Bayer, Gerd. "After Postmemory: Holocaust Cinema and the Third Generation." *Shofar: An Interdisciplinary Journal of Jewish Studies* 28, no. 4 (2010): 116–32.
Berger, Alan L. *Children of Job: American Second-Generation Witnesses to the Holocaust*. Albany: State University of New York Press, 1997.
Berger, Naomi. "Coming Full Circle." In *Second Generation Voices: Reflections by Children of Holocaust Survivors and Perpetrators*, edited by Alan L. Berger and Naomi Berger, 92–109. Syracuse, NY: Syracuse University Press, 2001.
Bergmann, Martin S., and Milton E. Jucovy. *Generations of the Holocaust*. New York: Columbia University Press, 1982.
Berlatsky, Eric L. *The Real, the True, and the Told: Postmodern Historical Narrative and the Ethics of Representation*. Columbus: The Ohio State University Press, 2011.
Bistritz, Janice F. "Transgenerational Pathologies in Families of Holocaust Survivors." In *The Psychological Perspectives of the Holocaust and of Its Aftermath*, edited by Randolph L. Braham, 129–44. New York: Columbia University Press, 1988.
Bosmajian, Hamida. "The Orphaned Voice in Art Spiegelman's *Maus*." In *Considering Maus: Approaches to Art Spiegelman's "Survivor's Tale" of the Holocaust*, edited by Deborah R. Geis, 26–43. Tuscaloosa: University of Alabama Press, 2003.
Bowlby, Rachel. "Domestication." In *Deconstruction: A Reader*, edited by Martin McQuillan, 304–10. New York: Routledge, 2001.
Boym, Svetlana. *The Future of Nostalgia*. New York: Basic Books, 2001.
Brennan, Teresa. *The Transmission of Affect*. Ithaca, NY: Cornell University Press, 2004.
Brown, Bill. *A Sense of Things: The Object Matter of American Literature*. Chicago: University of Chicago Press, 2003.
———. "Thing Theory." *Critical Inquiry* 28, no. 1 (2001): 1–22.
Budick, E. Miller. *The Subject of Holocaust Fiction*. Bloomington: Indiana University Press, 2015.
Bukiet, Melvin J. Introduction to *Nothing Makes You Free: Writings by Descendants of Jewish Holocaust Survivors*, edited by Melvin J. Bukiet, 11–23. New York: W. W. Norton, 2002.
Buttimer, Anne. "Home, Reach, and the Sense of Place." In *The Human Experience of Space and Place*, edited by Anne Buttimer and David Seamon, 166–96. New York: St. Martin's Press, 1980.
Caruth, Cathy. *Literature in the Ashes of History*. Baltimore: Johns Hopkins University Press, 2013.
———. "Lost in Transmission: Studies of Trauma across Generations." *International Journal of Psychoanalysis* 95, no. 2 (2014): 402–7.
———. *Unclaimed Experience: Trauma, Narrative, and History*. Baltimore: Johns Hopkins University Press, 1996.
Chute, Hillary. "'The Shadow of a Past Time': History and Graphic Representation in 'Maus.'" *Twentieth Century Literature* 52, no. 2 (2006): 199–230.
Cooper, Howard. "The Second Generation 'Syndrome.'" *Journal of Holocaust Education* 4, no. 2 (1995): 131–46.

Csikszentmihalyi, Mihaly, and Eugene Rochberg-Halton. *The Meaning of Things: Domestic Symbols and the Self.* Cambridge: Cambridge University Press, 1981.

Danieli, Yael. "The Heterogeneity of Postwar Adaptation in Families of Holocaust Survivors." In *The Psychological Perspectives of the Holocaust and of Its Aftermath*, edited by Randolph L. Braham, 109–27. New York: Columbia University Press, 1988.

Derrida, Jacques. *Archive Fever: A Freudian Impression.* Translated by Eric Prenowitz. Chicago: University of Chicago Press, 1998.

Després, Carole. "The Meaning of Home: Literature Review and Directions for Future Research and Theoretical Development." *Journal of Architectural and Planning Research* 8, no. 2 (1991): 96–115.

Des Pres, Terrance. *The Survivor: An Anatomy of Life in the Death Camps.* New York: Oxford University Press, 1976.

Diner, Hasia. "Post-World-War-II American Jewry and the Confrontation with Catastrophe." *American Jewish History* 91, no. 3–4 (2003): 439–67.

Douglas, Mary. "The Idea of Home: A Kind of Space." *Social Research* 58, no. 1 (1991): 287–307.

———. *Purity and Danger: An Analysis of the Concepts of Pollution and Taboo.* New York: Routledge, 1966.

Dres, Jérémie. *We Won't See Auschwitz.* Translated by Edward Gauvin. London: SelfMadeHero, 2012.

Eisenstein, Bernice. *I Was a Child of Holocaust Survivors.* Toronto: McClelland and Stewart, 2006.

Elmwood, Victoria. "'Happy, Happy Ever After': The Transformation of Trauma between the Generations in Art Spiegelman's 'Maus: A Survivor's Tale.'" *Biography* 27, no. 4 (2004): 691–720.

Epstein, Helen. *Children of the Holocaust: Conversations with Sons and Daughters of Survivors.* New York: Penguin, 1988.

———. *Where She Came From: A Daughter's Search for Her Mother's History.* Teaneck, NJ: Holmes and Meier, 2005.

Evoy, Jacob. "LGBTQ Children of Holocaust Survivors." *Perspectives: The Magazine of the Association for Jewish Studies*, Spring 2019, 71–72.

Fischer, Nina. *Memory Work: The Second Generation.* London: Palgrave, 2015.

Fivush, Robyn. "Remembering and Reminiscing: How Individual Lives Are Constructed in Family Narratives." *Memory Studies* 1, no. 1 (2008): 49–58.

Flem, Lydia. *The Final Reminder: How I Emptied My Parents' House.* London: Souvenir Press, 2005.

Foer, Jonathan Safran. *Everything Is Illuminated: A Novel.* New York: Penguin Books, 2002.

Freud, Sigmund. *Beyond the Pleasure Principle.* Translated by James Strachey. New York: W. W. Norton, 1961.

———. *Civilization and Its Discontents.* Translated by James Strachey. New York: W. W. Norton, 1962.

Friedmann, Thomas. *Damaged Goods.* Sag Harbor, NY: The Permanent Press, 1984.

Furman, Andrew. *Contemporary Jewish American Writers and the Multicultural Dilemma: The Return of the Exiled.* Syracuse, NY: Syracuse University Press, 2000.

Gorrara, Claire. "Not Seeing Auschwitz: Memory, Generation and Representations of the Holocaust in Twenty-First Century French Comics." *Journal of Modern Jewish Studies* 17, no. 1 (2018): 111–26.

Grimwood, Marita. *Holocaust Literature of the Second Generation*. London: Palgrave, 2007.
Halbmayr, Brigitte. "Sexualized Violence against Women during Nazi 'Racial' Persecution." In *Sexual Violence against Jewish Women during the Holocaust*, edited by Sonja M. Hedgepeth and Rochelle G. Saidel, 29–44. Waltham, MA: Brandeis University Press, 2010.
Hass, Aaron. *The Aftermath: Living with the Holocaust*. Cambridge: Cambridge University Press, 1995.
———. *In the Shadow of the Holocaust: The Second Generation*. Ithaca, NY: Cornell University Press, 1990.
Hirsch, Marianne. *Family Frames: Photography, Narrative, and Postmemory*. Cambridge, MA: Harvard University Press, 1997.
———. "Family Pictures: *Maus*, Mourning, and Post-Memory." *Discourse* 15, no. 2 (1992–1993): 3–29.
———. *The Generation of Postmemory: Writing and Visual Culture after the Holocaust*. New York: Columbia University Press, 2012.
———. "Objects of Return." In *After Testimony: The Ethics and Aesthetics of Holocaust Narrative for the Future*, edited by Jakob Lothe, Susan R. Suleiman, and James Phelan, 198–220. Columbus: The Ohio State University Press, 2012.
———. "Surviving Images: Holocaust Photographs and the Work of Postmemory." *Yale Journal of Criticism* 14, no. 1 (2001): 5–37.
Hirsch, Marianne, and Leo Spitzer. *Ghosts of Home: The Afterlife of Czernowitz in Jewish Memory*. Berkeley: University of California Press, 2010.
Hofmann, Bettina, and Ursula Reuter, eds. *Translated Memories: Transgenerational Perspectives on the Holocaust*. Lanham, MD: Lexington Books, 2020.
Hoffman, Eva. *After Such Knowledge: Memory, History, and the Legacy of the Holocaust*. New York: PublicAffairs, 2004.
———. *Lost in Translation: A Life in a New Language*. New York: Penguin Books, 1990.
Horowitz, Sara R. "Nostalgia and the Holocaust." In *After Representation? The Holocaust, Literature, and Culture*, edited by R. Clifton Spargo and Robert M. Ehrenreich, 41–58. New Brunswick, NJ: Rutgers University Press, 2010.
———. "What We Learn, at Last: Recounting Sexuality in Women's Deferred Autobiographies and Testimonies." In *The Palgrave Handbook of Holocaust Literature and Culture*, edited by Victoria Aarons and Phyllis Lassner, 45–63. Cham, Switzerland: Palgrave Macmillan, 2020.
Jacobowitz, Susan. "The Holocaust at Home: Representations and Implications of Second Generation Experience." PhD diss., Brandeis University, 2004.
Jacobs, Janet. "The Cross-Generational Transmission of Trauma: Ritual and Emotion among Survivors of the Holocaust." *Journal of Contemporary Ethnography* 40, no. 3 (2011): 342–61.
———. *The Holocaust across Generations: Trauma and Its Inheritance among Descendants of Survivors*. New York: New York University Press, 2016.
Jilovsky, Esther. *Remembering the Holocaust: Generations, Witnessing and Place*. New York: Bloomsbury Academic, 2015.
Kaminsky, Leah. *The Waiting Room: A Novel*. New York: Harper Perennial, 2016.
Kaplan, Louise. *No Voice Is Ever Wholly Lost: An Exploration of the Everlasting Attachment between Parent and Child*. New York: Simon and Schuster, 1995.

Karpf, Anne. *The War After: Living with the Holocaust*. London: William Heinemann, 1996.
Kern, Stephen. *The Culture of Time and Space: 1880–1918*. Cambridge, MA: Harvard University Press, 2003.
Kestenberg, Judith S. "A Metapsychological Assessment Based on an Analysis of a Survivor's Child." In *Generations of the Holocaust*, edited by Martin S. Bergman and Milton E. Jucovy, 137–58. New York: Basic Books, 1982.
———. "Survivor-Parents and Their Children.'" In *Generations of the Holocaust*, edited by Martin S. Bergman and Milton E. Jucovy, 83–102. New York: Basic Books, 1982.
Klein, Hillel. *Survival and Trials of Revival: Psychodynamic Studies of Holocaust Survivors and Their Families in Israel and the Diaspora*. Boston: Academic Studies Press, 2012.
Koerfer, Katharina. "Legacies of Survival and Perpetuation in Elizabeth Rosner's Second Generation Holocaust Fiction." Master's thesis, Technische Universität Dortmund, 2013.
Krasner, James. *Home Bodies: Tactile Experience in Domestic Space*. Columbus: The Ohio State University Press, 2010.
LaCapra, Dominick. *History and Memory after Auschwitz*. Ithaca, NY: Cornell University Press, 1998.
Laga, Barry. "*Maus*, Holocaust, and History: Redrawing the Frame." *Arizona Quarterly* 57, no. 1 (2001): 61–90.
Lang, Jessica. *Textual Silence: Unreadability and the Holocaust*. New Brunswick, NJ: Rutgers University Press, 2017.
Langer, Lawrence L. *The Holocaust and the Literary Imagination*. New Haven, CT: Yale University Press, 1975.
———. *Holocaust Testimonies*. New Haven, CT: Yale University Press, 1991.
Latour, Bruno. *Reassembling the Social: An Introduction to Actor-Network-Theory*. Oxford: Oxford University Press, 2005.
Laub, Dori. "Bearing Witness or the Vicissitudes of Listening." In *Testimony: Crises of Witnessing in Literature, Psychoanalysis, and History*, edited by Shoshana Felman and Dori Laub, 57–74. New York: Routledge, 1991.
———. "An Event without a Witness: Truth, Testimony and Survival." In *Testimony: Crises of Witnessing in Literature, Psychoanalysis, and History*, edited by Shoshana Felman and Dori Laub, 75–92. New York: Routledge, 1991.
Lehrer, Erica T. *Jewish Poland Revisited: Heritage Tourism in Unquiet Places*. Bloomington: Indiana University Press, 2013.
Lentin, Ronit. "Re-occupying the Territories of Silence: Israeli Daughters of Shoah Survivors between Language and Silence." In *Women and the Holocaust: Narrative and Representation*, edited by Esther Fuchs, 47–61. Lanham, MD: University Press of America, 1999.
Levine, Michael. "Necessary Stains: Art Spiegelman's *Maus* and the Bleeding of History." In *Considering* Maus*: Approaches to Art Spiegelman's "Survivor's Tale" of the Holocaust*, edited by Deborah R. Geis, 63–104. Tuscaloosa: University of Alabama Press, 2003.
Lipstadt, Deborah E. *Holocaust: An American Understanding*. New Brunswick, NJ: Rutgers University Press, 2016.
Luckhurst, Roger. *The Trauma Question*. New York: Routledge, 2008.

Mallett, Shelley. "Understanding Home: A Critical Review of the Literature." *The Sociological Review* (2004): 62–89.

Malpas, Jeff E. *Place and Experience: A Philosophical Topography*. Cambridge: Cambridge University Press, 1999.

Mason, Edward A., and Eva Fogelman, directors. *Breaking the Silence: The Generation after the Holocaust*. 1984. Waltham, MA: National Center for Jewish Film, 2008. DVD.

McCloud, Scott. *Understanding Comics*. New York: Harper Perennial, 1993.

McGlothlin, Erin H. "No Time like the Present: Narrative and Time in Art Spiegelman's 'Maus.'" *Narrative* 11, no. 2 (2003): 177–98.

Milbauer, Asher Z. "Teaching to Remember." In *Second-Generation Voices: Reflections by Children of Holocaust Survivors and Perpetrators*, edited by Alan L. Berger and Naomi Berger, 30–45. Syracuse, NY: Syracuse University Press, 2001.

Moos, Merilyn. *Breaking the Silence: Voices of the British Children of Refugees from Nazism*. Lanham, MD: Rowman and Littlefield, 2015.

Moskowitz, Golan. "Claustrophobic in the Gaps of Others: Affective Investments from the Queer Margins." In *The Palgrave Handbook of Holocaust Literature and Culture*, edited by Victoria Aarons and Phyllis Lassner, 553–73. Cham, Switzerland: Palgrave Macmillan, 2020.

———. "Grandsons Who Remember: Intersections of Holocaust Heritage and Contemporary Male Positioning." Master's thesis, Brandeis University, 2012.

———. "Like Daughter, Like Grandson: Queering Post-Traumatic Memory." *Memory Studies* 16, no. 4 (2021): 1–25.

———. *Wild Visionary: Maurice Sendak in Queer Jewish Context*. Redwood City, CA: Stanford University Press, 2020.

Nouvet, Claire. "The Inarticulate Affect: Lyotard and Psychoanalytic Testimony." *Discourse* 25, no. 1–2 (2018): 231–47.

Novick, Peter. *The Holocaust in American Life*. Boston: Mariner Books, 2000.

Orvell, Miles. "Writing Postmemory: *Krazy Kat*, *Maus*, and the Contemporary Fiction Cartoon." *American Literary History* 4, no. 1 (1992): 110–28.

Parker, Miriam. "Holocaust Survivors Give Legacy to the World." *The American Israelite*, May 1984.

Patt, Avinoam, and Jeff I. "In Our Own Words Interview Project," University of Hartford, Greenberg Center Special Collections, November 25, 2013.

Pattison, Dale. "Writing Home: Domestic Space, Narrative Production, and the Homeland in Roth's *American Pastoral*." *Twentieth Century Literature* 60, no. 2 (2014): 222–42.

Pilcer, Sonia. *The Holocaust Kid: Stories*. New York: Persea Books, 2001.

Pint, Kris. "Bachelard's House Revisited: Toward a New Poetics of Space." *Interiors* 4, no. 2 (2013): 109–23.

Pisano, Nirit G. *Granddaughters of the Holocaust: Never Forgetting What They Didn't Experience*. Brighton, UK: Academic Studies Press, 2013.

Plath, Sylvia. "The Colossus." Accessed March 16, 2022. https://www.poetryfoundation.org/poems/89119/the-colossus.

Prince, Robert M. *The Legacy of the Holocaust: Psychohistorical Themes in the Second Generation*. Ann Arbor, MI: UMI Research Press, 1999.

Rakoff, Vivian M., J. J. Sigal, and N. B Epstein. "Children and Families of Concentration Camp Survivors." *Canada's Mental Health* 14 (1966): 24–26.

Raphael, Lev. "Caravans." In *Dancing on Tisha B'Av*, 69–82. New York: St. Martin's Press, 1990.

Ribbat, Christoph. "Nomadic with the Truth: Holocaust Representation in Michael Chabon, James McBride, and Jonathan Safran Foer." In *Twenty-First Century Fiction: Readings, Essays, and Conversations*, edited by Christoph Ribbat, 199–218. Heidelberg: Universitätsverlag Winter, 2005.

Rosenbaum, Thane. "Cattle Car Complex," in *Elijah Visible*, 196–205. New York: St. Martin's Press, 1996.

Rosner, Elizabeth. "Bio." Accessed January 15, 2022. http://elizabethrosner.com/bio/.

———. *The Speed of Light*. New York: Ballantine, 2001.

———. *Survivor Café: The Legacy of Trauma and the Labyrinth of Memory*. Berkeley, CA: Counterpoint, 2017.

Rotenberg-Schwartz, Michael. "Looking at/in *Maus*: A Survey of Critical Approaches." In *Critical Insights: Holocaust Literature*, edited by Dorian Stuber, 63–81. New York: Salem Press, 2016.

Rothberg, Michael. *Multidirectional Memory: Remembering the Holocaust in the Age of Decolonization*. Redwood City, CA: Stanford University Press, 2009.

Safer, Elaine. "Illuminating the Ineffable: Jonathan Safran Foer's Novels." *Studies in American Jewish Literature* 25 (2006): 112–32.

Scherr, Rebecca. "The Uses of Memory and Abuses of Fiction: Sexuality in Holocaust Film, Fiction, and Memoir." In *Experience and Expression: Women, the Nazis, and the Holocaust*, edited by Elizabeth R. Baer, 278–97. Detroit: Wayne State University Press, 2003.

Schwarz, Daniel R. *Imagining the Holocaust*. New York: St. Martin's Press, 1999.

Seidler, Victor J. *Shadows of the Shoah: Jewish Identity and Belonging*. Oxford: Berg, 2000.

Shmotkin, Dov, Amit Shrira, Shira C. Goldberg, and Yuval Palgri. "Resilience and Vulnerability among Aging Holocaust Survivors and Their Families: An Intergenerational Overview." *Journal of Intergenerational Relationships* 9 (2011): 7–21.

Sicher, Efraim. *The Holocaust Novel*. New York: Routledge, 2005.

Smith, Philip. *Reading Art Spiegelman*. New York: Routledge, 2016.

Somerville, Peter. "Homelessness and the Meaning of Home: Rooflessness and Rootlessness?" *International Journal of Urban and Regional Research* 16, no. 4 (1992): 529–39.

Spiegelman, Art. "Mad Youth." In *Comix, Essays, Graphics and Scraps: From MAUS to Now*, edited by Art Spiegelman, 21–22. New York: Raw Books and Graphics, 1999.

———. *Maus I: A Survivor's Tale: My Father Bleeds History*. New York: Knopf, 1986.

———. *Maus II: A Survivor's Tale: And Here My Troubles Began*. New York: Knopf, 1992.

Spiegelman, Art, and Hillary Chute. *MetaMaus*. New York: Pantheon Books, 2011.

Stanger, Judy E. "Children of Holocaust Survivors: A Life History Study." PhD diss., State University of New York at Albany, 2004.

Stein, Arlene. *Reluctant Witnesses: Survivors, Their Children, and the Rise of Holocaust Consciousness*. Oxford: Oxford University Press, 2014.

Stier, Oren B. *Holocaust Icons: Symbolizing the Shoah in History and Memory*. New Brunswick, NJ: Rutgers University Press, 2015.

Sutin, Lawrence. "An Afterword on the 'Second Generation." In *Jack and Rochelle: A Holocaust Story of Love and Resistance*, edited by Lawrence Sutin, 205–18. Minneapolis: Graywolf Press, 2008.

Tuan, Yi-Fu. *Space and Place: The Perspective of Experience*. Minneapolis: University of Minnesota Press, 2011.
Wardi, Dina. *Memorial Candles: Children of the Holocaust*. London: Routledge, 1992.
Wiseman, Hadas, and Jacques P. Barber. *Echoes of the Trauma: Relational Themes and Emotions in Children of Holocaust Survivors*. Cambridge: Cambridge University Press, 2008.
Williams, Tennessee. *The Glass Menagerie*. New York: New Directions, 1999.
Wilson, Lucas F. W. "Dismantling Christian Readings of Jewish American Literature in the Christian College: A. M. Klein's *The Second Scroll*." In *Teaching Jewish American Literature*, edited by Roberta Rosenberg and Rachel Rubenstein, 58–62. New York: Modern Language Association of America, 2020.
———. "Inherited Traumatic Threads: Postmemory and the Dis/function of Hand-Me-Downs in Bernice Eisenstein's *I Was the Child of Holocaust Survivors*." *Canadian Jewish Studies* 32 (2021): 86–98.
———. "Jewish Heritage Collection: Oral History Interview with Evaline E. Kalisky Delson." 2019. https://lcdl.library.cofc.edu/lcdl/catalog/246432.
———. "Pre/Occupied Longing: Toward a Definition of Postnostalgia in Jonathan Safran Foer's *Everything Is Illuminated*." *Studies in American Jewish Literature* 42, no. 2 (2023): 121–40. https://doi.org/10.5325/studamerijewilite.42.2.0121.
———. "'Remember, my house it's also your house too': Survivor-Family Homes as Postmemorial Structures in Art Spiegelman's *Maus*." *Modern Language Studies* 52, no. 2 (2023): 10–33.
———. "Unlearning Evangelicalism: What a Poor Education Taught Me." In *Becoming: Transformative Storytelling for Education's Future*, edited by Laura Colket, Tracy Penny Light, and M. Adam Carswell, 27–34. New York: DIO Press, 2021.
Wilson, Lucas F. W., and Alex Anderson. "'I Was a Prisoner. Jew. Whore': Inherited Sexualized Trauma in Sonia Pilcer's *The Holocaust Kid*." *Journal of Jewish Identities* 16, no. 1–2 (2023): 5–21.
Yehuda, Rachel, and Linda M. Bierer. "The Relevance of Epigenetics to PTSD: Implications for the DSM-V." *Journal of Traumatic Stress* 22 (2009): 427–34.
Yehuda, Rachel, Linda M. Bierer, James Schmeidler, Daniel H. Aferiat, Ilana Breslau, and Susan Dolan. "Low Cortisol and Risk for PTSD in Adult Offspring of Holocaust Survivors." *American Journal of Psychiatry* 157, no. 8 (2000): 1252–59.

Index

Aarons, Victoria, 28, 31
Adams, Jenni, 158n57
affect: of childhood home, 48; material culture and, 28–29; *Maus* and, 34; parents' traumatic pasts and, 33; postmemorial structures and, 39–40; second generation and, 23, 37; transmission, 24; trauma and, 23
archive(s): Holocaust and, 30, 106; home as, 20; oral histories, 11; survivor-family homes as, 31; as term, 20
Arendt, Hannah, 3
Ascher, Carol, 7
assemblages, 48
Auschwitz: in *The Holocaust Kid*, 62–63, 71, 77; in *Maus*, 35, 37–38, 46, 49, 52, 54, 55; in other works, 111; postmemory and, 87; in second generation's views on, 30; *The Speed of Light*, 79, 81–83, 87, 88. *See also* Holocaust

Bachelard, Gaston, 6, 18–19, 47, 85
Baldwin, James, 46
Bar-On, Dan, 22–23
Bayer, Gerd, 107
belongings, 28–29. *See also* material culture; postmemory: material culture and
Berger, Naomi, 23

body, the: as archive, 106; body language, 40; fragility of, 81–82, 116–17; time and, 88
books, 37
Bosmajian, Hamida, 41
boundaries, 64–65, 88–89, 91–92, 94, 145n54
bourgeois society, 17, 19
Bowlby, Rachel, 52, 66
Boym, Svetlana, 108–9, 118
Brennan, Teresa, 24
Brown, Bill, 29, 92
Bukiet, Melvin J., 111
Buttimer, Anne, 102

Caruth, Cathy, 7–8, 106
"Cattle Car Complex" (Rosenbaum), 15–16, 24, 27
children of survivors: children of, 73–74; displacement (feelings of), 103; haunting by past, 24, 96–97; homeland and, 101–3; homes of, 63–64, 66, 69, 78, 84–93; independence from parents, 57–59, 60–61, 62, 63–64, 72–73; living with parents, 38; parents' control over, 64–66; parents' traumatic pasts and, 16, 20, 21–22, 54–55, 66–67, 141n32; play outside, 61; postmemorial structures and, 6, 27, 53–63; relationship with parents, 43–44; silence about Shoah, 22–23;

children of survivors (cont.)
  trauma and, 20, 105; writings by
  (generally), 112. *See also* second
  generation; third generation
Chute, Hillary, 42
claustrophobia, 15, 39, 58, 84
cleanliness, 55, 91
clothing: Holocaust and, 28, 30; in *The Holocaust Kid*, 13, 52, 55–57, 69, 70, 71, 74; in *Maus*, 39, 41–42
colonization as domestication, 66
"The Colossus" (Plath), 66
concentration camps, 37–38, 39, 55
Csikszentmihalyi, Mihaly, 18, 33, 57, 91

Dancing on Tisha B'Av (Raphael), 18
Danieli, Yael, 21
dark, fear of the, 15
death: fear of, 60; in the home, 21, 43–45, 46, 49; by suicide, 39, 41–42
Delson, Evaline E., 58–61, 84
desire, 92
Despres, Carole, 17–18
Des Pres, Terrence, 30
destabilization, 42–43
detachment, 93
dirt, 91, 117–18
displaced persons (DP) camps, 51, 140n10
domestication: colonization as, 66; generally, 51–52; in *The Speed of Light*, 78. *See also* postmemorial domestication
double consciousness, 108
Douglas, Mary, 19, 63, 91
dream life, 25
dust, 91

Eichmann, Adolf, trial of, 3
Elmwood, Victoria, 42
emotional labor, 34–35
Epstein, Helen, 4, 7, 23–24, 43, 82, 89, 90, 145n43
everyday, the, 81, 150n12
Everything Is Illuminated (Foer), 10, 14, 101–23; generally, 114; plot details, 115–20, 158n57; postnostalgia and, 104, 105, 108, 116, 118, 120–21, 122
Evoy, Jacob, 160n9

family: material culture and, 28, 105–6; memories of passed relatives, 73; narratives, 21–22, 110–12, 115, 122–23; possession within, 56–57; pre-Shoah family, 14; roles within, 44; structure, 6
fashioning, 52, 56, 74–75
fathers: in *Maus*, 35–37, 43–44, 45–47; in *The Speed of Light*, 79–80, 81, 86, 87, 93, 95–96, 99
fear: of atrocity, 25; of the dark, 15
fiction, 10
Finkelstein, Barbara, 7
fire, 62
Fischer, Nina, 5, 10, 31, 52–53, 68
Fivush, Robyn, 21
flies, 49–50
Foer, Jonathan Safran, 114. *See also Everything Is Illuminated* (Foer)
Freud, Sigmund, 23, 24, 45, 46
Friedmann, Thomas, 7, 80; *Damaged Goods*, 143n12

games, 36
Glass Menagerie, The (Williams), 62
Golems of Gotham, The (Rosenbaum), 18

Halbmayr, Brigitte, 67–68
Hass, Aaron, 26, 113
haunting, 24, 47–48, 73, 96–98, 143n15
Hirsch, Marianne: on homeland, 112–13; on nostalgia, 103–4, 105, 109; on past generations, 108; on postmemory, 4, 6, 10, 31; on the punctum, 156n96; self-in-relation, 40; on technologies, 29, 101
Hoffman, Eva, 25, 103, 104, 107, 110, 111
Hofmann, Bettina, 7
Holocaust: archives and, 30, 106; being at home with, 1–2; the body and, 116–17; concealment of, 20–21; as domestic, 22; as family origin, 110; in the home, 23, 25–26, 37; life before, 115, 116, 118, 120, 121; literature on, 142n33; material culture and, 28–29, 30; in *Maus*, 48; memories of, 82–83; nostalgia and, 104; postmemory and, 42, 87; as psychic reality, 4; public consciousness of, 2; representations, 2–3, 7–8, 10; second generation and, 15, 20, 27–28, 29, 66, 69, 150n12, 150n25; sharing

with children, 16, 21; silence about, 22; symbolism and, 54–55, 70, 73–74; as term, 2, 62, 140n9; third generation's connection with, 106–7, 108; trauma and, 45. *See also* Auschwitz

Holocaust Kid, The (Pilcer), 51–75; clothing in, 52; domestication qua colonization, 13, 66; Holocaust in, 151n50; home in, 10, 28; postmemorial domestication and, 51–52, 54–55, 58, 59–60, 61–62, 63, 64, 65–66, 67, 72; reception of work, 52–53; self and (m)other in, 68–69, 70–72, 73, 153n67; trauma in, generally, 53

homelands: children of survivors and, 101–3; displacement and, 103, 112, 113; nostalgia for, 104, 108–9; returning to, 105–6, 109, 114–16, 117–18, 122–23

home(s): as archive, 20; of children of survivors, 63–64, 66, 69, 78, 84–93; concentration camp and, 37–38, 39; control and, 57–59, 60–61, 62, 63; cooking meat in, 82; dark presence in, 19, 23; death in, 21; decorating, 26–27; descriptions of, 61, 77; feeling at home, 45; generally, 17–18; Holocaust in, 23, 25–26, 37; inside vs. outside, 26, 86; invasions, 26; in *Maus*, 34, 38–50; mothers and, 45; notions of, 14; as postmemorial structure, 41, 58, 59, 60; postmemory and, 35, 39; psyche and, 17, 18–19, 33, 39, 46, 89–91, 95; representations of, 8, 10, 14, 18, 39, 47, 143nn13–14; in *The Speed of Light*, 79–84; spending time outside, 27, 28; time and space's destabilization in, 42; trauma and, 25, 52, 82; as womb, 44

Horowitz, Sara, 103, 109
Hungary, 97

imagination: memory and, 36; parents' traumatic pasts and, 33, 34, 36, 68; vs. reality, 53
inside vs. outside, 26
Israel, 9–10

Jacobowitz, Susan, 102–3
Jacobs, Janet, 5, 68, 109–10
Jung, Carl, 18

Kaplan, Louise, 80
Karpf, Anne, 21, 22, 23, 24, 28, 84
Kern, Stephen, 65, 88
Kestenberg, Judith, 54, 68
Koerfer, Katharina, 82
Krant, Dientje, 58
Krasner, James, 6, 86

Lang, Jessica, 20, 111
language: in *Everything Is Illuminated*, 120–21; imperative tense, 56; mother tongue, 95; subjunctive, 72; trauma and, 95
Latour, Bruno, 145n62
Laub, Dori, 8
Lehrer, Erica T., 113
Levine, Michael, 38–39
light, 73–74
linear temporality, 21
Lyotard, Jean-François, 23

Malpas, Jeff E., 141n21
material culture: affect and, 28–29; postmemory and, 28–31; second generation and, 105–6; in *The Speed of Light*, 87, 91–93, 95–96
Maus (Spiegelman), 32–50; adulthood home in, 47–50; affect and, 34; childhood home in (as adult), 38–47; childhood home in (as child), 34–38; compilation, 32–33, 36; death in, 39, 41–42, 43–45, 46, 49; family in (generally), 45–46; flies in, 49–50; generally, 7, 146n3; "Hell Planet," 38; Holocaust in, 48; home in, 73; parents' traumatic pasts and, 34–35; photography in, 40–41; plot details, 28, 34–38, 39–42, 43–46, 47–50; postmemorial structures and, 11; postmemory and, 34, 35–36, 37, 47, 48, 50; reception of work, 32, 147nn5–6; scholarship on, 33; space in, 12–13, 33; text as testimony/witness, 10
McCloud, Scott, 42, 43
McGlothlin, Erin, 49
mediators, 145n62
memory: imagination and, 36; memory work, 113; vs. postmemory, 4
mental health, 3–4, 60

mothers and home, 45
music, 98

names, 26
Nazis, 116; postmemory fear of, 60
nonlinear temporality, 25
nonverbal communication, 9, 20, 23, 24, 40
nostalgia, 14, 103–4, 109–10; for homeland, 104, 108–9. *See also* postnostalgia
Nouvet, Claire, 23

Oedipal conflict, 45
oral histories, 11, 32, 46
outside vs. inside, 26

parents: children's relationship with, 43–44, 54, 57; living with, 38; as memorials to Holocaust, 66; parenting parents, 43, 44
parents' traumatic pasts: affect and, 33; belongings and, 28; children re-enacting, 28, 52, 68–69, 70–72, 97; control over children, 64–66; haunting by, 97–98; imagination and, 33, 34, 36, 68, 71, 98; mental health and, 3–4; postmemory and, 36, 62, 93–99, 110–11; the present and, 34; re-enactment and, 68–69; remembering constantly, 57, 62; silence about, 22–23, 79, 84, 111; telling children about, 16, 20, 21–22, 34–35, 52, 54, 66–67
Patt, Avinoam, 11
phone calls, 65
photographs, 4, 40–41, 44
Picasso, Pablo, 48
Pilcer, Sonia, 51, 149n2
pilgrimages, 105–6, 109, 114–16, 117–18, 122
place and postmemory, 101. See also *Everything Is Illuminated* (Foer)
Plath, Sylvia: "The Colossus," 66
postmemorial divergences, 78, 93–99
postmemorial domestication, 51, 52, 56, 74–75
postmemorial structure(s): adulthood and, 63–74; affect and, 39–40; childhood and, 53–63; in *The Holocaust Kid*, 53–74; home as, 41, 58, 59, 60; in *Maus*, 35–36, 47, 48, 50; parents' traumatic pasts and, 36; sizes of, 36; in *The Speed of Light*, 83, 86, 98, 100

postmemory: clothing and, 55–56; control over, 96; defined, 4, 6; dreams vs. life and, 25; emancipation and, 96; haunting and, 73; Holocaust and, 42; home and, 35, 39; material culture and, 28–31, 87, 91–93, 95–96; *Maus* and, 34, 35–36, 37; nostalgia and, 108–9; parents' traumatic pasts and, 36, 62, 93–99, 110–11; place and, 101; psychosomatic responses to, 60; stories and, 37; structures of, 6, 11, 12, 13, 14, 20, 22, 23, 24–25, 26, 28; stuff of, 6–7, 28–31; survivor-family homes and, 4–5, 9, 12; trauma and, 33
postnostalgia, 107; *Everything Is Illuminated* and, 104, 105, 108, 116, 118, 120–21, 122; second-generation postnostalgia, 110–14; as term, 109–10. *See also* nostalgia
presence and absence, 22
present, the, 34, 49–50, 81, 87–88, 98
Prince, Robert M., 90
psyche: home and, 17, 18–19, 33, 39, 46, 89–90, 91, 95; representations of, 42
psychoanalysis, 45
psychological disturbances, 3–4

Raphael, Lev: *Dancing on Tisha B'Av*, 18
reality: vs. imagination, 53; second generation's experience of, 53–54
re-enactment: homes and, 25, 28, 52; parents' traumatic pasts and, 68–69; the past and, 97; sexually, 70–72; and the trace, 8
Reluctant Witnesses (Stein), 11
retraumatization, 35
Reuter, Ursula, 7
Ribbat, Christoph, 104
Rochberg-Halton, Eugene, 18, 33, 57, 91
Rosenbaum, Thane: "Cattle Car Complex," 15–16, 24, 27; *The Golems of Gotham*, 18
Rosh Hashanah, 57
Rosner, Elizabeth, 76, 78, 153n1. See also *Speed of Light, The* (Rosner)

Safer, Elaine, 116
Schwartz, Daniel R., 37
second generation: affect and, 23, 37; anxiety over home invasions, 26; belongings/things and, 29; defined, 140n6, 140n10; Holocaust and, 15, 20, 27–28, 29; homes

of (generally), 8–9; literature and oral history, 7–10, 147n6, 152n51; material culture and, 105–6; mental health, 4; names, 26; oral history, 11; psyches of, 9, 90–91; temporality (experience of), 25; trauma and, 1, 3, 26–27, 30
Seidler, Victor J., 26–27
self, the, and the home, 18
self-in-relation (Hirsch), 40
sexual violence, 52, 64, 67–69
Shoah. *See* Holocaust
signification, 30
silence, 22–23, 66, 77, 79, 80–81, 82–83, 93, 111
Six-Day War, 3
social class, 17
Somerville, Peter, 102
Sonderkommandos, 77, 82, 97, 98, 154n4
space: awareness of, 15; domestic space, 47; in *The Holocaust Kid*, 53–55, 62, 67, 75; inheriting perceptions of, 15, 16; inside vs. outside, 26; in *Maus*, 12–13, 33; perception of, 26; poetics of, 47; of postmemory, 20–28; as speaking, 14; in *The Speed of Light*, 93–94; vs. time, 53; time and, 42–43, 79, 81. *See also Everything Is Illuminated* (Foer)
speaking, 14
Speed of Light, The (Rosner): adulthood homes in, 84–93; family home in, 79–84, 86; generally, 10, 18, 28; plot details, 76–78, 85–86, 88–90, 93, 94–95, 96–97, 98–99; postmemorial structures and, 76, 83, 86, 98–99, 100; reception of work, 13–14, 153n3
Spiegelman, Art, 32–33, 146n3. *See also Maus* (Spiegelman)
Spitzer, Leo, 10, 105, 109, 113
Star of David, 73–74
Stein, Arlene: *Reluctant Witnesses*, 11
Steinitz, Lucy Y., 7
Stier, Oren B., 28
stories: family stories, 21–22, 110–12, 115, 122–23; postmemory and, 37; reconstructing, 36–37; of trauma, 8
stuff of postmemory, 28–31
survivor-family homes: as archives, 31; dark presence of, 19; death in, 21; literary representations, 10, 12–14, 18; physical aspects, 9, 12; postmemory and, 4–5, 9, 12; scholarship on, 5; trauma and, 16, 28
survivors, as term, 139n1
Szony, David M., 7

talismans, 28–29
tattoos, 46
telephones, 65
televisions, 2–3, 87, 91–92, 95–96
temporality: the body and, 88; of flies, in *Maus*, 49–50; linear temporality, 21; in *Maus*, 42; nonlinear temporality, 25; the past, 36, 118; past and present colliding, 81, 87–88, 98; postmemory and, 90; the present, 34; second generation's experience of, 25, 53–54; space and, 42–43, 53, 79, 81; trauma and, 10
testimony, 10
things. *See* belongings; material culture
third generation, 14, 106–7, 108, 121–23
Third Reich, 1–2, 31
trauma: affect and, 23; children and, 20; defined, 7–8; expression of, 60; home and, 25, 52, 82; imagining, 22; intergenerational transmission, 4, 8, 64, 67, 84; language and, 95; narratives of, 8; postmemory and, 33; repression of, 67; retraumatization, 35; second generation and, 1, 3, 26–27, 30; Shoah and, 45; survivor-family homes and, 28; survivors of Holocaust and, 1; temporality and, 25; third generation and, 106–7; the womb and, 44
Tuan, Yi-Fu, 45

Ukraine, 103, 115, 117–18
uniforms, 30

violence, sexual, 52, 64, 67–69

wars: Six-Day War, 3; Yom Kippur War, 3
Wiesel, Elie, 7, 111
Williams, Tennessee: *The Glass Menagerie*, 62
windows, 22, 48, 88, 94–95, 99

Yom Kippur War, 3

About the Author

LUCAS F. W. WILSON, previously the Justice, Equity, and Transformation Postdoctoral Fellow at University of Calgary (2022–2024), is a Social Sciences and Humanities Research Council Postdoctoral Fellow at University of Toronto Mississauga. His academic work has appeared in *Modern Language Studies*, *Canadian Jewish Studies*, *Flannery O'Connor Review*, *Journal of Jewish Identities*, *Studies in American Jewish Literature*, and in several edited collections. He is the editor of *Shame-Sex Attraction: Survivors' Stories of Conversion Therapy*, as well as coeditor, with Alan L. Berger, of *Emerging Trends in Third-Generation Holocaust Literature*. He is currently working on two interrelated monograph projects that examine evangelical homophobia and transphobia in the United States.